women's best spiritual travel writing

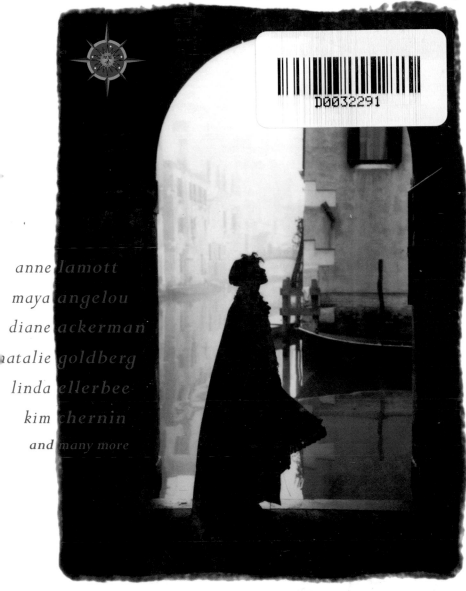

anne *lamott*

maya angelou

diane *ackerman*

natalie goldberg

linda *ellerbee*

kim *chernin*

and *many more*

A WOMAN'S PATH

edited by lucy mccauley, amy g. carlson & jennifer leo

CRITICAL ACCLAIM
FOR *A WOMAN'S PATH*

"Thirty-two women writers lend their distinctive voices to this moving chorus of essays in which their physical journey sometimes reflects, often impacts their spiritual unfolding."

—Book Sense 76

"A sensitive exploration of women's lives that have been unexpectedly and spiritually touched by travel experiences...highly recommended."

—*Library Journal*

"In *A Woman's Path* readers are presented with essays by women who pour their honesty and personal spiritual journeys onto the page with the fervor of someone who must.... Some essays give one pause, others bring clarity to matters of the soul, yet as a whole the voyage is worth the price of the fare."

—*ForeWord*

"This book helps you see that travel can have a higher purpose than just collecting snapshots."

—Judy Wylie, *Chicago Herald*

"An inspiring book, and worth a place in your heart as well as your bookshelf."

—*Herspace.com*

"The women who share these stories dance and drink and worry and wonder at the crossroads of spirit, self, heart, and mind."

—Linda Watanabe McFerrin, *San Francisco Examiner*

"Follow the call of some of our finest women writers as they share their impressions, perspectives, challenges and inspirations from the spiritual path."

—*NAPRA ReView*

"This is no ordinary collection. These are not destination pieces describing what to see and do, but rather thoughtful, meditative accounts of both inner and outer journeys."

—June Sawyers, *Chicago Tribune*

TRAVELERS' TALES

A
WOMAN'S
PATH

WOMEN'S BEST SPIRITUAL
TRAVEL WRITING

Edited by

LUCY MCCAULEY, AMY G. CARLSON,
AND JENNIFER LEO

TRAVELERS' TALES
SAN FRANCISCO

Travelers' Tales and *Travelers' Tales Guides* are trademarks of Travelers' Tales, Inc.

Credits and copyright notices for the individual articles in this collection are given starting on page 251.

We have made every effort to trace the ownership of all copyrighted material and to secure permission from copyright holders. In the event of any question arising as to the ownership of any material, we will be pleased to make the necessary correction in future printings. Contact Travelers' Tales, Inc., 330 Townsend Street, Suite 208, San Francisco, California 94107. www.travelerstales.com.

Art Direction: Michele Wetherbee
Interior design: Susan Bailey and Kathryn Heflin
Cover photograph: Copyright © Theo Westenberger/Images.com, Inc. Woman Standing in Archway, Venice.
Research editor: Lisa Bach
Page layout: Cynthia Lamb using the fonts Bembo and Boulevard

Distributed by Publishers Group West, 1700 Fourth Street, Berkeley, California 94710.

Library of Congress Cataloging-in-Publication Data
A woman's path : women's best spiritual travel writing / edited by Lucy McCauley, Amy G. Carlson, and Jennifer Leo. — 1st ed.
    p. cm.
Includes bibliographical references.
    ISBN 1-932361-00-6 (pbk.)
    1. Women travelers. 2. Voyages and travels. 3. Women—religious life. 4. Pilgrims and pilgrimages. I. McCauley, Lucy. II. Carlson, Amy Greimann. III. Leo, Jennifer.
G465 .W646 2003
910.4—dc22
                                                                        2003014900

First Edition
Printed in the United States of America
10 9 8 7 6 5 4

I, the fiery life of divine essence, am aflame beyond the beauty of the meadows. I gleam in the waters, and I burn in the sun, moon, and stars. With every breeze, as with invisible life that contains everything, I awaken everything to life.

—HILDEGARD OF BINGEN (1098–1179),
The Book of Divine Works

In memory of Kyle E. McHugh,
Travelers' Tales author and friend,
whose pilgrimage through life
ended far too soon.
We will miss her.

Table of Contents

Part Three
TRANSFORMING THE SELF

Part Four
WALKING THE SHADOW SIDE

A Woman's Path: An Introduction

How difficult it can be to talk about what is spiritual. We experience moments of "connection" to a "higher power"; times of "communion" with what we sometimes call our "soul." Yet the language we use doesn't come close to capturing the depth of the experiences themselves. Almost by definition, what takes place in the spiritual realm eludes description.

The stories in this collection nevertheless attempt to initiate a conversation, at least, about those elusive moments—in the context of travel. In some ways, one could say that all journeys are spiritual; by its very nature, journeying involves a leap of faith. We climb onto a train, strap ourselves into an airplane seat, or step onto a winding path with the fullest of hopes—and yet knowing nothing for certain about where the venture might actually lead us.

Perhaps that leap of faith is what makes our spiritual center so accessible when we travel. In the act of moving from one place to another, somehow a space is created where, if we're lucky, a moment of clarity alights on us and offers a window into our natures, and the nature of everything around us. Travel to distant places has a way of opening a path inward, to possibility—to memory, even. After a while, the physical experience of travel somehow becomes less significant than the inner transformations we undergo: when, by moving through space, bumping up against strangeness and being changed by it, we somehow become more of who we are meant to be.

Ancient philosophers and contemporary mystics alike have proposed that we are conceived in the womb with a deep knowledge of everything, of all the secrets and mysteries of the universe, and that life is a process of "remembering": As we live and learn, we reconnect with knowledge that we already have; it is as if we simply draw back a veil so that we can see and understand it all anew. The stories in this volume have convinced my coeditors and me that the act of travel is a potent way indeed of calling forth that inner knowledge. To relearn what we already know on the deepest level; to wake up to it and allow it to change us. Such is the power of the spiritual journey.

But for women, the path of that journey takes on yet another dimension. Many of our childhood experiences of spirituality revolved around the sacred male image found in the Judeo-Christian tradition—which, implicitly and explicitly, often excluded us as females. Yet we know that other religions reject that focus on a wholly male God: Native American, Hindu, and African traditions are rich with imagery of female deities, and archaeological evidence has pointed to long traditions of Goddess worship in ancient cultures all over the world.

The collection of essays that follows attempts to provide a forum in which, through our unique experiences as women, we might begin to find ways to reclaim, honor, and celebrate our spiritual power and wisdom: to explore what might be called the sacred feminine. You will read here of many kinds of women's excursions of the spirit—some in the context of faiths like Judaism, Christianity, Islam, and Buddhism, while others venture into the realms of Goddess spirituality, shamanism, and African and Native American traditions. Still, many of these essays describe journeys that have less to do with worship than with explorations of inner spiritual strength, or even of deep connections to the spirit of particular places.

We begin and end with stories set along the classic pilgrim's trail, in which the traveler undertakes a spiritual quest by walking many weeks or months along a well-worn path. The first of these, Abigail Seymour's "Go Beyond!" takes place along Spain's Camino de Santiago that dates back to the Middle Ages; the last, Kelly Winters's "Trusting the Trail," occurs on the Appalachian Trail that runs 2,000 miles, from Georgia to Maine. Both lead the traveler to a kind of introspection and reckoning with herself and her beliefs that is nothing short of transformative.

But there are other ways of connecting to one's spirit than by setting out on a walking pilgrimage. Some of the women in these stories partake of the religious rites and rituals of wholly foreign cultures, such as Emily Zuzik does in "Going Without at Ramadan." Some women, like Sue Bender in "Sweat Lodge," do it by venturing into darkness, metaphorically and literally, in order to touch their own luminous centers. Some use travel as a way of healing physical and emotional wounds, or to test and push their inner strengths and limits, as Linda Ellerbee does in "No Shit! There I Was…". Others, like Maya Angelou in "Return to Keta," travel to foreign lands that they find strangely familiar, and where they encounter ancestors—or past lives—long forgotten by the conscious mind. And still others, like Jill Jepson in "Cave Temple of the Goddess," embark on their journeys as skeptical pilgrims—only to return with a new kind of faith.

What all of these journeys share, however, is their ability to convey the power of feminine spiritual transformation—of its possibilities and direction, of its contingencies and freedom, of its poetry and joy. And although this book cannot provide any fixed direction-markers for other cartographers of the spirit, it is our hope that the stories here will serve as gentle spurs for those who desire to embark on such a journey for themselves.

—LUCY MCCAULEY

PART ONE

AWAKENING

ABIGAIL SEYMOUR

✦ ✷ ✦

Go Beyond!

A pilgrimage to Santiago initiates
a search for "home."

A MAN SLEEPING IN THE COT NEXT TO MINE WAS SNORING. HE HAD a kerchief over his face that flapped each time he let out a breath. It was 2:30 in the morning. The other fifty or so people in the musty room of the monastery were sound asleep. I felt pale and soft and timid, among people who seemed to sleep the sound sleep of certainty. Roncesvalles, the monastery where we were all staying in the Pyrenees, is the gateway into Spain from France on the Camino de Santiago. It was my first night on the pilgrimage; I was the only American and one of the few women in the group, as far as I could tell. Most of the people were traveling in groups of three or four, some were couples. I was alone.

Sleepless, I walked down the three flights of wooden stairs, worn in a rut down the middle. They led me to a stone entryway, the spot that in a few hours would be the start of my walk to Santiago de Compostela, 500 miles away. There was a ring around the moon. The road faded into a gray, gauzy haze.

"Lord, hear my prayer."

The sound of my own voice, hollow and thin, startled me. I had long ago given up the idea that anyone or anything could hear me. Feeling chilled, I went back inside.

When I awoke the next morning, most of the beds were empty. My fellow pilgrims had already set out before 5:00, before it was even light. I left two and a half hours later than they did and had the path to myself, sure that I had beaten the system. But by noon I was caught in the blazing sun with 4 more miles to the next refuge.

> My desire to slip away from the stories and the choices we make to secure our identity in everyday life has borne fruit again and again. To go on a pilgrimage, I discovered, you do not need to know what you are looking for, only that you are looking for *something*, and need urgently to find it. It is the urgency that does the work, a readiness to receive that finds the answers.
>
> —Janine Pommy Vega,
> *Tracking the Serpent:*
> *Journeys to Four Continents*

As I clumped down the mountain, trying to gauge how much my legs hurt, I came upon Burguete, a tiny whitewashed town where Hemingway stayed during the bullfight season. No sign of any fiestas, just windows shuttered against the heat and a lone bar open. Just outside of town was a series of wooden signs with just one word: ¡*Ultreya!* My guidebook told me that it was a cognate of the Latin "*ulter*," the same root as the English "ultra." It was the ancient greeting exchanged by medieval pilgrims. "Beyond!" they cried to one another. "Go beyond!"

Their destination, and mine, was the cathedral in Santiago de Compostela, Spain. Inside is a marble pillar carved into a Jesse Tree, the depiction of the prophecy of Jesus's birth from the book of Isaiah: "A shoot shall come from the stump of Jesse, and a branch shall grow out of its roots." The marble tree's trunk bears an indentation in the shape of a human hand that has been worn over a millennium by millions of pilgrims. Legend says that if you put your right hand against the pillar and touch your forehead three times to the statue just below it, you will be blessed.

This act of faith is the culmination of a 500-mile walk from the

Spanish border with France to the spot where the remains of Apostle James were said to have been unearthed. The story goes that Saint James was beheaded in Jerusalem and his body was carried in a divinely guided boat to the western coast of Spain, where he lay undiscovered for 750 years. One night, an old hermit named Pelayo saw a series of bright lights floating in the sky above a field. He began digging on the spot and discovered a well-preserved body and a note identifying the remains as Santiago—Saint James himself.

Soon after Pelayo's revelation, people began walking across Europe to venerate Saint James. At the height of the shrine's popularity in the eleventh century, more than half a million people a year walked to Santiago de Compostela. The route, which crosses the Pyrenean mountains, Navarre, the plains of Castile, and ends in the lush hills of Galicia, became an important trade road. Merchants set up shop to cater to the crowds of people pouring in, and churches and monasteries were erected to house them. "Santiago," wrote Goethe, the German philosopher, "built Europe."

The pilgrimage never died out; in fact, its popularity has surged since the Camino was named a UNESCO World Heritage Site in 1985.

It remains largely unchanged since the Middle Ages, with the exception of a long, ugly stretch along a busy highway in the middle of the country. Friends of the Camino associations across Spain is working hard to divert the footpath in a safer direction without losing any of its authenticity. Pilgrim refuges have been built for modern-day seekers providing bunk beds, cold showers, and kitchens, all staffed by former pilgrim volunteers. During the Holy Year in 1993 (when the Feast of Saint James, July 25, fell on a Sunday), 100,000 people walked, bicycled, or rode horseback the length of the Camino.

I never thought I would be one of them. I am not Spanish. I was raised a Protestant. And I am not hardy by nature. I was the sort of timid child who kept her white Keds on throughout the summer for fear of stepping on a bee. I honestly can't say for what or for whom I decided to walk to Santiago myself. All I know is that I did walk it, all the way, and that it changed me.

I was twenty-eight years old and had just gone through a divorce. I had left Manhattan with the notion of shedding my possessions and disappearing overseas. Maybe I could create myself anew, I thought, become someone more varied and textured. I came to Europe with a list of all the cities I planned to visit. Paris, Moscow, Munich, Prague, Barcelona, Athens—I never wanted to stop moving. I got a job in Madrid teaching English to businesspeople and lived in a small apartment in the center of the city. After a few months there, a creeping loneliness had tracked me down again, and it was time to start moving, but I didn't know where.

I spent my first Spanish Thanksgiving dinner sitting across the table from a clean-cut young American student in a bowtie. He was thin and eager and soft around the edges. I forgot his name before the end of the evening, and then forgot about him entirely. Six months later I was introduced at a party to an earthy, handsome man in faded jeans and sandals. He had long hair, an earring, and a scallop shell pendant around his neck. It took me a few minutes to recognize him without his bow tie—it was my Thanksgiving dinner companion, utterly transformed. "I have walked across Spain," Jamie told me, "along the Camino de Santiago." In those words I found what I had been looking for—whatever had changed him could change me, too.

So I set out that August for the monastery of Roncesvalles in the Pyrenees, the beginning of the walk on Spanish soil. The Camino appealed to me because I would never have to stop moving—I even thought maybe I would just stay on it forever, live on it, walking back and forth, becoming one of its eccentric fixtures, another character people would meet along the way.

That was how I ended up sleepless that first night among strangers near the border of France, ready to walk through the wilderness—Spain's and my own.

The Camino is as varied as the people who travel it. It is moody and changeable, sometimes a dripping forest path of overhanging trees and not a soul in sight, other times an exhaust-filled highway with semis whizzing by and crowds of people clogging the way. It has bridges and hills and rivers—things to cross and climb and navigate. After about a week of walking alone, I fell in with a group of people who, although we never actually declared our allegiance, remained more or less together for the rest of the trip. There were about twenty of us disbanding and reforming each night and morning. They included Manuel, a big, lumbering, mustachioed man who worked as a cobbler in Valencia and laughed so hard at his own jokes that he would have to stop walking. He warned us that sometimes he talked and sang in his sleep, and indeed a few nights later he sat bolt upright shouting, "Chickens for sale! Chickens for sale!"

I n many religious traditions the way to spiritual growth and development is seen as a path, traveled by many people over time. The spiritual path is one route to awakening from the sleep of unconsciousness that plagues human beings. A pilgrimage is a more intensified part of the journey, a time to be tested by the unexpected, to ask questions of meaning, and to gain strength and merit.

—Stephanie Kaza,
The Attentive Heart

His constant companion was Sergio, a quiet vending machine salesman from the south of Spain, who revealed one night after dinner that he had been diagnosed with cancer two years before at age thirty-two. When his cancer went into remission, Sergio made a vow to walk the Camino in thanksgiving—and there he was. *"A Santiago nunca se llega, solo se va,"* he said. "You never get to Santiago, you only set out for it." Then there was Geert, a Dutch bus driver with no front teeth, who enjoyed a breakfast each morning of two yogurts and a Heineken. Christine was a doctoral candidate from Switzerland who wrote in her journal every night by flashlight.

We compared blisters and bandaged joints, pored over each other's maps, and listened wide-eyed to Camino veterans tell of what lay in store for us. We were advised to ask for Pablo in a

village up ahead. The old man, they said, would give us each a
perfectly whittled walking stick. I heard about Tomás, a self-
proclaimed Knight Templar, who lived in the mountains, carrying
on the tradition of his defunct monastic order to protect the pilgrims. I heard about a fountain that spouted wine instead of
water, and about a stained glass window, made of every color in
the rainbow, where the light nonetheless shone through white instead of tinted. I was urged to stop in at Molinaseca, a town so
inviting that swimming pool ladders were installed on its riverbanks. I was given a scallop shell, the traditional symbol of the
Camino, to wear around my neck. Its magical properties would
protect me from evil.

I happened to be walking alone on the fourth day when I entered the little village of Zariquiegui, near Pamplona. Every window and door was shuttered against the midafternoon heat, but
three backpacks were propped against the wall of the village
church. I peered inside toward the darkened nave and all was quiet.
Light angled down through a window near the ceiling in dusty
rays, and I stood with the cool wood of the door against my back
as it closed. It was completely quiet—and then I heard someone
take a breath. Out of the darkness near the altar came three voices
singing in a cappella harmony. The hair stood up on the back of
my sweaty arms. I crept into the last pew and listened. As my eyes
came into focus I saw that the singers were fellow pilgrims; two
men and a woman in their twenties, wearing hiking boots, t-shirts,
and shells around their necks. When they finished, I followed them
back outside. They were German students who were walking to
Santiago in segments, one week each year. They stopped in at
every unlocked church along the way to sing.

"Why do you sing when no one else will hear you?" I asked.

"God can hear us," the woman said.

I found Pablo the whittler in the village of Ázqueta. He shyly
handed me a walking stick and wouldn't take any money. The river
in Molinaseca also lived up to its reputation—the water was cool
and sweet, and I lingered during the hottest part of the afternoon.

In the little town of Irache I actually found the fountain of wine. It turned out to be a marketing ploy on the part of a local vintner, who hooked up a tap to barrels of his house red. I never did find the miraculous stained glass window.

In the tenth-century village of Manjarín I found Tomás the Templar. He was the only dweller left in that ghost town, living in a chaotic camp in an old, partly roofed stone house. Tomás blessed me with a steel sword on both shoulders "*El Camino es un río,*" he said. "The Camino is a river—just ride it."

I found it easier to ride as I went. Even my nationality started to fade from me like something left in the sun too long. I got browner and my Spanish improved. If anything, people thought maybe I was British or German—never American, never me.

I walked for twenty-eight days in all, from one full moon to the next, starting out with a backpack full of prissy toiletries, trendy halter tops, Band-Aids, and traveler's checks. By the time I wriggled out of my dinged-up pack for the last time, I had pared down to one change of clothes and a toothbrush.

On the last day I reached the hilltop of Monte de Gozo, where pilgrims used to dance and weep and hold each other at the first glimpse of the cathedral spires. It is now a touristy park with a view of the football stadium, a superhighway, and a rest stop. I had to ask someone to point out the spires, and could barely make out three gray needles above the skyline. I wended my way through the old part of the city, still following the crude yellow arrows which had guided me that far, and suddenly rounded a corner and there it was. I looked up at the spires and the sun shone right into my eyes. I continued on through an archway and into the grand plaza that faces the astonishing, ornate facade.

Inside the cathedral, the marble Jesse Tree supports an entire carved entryway. In the middle of this tall "Doorway of Glory," Santiago is seated peacefully. As I waited in line, leaning on the walking stick that Pablo had made me, it became clear that everyone up ahead followed exactly the same ritual, although slightly different from the version I was prepared for: they put their hand to the pillar, reached into a stone lion's mouth to the right, and *then* bent to tap their foreheads three times. It got to be my turn and I did the same thing. Eyes closed, lion's mouth, forehead, tap, tap, tap. I looked up and noticed a uniformed guard standing nearby, his eyes at a bored half-mast, arms folded across his chest. "Excuse me," I said. "What is the significance of the lion's mouth?"

He shrugged. "Nothing. Some kid reached in there this morning and everybody who came after him's been doing it ever since."

And, for all I know, they still are. I like to think so, to imagine that I was another tiny thread in this rich fabric of tradition. Are the threads mere gossamer of fact? Skeptics will tell you that the scallop shell that protected me en route was the membership badge of an ancient Venus cult. Its members dwelt in the Celtic forests and practiced rituals that Christians would find shocking. Some scholars say that the divine revelation of the tomb's location was mistranscribed by a monk with poor eyesight. They say he probably looked at an early account of Saint James's burial site whose Latin script said *Hierosolyma,* Jerusalem, and mistakenly wrote *Hispania,* Spain. There are those who try to explain away the hermit Pelayo's vision, pointing to current astronomical phenomena. I doubt that any of them have been pilgrims. On the Camino there is a much finer line between an astronomical phenomenon and a miracle.

If I was expecting something miraculous in myself, though, it had yet to happen. I didn't feel anything except tired, and sad that it was over. I said goodbye to Manuel, Sergio, Christine, Geert, and the singing Germans, and returned to Madrid.

I spent several weeks going over my snapshots and watching the blisters on my feet heal and disappear. My walking stick rested in the corner of the living room. I rode the subway and taught grammar classes and wrote, but I felt as though I had been separated from a loved one. I thought about the Camino all year, wondering what winter was like in the mountains of León and how they might celebrate Easter in Santiago. You might say I was homesick, if a journey can be a home.

So when it got warm again, I went back. I worked as a volunteer at one of the Camino refuges. I cleaned toilets and kept house for more than 1,000 people in two weeks. I was restless and wanted to be among them. The day before I planned to begin my second pilgrimage, I started to feel strange. I was prickly with fevered goose bumps and everything seemed too bright and too loud.

I set out at dawn with a ringing in my right ear. By nightfall it was completely deaf. I was losing sensation in my cheek and temple, but I kept walking. León, Astorga, Ponferrada, Triacastela, mile after mile. "Beyond," I told myself. "Go beyond."

I kept walking until I couldn't stand the pain and pressure in my head. My hearing was shot, and I was angry that the one thing that had ever brought me peace—the Camino—was the very thing that was hurting me now.

Eight days away from Santiago I boarded a bus for Madrid. The doctor there told me that it was a good thing I'd come to him, since I was about eight days away from being dead—a staph infection I'd caught back at the refuge had been spreading through my ear on its way to my brain and spinal cord. Although grateful to be alive, I still felt that I had failed. When I called my Camino-mates to tell them I hadn't made it the second time, Sergio just laughed: "Don't you remember? *A Santiago nunca se llega.*"

I thought about what he said as I tried to stitch my life back together and recover from the trip. My loss of hearing took on new meaning for me—I had always thought that nothing or no one could hear me; maybe I was the one not listening. I sat in a rocking chair near the window in my apartment on Calle Huertas and finally understood the obvious: "beyond" isn't about distance or the capacity to endure. And so I left the Camino permanently and began an altogether different journey, the search for a real home. After three years in Spain, I accepted a job offer in the United States, where I am living now. My hearing is fully restored, and I try to be more open to what I hear. I have gone beyond.

I like to remember my last night in Santiago after I finished the Camino. I was lying on my back in the middle of the deserted Plaza Obradoiro, gazing up at the cathedral. Suddenly I heard someone chattering at me from the far side of the plaza. I couldn't quite hear what she was saying, but I assumed it was along the lines of "Get up off the street, young lady." Instead, the woman came over and sat beside me, then spun around and gestured for me to do the same.

"¡*Al revés!* ¡*Al revés!*" she commanded. "Turn around—the view is much better the other way."

The two of us lay back side by side and looked at the cathedral upside down. She was right: the spires of Santiago no longer looked rooted to the earth, but seemed to rise up out of the sky.

Abigail Seymour lived in Spain for three years. She is now an editor and writer in North Carolina, where she hikes with her husband, whom she met while walking a local watershed trail.

ANNE LAMOTT

* * *

Knocking on Heaven's Door

A harrowing flight prompts a miracle of sorts.

SO THERE I WAS ON A PLANE RETURNING HOME FROM ST. LOUIS. Or rather, there I was in a plane on the runway at the airport in St. Louis with, I think, the not unreasonable expectation that we would be in the air soon, as our flight had already been delayed two hours. I was anxious to get home, as I had not seen my son Sam in several days, but all things considered, I thought I was coping quite well, especially because I am a skeptical and terrified flier. In between devouring Hershey's chocolate and thirteen dollars' worth of trashy magazines, I had spent the two hours of the delay trying to be helpful to the other stranded passengers: I distributed all my magazines and most of my chocolates; I got an old man some water; I flirted with the babies; I mingled, I schmoozed. I had recently seen what may have been a miracle at my church and had been feeling ever since that I was supposed to walk through life with a deeper faith, a deeper assurance that if I took care of God's children for God, he or she would take care of me. So I took care of people and hoped that, once we were on board, everything would go smoothly.

My idea of everything going smoothly on an airplane is (*a*) that I not die in a slow-motion, fiery crash or get stabbed to death by

13

terrorists and (*b*) that none of the other passengers try to talk to
me. All conversation should end at the moment the wheels leave
the ground.

Finally we were allowed to board. I was in row thirty-eight, between a woman slightly older than I, with limited language skills,
and a man my own age who was reading a book by a famous
right-wing Christian novelist about the Apocalypse. A newspaper
had asked me to review this book when it first came out, because
its author and I are both Christians—although as I pointed out in
my review, he's one of those right-wing Christians who thinks that
Jesus is coming back next Tuesday right after lunch, and I am one
of those left-wing Christians who thinks that perhaps this author
is just spiritualizing his own hysteria.

"How is it?" I asked, pointing jovially to the man's book, partly
to be friendly, partly to gauge where he stood politically.

"This is one of the best books I've ever read," he replied. "You
should read it." I nodded. I remembered saying in the review that
the book was hard-core right-wing paranoid anti-Semitic homo-
phobic misogynistic propaganda—not to put too fine a point on
it. The man smiled and went back to reading.

I couldn't begin to guess what country the woman was from,
although I think it's possible that she had one Latvian parent and
one Korean. She sounded a little like Latka Gravas, the Andy
Kaufman character on *Taxi*, except after things began to fall apart
when she sounded just like the Martians in *Mars Attacks*. "Ack ack
ack!" she'd cry. But I'm getting ahead of myself.

As we sat there on the runway, the man with the book about
the Apocalypse commented on the small gold cross I wear.

"Are you born again?" he asked, as we taxied down the runway.
He was rather prim and tense, maybe a little like David Eisenhower
with a spastic colon. I did not know how to answer for a moment.

"Yes," I said, "I am."

My friends like to tell each other that I am not really a born-
again Christian. They think of me more along the lines of that old
Jonathan Miller routine, where he said, "I'm not really a Jew—I'm
Jew-ish." They think I am Christian-ish. But I'm not. I'm just a

bad Christian. A bad born-again Christian. And certainly, like the apostle Peter, I am capable of denying it, of presenting myself as a sort of leftist liberation-theology enthusiast and maybe sort of a vaguely Jesus-y bon vivant. But it's not true. And I believe that when you get on a plane, if you start lying you are totally doomed.

So I told the truth: that I am a believer, a convert. I'm probably about three months away from slapping an aluminum Jesus-fish on the back of my car, although I first want to see if the application or stickum in any way interferes with my lease agreement. And believe me, all this boggles even *my* mind. But it's true. I could go to a gathering of foot-wash Baptists and, except for my dreadlocks, fit right in. I would wash their feet; I would let them wash mine.

But as the plane taxied out to the runway, the man on my right began telling me how he and his wife were home-schooling their children, and he described with enormous acrimony the radical, free-for-all, feminist, touchy-feely philosophy of his county's school system, and I knew instantly that this description was an act of aggression against me—that he was telepathically on to me, could see that I was the enemy, that I will be on the same curling team in heaven as Tom Hayden and Vanessa Redgrave. And then suddenly the plane braked to a stop.

We all looked around for a moment, before the captain came on the PA system and announced calmly that two passengers wanted to get off the plane, right then and there. We were headed back to the gate. "What?" we all cried. The good news was that this was only going to take a minute or so, since in the past two hours we had only traveled about five hundred feet. The bad news was that FAA regulations required that security go over all of the stowed luggage to make sure these two people had not accidentally left behind their pipe bombs.

The Latvian woman stared at me quizzically. I explained very slowly and very loudly what was going on. She gaped at me for a long moment. "Ack," she whispered.

Eventually the three of us in row thirty-eight began to read. The other two seemed resigned, but I felt frantic, like I might develop a blinky facial tic at any moment. Time passed underwater.

An hour later the plane finally took off.

We, the citizens of row thirty-eight, all ordered sodas. The Latvian woman put on a Walkman and began to listen with her eyes closed; the Christian man read his book about the Apocalypse; I read *The New Yorker*. Then the seat-belt sign came on, and the pilot's voice came back over the PA system. "I'm afraid we are about to hit some heavy turbulence," he said. "Please return to your seats."

The next minute the plane was bouncing around so hard that we had to hold on to our drinks. "Ack ack ack!" said the Latvian, grabbing for her Sprite.

"Everyone take your seat," the pilot barked over the PA system. "We are in for some rough going." My heart thumped around my chest like a tennis shoe in the dryer.

The plane rose and fell and shook, and the pilot came back on and said sternly, like an angry dad, "Flight attendants, sit down *now!*" And the plane hit huge waves and currents on the choppy sea of sky, and we bounced and moaned and gasped. "Whhhoooooaaa!" we're going down, I thought. I know that a basic tenet of the Christian faith is that death is really just a major change of address, but I had to close my eyes to squinch back tears of terror and loss. Oh, my God, I thought, oh, my God: I'll never see Sam again. This will kill me a second time. The plane bucked and shook without stopping, and the Christian man read calmly, stoically, rather pleased with his composure, it seemed to my tiny, hysterical self. The Latvian closed her eyes and turned up her Walkman. I could hear it softly. And I, praying for a miracle, thought about the miracle I had seen in church.

One of our newer members, a man named Ken Nelson, is dying of AIDS, disintegrating before our very eyes. He came in a year ago with a Jewish woman who comes every week to be with us, although she does not believe in Jesus. Shortly after the man with AIDS started coming, his partner died of the disease. A few weeks later Ken told us that right after Brandon died, Jesus had slid into the hole in his heart that Brandon's loss left, and had been there ever since. Ken has a totally lopsided face, ravaged and emaciated, but when he smiles, he is radiant. He looks like God's crazy nephew Phil. He says that he would gladly pay any price for what he has now, which is Jesus, and us.

There's a woman in the choir named Ranola who is large and beautiful and jovial and black and as devout as can be, who has been a little standoffish toward Ken. She has always looked at him with confusion, when she looks at him at all. Or she looks at him sideways, as if she wouldn't have to quite see him if she didn't look at him head on. She was raised in the South by Baptists who taught her that his way of life—that he—was an abomination. It is hard for her to break through this. I think she and a few other women at church are, on the most visceral level, a little afraid of catching the disease. But Kenny has come to church almost every week for the last year and won almost everyone over. He finally missed a couple of Sundays when he got too weak, and then a month ago he was back, weighing almost no pounds, his face even more lopsided, as if he'd had a stroke. Still, during the prayers of the people, he talked joyously of his life and his decline, of grace and redemption, of how safe and happy he feels these days.

So on this one particular Sunday, for the first hymn, the so-called Morning Hymn, we sang "Jacob's Ladder," which goes, "Every rung goes higher, higher," while ironically Kenny couldn't even stand up. But he sang away sitting down, with the hymnal in his lap. And then when it came time for the second hymn, the Fellowship Hymn, we were to sing "His Eye Is on the Sparrow." The pianist was playing and the whole congregation had risen—

Each time we heard the music we marveled again at the beautiful and often familiar melodies, at the purity of sound, at this miracle that was happening to us amid the cockroaches, the rats, the bedbugs, and the stink of the latrines. The music renewed our sense of human dignity. We had to live under bestial conditions but, by Jove, we could rise above them!
—Helen Colijn, *Song of Survival: Women Interned*

only Ken remained seated, holding the hymnal in his lap—and we began to sing, "Why should I feel discouraged? Why do the shadows fall?" And Ranola watched Ken rather skeptically for a moment, and then her face began to melt and contort like his, and she went to his side and bent down to lift him up—lifted up this white rag doll, this scarecrow. She held him next to her, draped over and against her like a child while they sang. And it pierced me.

I can't imagine anything but music that could have brought about this alchemy. Maybe it's because music is about as physical as it gets: your essential rhythm is your heartbeat; your essential sound, the breath. We're walking temples of noise, and when you add tender hearts to this mix, it somehow lets us meet in places we couldn't get to any other way.

Meanwhile, little by little, the plane grew steadier, and the pilot announced that everything was OK. I was so excited that we were not going to crash and that I might actually get to see Sam again that I started feeling mingly, suddenly wanted the Christian man to be my new best friend. But just as I opened my mouth, the pilot came back once more to ask if there was a doctor on board.

The woman behind us, who turned out to be a nurse, got up and went back to investigate. The Christian man prayed; I tried to rubberneck, but I couldn't see a thing. I went back to thinking about Ken and my church and how on that Sunday, Ranola and Ken, of whom she was so afraid, were trying to sing. He looked like a child who was singing simply because small children sing all the time—they haven't made the separation between speech and music. Then both Ken and Ranola began to cry. Tears were pouring down their faces, and their noses were running like rivers, but as she held him up, she suddenly lay her black weeping face against his feverish white one, put her face right up against his and let all those spooky fluids mingle with hers.

When the nurse sitting behind us returned, she offered the news that a woman in the back was having a heart attack. A heart attack! But there were doctors on hand, and the nurse thought the woman was going to be OK. ·

"Good Lord," said the Christian man. We looked at each other and sighed, and shook our heads, and continued to look at each other.

"God," I said. "I just hope the snakes don't get out of the cargo hold next." The prim apocalyptic man smiled. Then he laughed out loud. The Latvian woman started laughing, although she still had her Walkman on, and while I hate to look like I'm enjoying my own jokes too much, I started laughing too. The three of us sat there in hysterics, and when we were done, the man reached over and patted the back of my hand, smiling gently. The Latvian woman leaned in close to me, into my Soviet air space, and beamed. I leaned forward so that our foreheads touched for just a second. I thought, I do not know if what happened at church was an honest-to-God little miracle, and I don't know if there has been another one here, the smallest possible sort, the size of a tiny bird, but I feel like I am sitting with my cousins on a plane eight miles up, a plane that is going to make it home—and this made me so happy that I suddenly thought, *This is plenty of miracle for me to rest in now.*

Anne Lamott is the author of numerous books, including Blue Shoes, Hard Laughter, Rosie, All New People, Operating Instructions, Crooked Little Heart, *and* Traveling Mercies, *from which this story was excerpted. She lives in Northern California.*

* * *

Awakening the Stone

Was everything she'd been told
about the universe wrong?

I RECALL A WINTER DAY LONG AGO. I WAS LIVING IN IRELAND. I HAD driven from Dublin up into the mountains, feeling depressed and despondent. I took no pleasure in my studies, was bored and restless during serious conversations with my friends.

Looking back, I recognize this urgent dissatisfaction as the beginning of initiation. It is a time of dislocation. One grows tired of one's favorite food, can't sleep at night, gives up on the books and music one loves best, loses interest in even the oldest and most loyal obsessions, stands up suddenly in the midst of conversations, walks about by oneself, writes down scraps of thought on scraps of paper, looks for counsel in familiar places, hears nothing worth listening to, frowns, alienates friends, eats too much or stops eating much at all, feels dreadfully tired and sick of it all and at the same time as if one were in a state of unbearable suspense, waiting for the phone to ring, for the mail to arrive, for that stranger to walk around the corner. And meanwhile nothing happens and everything is just about to happen and you are, you think, too old for this sort of thing and then the despondency starts to grow and the anxiety becomes more acute and you know you're up against it, whatever it is. You can't turn back. Have you gone forward? You can't go forward. Where is there to go?

It was a cold day, I remember clearly. There was frost on the ground. Up in the mountains the trees were covered with a thin coating of ice. I was on my way to a spot my friends and I visited frequently, where we would go for picnics and drink stout and wrap ourselves in blankets and shiver, even in summer, in the cold. To get there, we had always driven past the Powerscourt Estate, but we had never stopped to visit. This time I stopped. I pulled over to the right and got out of the car, stamping my feet, slapping my hands against my thighs.

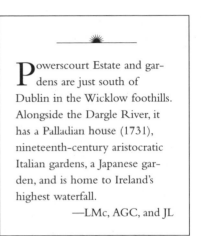

Powerscourt Estate and gardens are just south of Dublin in the Wicklow foothills. Alongside the Dargle River, it has a Palladian house (1731), nineteenth-century aristocratic Italian gardens, a Japanese garden, and is home to Ireland's highest waterfall.

—LMc, AGC, and JL

An old man came out of the gatehouse; he was surprised to see me, touched his finger to his cap, showed me the bell on the gate. A scrappy dog growled and came toward me, tugging at his rope. I had several cookies in my pocket. I threw one to him. He jumped up and caught it in the air, his stump of a tail wagging furiously. The gate swung back a few feet; I walked through and turned to wave at the old man, who locked it behind me.

So there I was, a visitor to the Powerscourt Estate, locked in until I rang the bell and threw cookies to the dog to make my way out again. Well, why not? This is why not. From the moment the old man disappeared into the gatehouse again I felt a panic of loneliness, as if I'd been left alone in a world of strangers. I wanted to run back to the car and head out for Dublin, but I was ashamed to face the old man again.

The road was smooth and level; it was kept free of rocks and ran along a slight incline on which trees were densely planted. Their leaves had turned yellow but had not dropped from the branches. They seemed strange and otherworldly, but I kept looking at them with a childlike curiosity. Whenever the breeze rose the leaves chimed together and made a desolate, frozen rattle.

Then, from out of my panic and despondency, there came an odd sensation. I felt as if I were a small girl, with little hands and legs. My entire body surged with delight, as if it had just discovered the pleasure of being a body. I jumped a fallen tree, climbed a rock, leaped down again, ran on. Soon, I came upon a flock of black sheep, grazing below me near a cluster of trees. There was not a single white sheep among them. All around me the colors were growing deeper and richer, the air was saturated with light. The flock of black sheep seemed to be grazing joyfully upon a grass so vibrant I could scarcely believe it was a material substance. Then I noticed the gray stones scattered about here and there in the field; they, too, were vibrating and pulsing with the same kind of intensity. "They're alive," I gasped. Nature, which I'd always imagined a brute dead stuff, had some kind of vivid life to it.

I had by then reached the valley's farthest edge. With every step I took, I was intending to go back. There was something uncanny in the place, bringing out something weird in me. I did not want to think that stones were alive. I did not want the logical categories through which I ordered the world to break down and desert me. I was addicted to what I then called rationality—to holding the world view the men of my time thought most plausible. Humans had consciousness and spirit and feelings. Trees and stones and sheep did not. I wanted to get out of anyplace that was teaching me anything else.

But then I noticed a waterfall pouring down a steep rock face that dropped precipitously into the river, and I was running toward it. Below me was a rock pool, churning and foaming with a peculiar gleefulness. I stood there laughing back at it and then, all at once, I had the strong desire to throw off my clothes and immerse myself in the pool. I looked around me. The valley was deserted. The sheep grazed quietly; from the distance I heard the rattle from the frozen leaves. "Do it, do it," something in me kept urging, from a child's sense of delight in what should not be done. But who had decided what was and was not permitted? Here I was, a woman of the twentieth century, capable of making my own way in the world, presumably liberated, but in reality chained by unquestioned assumptions about the way thinking was to take place and the world was to be experienced and I, myself, was to behave.

I turned back toward the valley. Light was pouring down over the black sheep and the green fields as if someone has just lifted a bucket and were watering everything in sight. I looked up and saw that this light was flooding down from a sky that was not any longer a sky. It was, as I looked, withdrawing behind shimmering veils of blue light. And now the whole valley became one great wave of light, rising and falling, shaping and dissolving. My idea that the sky was a sky and the tree a tree, separate and distinguishable from one another, had to be questioned. Here they were dissolving into one another. Was it possible everything I had been told about the universe was simply an assumption, a style of perception, rather than truth?

It was too late to flee from the place. I, the rationalist, was in the grip of extreme emotion. I could fight it off, run away, or surrender and find out what it meant. I found myself before an immense tree. Near the bottom it had been split almost in two by lightning and in the charred, concave base, a brilliant green-and-yellow lichen was growing. I stared at the tree, a natural altar. I wondered, had the Druids worshipped this tree? I tried to distract myself with this thought and meanwhile my body was doing something peculiar. I noticed it, thought I should fight it, was doing it anyway. Then it was done. There I was, on the ground in front of the tree. Tears streaming down my face. I, raised in a family of Marxist atheists, down on my knees, worshipping?

Kim Chernin is a novelist, a poet, and the author of several nonfiction books, including The Hungry Self, The Woman Who Gave Birth to Her Mother: Tales of Transformation in Women's Lives, In My Mother's House, *and* Reinventing Eve: Modern Woman in Search of Herself, *from which this story was excerpted. She lives in the San Francisco Bay Area, where she is a psychoanalyst in private practice.*

CHERILYN PARSONS

✦ ✦ ✦

Mother to the World

Not all mothers bear children.

I AM FEEDING A CHILD IN SHISHU BHAVAN, MOTHER TERESA'S orphanage in Calcutta. I give him tiny spoonfuls so he won't choke on this stew of rice, carrots, peas, and curry that the Missionaries of Charity have prepared. I cut the carrots, keep the food toward the end of the spoon, and wait until he swallows before giving him another bite. It is taking over an hour to feed him.

His giant brown eyes, fringed with lashes, move from the food to my face as if he needs my gaze as much as the rice. I'm keeping tears down, intent on doing this work. He has a huge belly from malnourishment, spindly limbs, and a tiny chest racked with advanced tuberculosis. Except for opening and closing his mouth, he is very still. It's impossible to tell his age. He looks about a year old, but I was told by the Sisters that he is probably four or five. He has no name.

It's the middle of heat season. I smell the fetid odor of this child's flesh. His urine flows like water through his body, which doesn't remember how to absorb. I smell my own body, damp and dirty in the sweltering humidity. Sweat drips between the crooks of my elbows and knees as I sit cross-legged in my cotton dress. I feel faint from this heat but keep lifting the spoon, my eyes riveted on this child who depends utterly on women he doesn't know.

This ageless, nameless boy was left abandoned on Mother Teresa's doorstep, as many children are. Perhaps this boy's biological mother is dead, or simply so poor that she couldn't care for him—except by leaving him where he might have a chance of life, or at least a more comfortable death.

My first days volunteering for Mother Teresa were spent playing with the older children before I was trusted in the nursery. The older children are long-term residents at Shishu Bhavan. They range from about three years old to twelve. A vibrant, demanding girl named Radha seemed determined to walk (and fall) in spite of her polio. Leaning over to hold her up, I walked her around the room so many times that my back ached. Then I carried other children whose polio was so bad that their legs hung thin, soft, and useless. I held Dasa at the window for hours, my arms cradling him carefully so I wouldn't crush his limp legs. He loved to play with the latch and figure out how it worked. Some of the children are mentally disabled, and they cry and hit when I set them back down after holding them. Two girls are blind and beat their fists on their heads and ears as if to stop a terrible din inside.

I've changed numerous diapers made of *lungis*, the triangular scraps of cloth that men all over India wear. No Pampers here, wicking away moisture to keep bottoms dry. The *lungis* are made of cloth woven at Titagarh, a nearby colony operated by Mother Teresa which houses people healing from leprosy.

Calcutta is the most intense, horrible, wonderful place in the world because it forces you to ask not only what life means, but what your responsibility is to life. When I walked into Shishu Bhavan for the first time, I was overwhelmed by tenderness, outrage, exhaustion, impotence at these problems, and anger at the parents and society which create such anguish. I was dazed at the complexity of issues that build this orphanage as surely as bricks do. I was appalled at the Catholic Church and Mother Teresa for resisting birth control. Stunned at the compassion of the nuns in serving these children. Upset at how limited their response could be: these still aren't happy kids.

Most of all, I was thrown back to stare at what my response should be to the world, especially as embodied in the lives of children. The fact that I am a childless woman doesn't matter; and if I were a man it wouldn't matter either. We all give birth to the world around us.

Sister Charmaine, who runs Shishu Bhavan, said to me, "What matters is for each of us to do what we can. And what is that? Isn't it love? Isn't that all? To do that however we can?"

But what does love mean? Why was I volunteering here? It had taken me a week after arriving in Calcutta, the halfway point on my round-the-world journey, to gather the courage to inquire about working for Mother Teresa. I felt shy about trying to love, if that's what I could call it—about believing that I, a young professional from Los Angeles, would have anything to give the struggling children in Shishu Bhavan. I couldn't presume to be a mother, much less a Missionary of Charity. Surely I was just assuaging guilt. My volunteering probably would help me far more than them. And my gift was nothing compared to the suffering that India makes you see.

But traveling itself makes

For millennia women have dedicated themselves almost exclusively to the task of nurturing, protecting, and caring for the young and the old, striving for the conditions of peace that favor life as a whole...to the best of my knowledge, no war was ever started by women. But it is women and children who have always suffered most in situations of conflict. Now that we are gaining control of the primary historical role imposed on us of sustaining life in the context of home and family, it is time to apply in the arena of the world the wisdom and experience thus gained in activities of peace over so many thousands of years.

—Aung San Suu Kyi, recipient of the 1991 Nobel Peace Prize, a speech given at the 1995 Beijing Women's Conference you see, too, not only what is outside but what is inside. Travel is about transformation. It is about discoveries of all sorts. It was easier for me to jump alone on a bus to a remote village—an act which many people would call courageous—than to travel the inner territory where my heart might be broken and I just might grow up. I had to try.

I walked through the congested, filthy streets toward "the Motherhouse" to inquire about volunteering. The street numbering wasn't clear, but everyone knew how to find "the Mother." I turned down a mud alley off a busy street. A little brass card saying "M. Teresa" and "Sisters of Charity" marked the door of an undistinguished three-story building with brown wooden shutters.

Sister Dolores, the Volunteer Coordinator, gave me a cordial and businesslike welcome. In the plain rooms, which were furnished only as much as needed, was serene activity. The house was built around a large courtyard where other Sisters were doing laundry in large buckets. Some of the women wore white cotton saris edged with blue, while others had plain white saris. The women themselves were brown, yellow, white, or black skinned.

Sister Dolores heard my concerns. The cloth draped over her head framed clear, dark eyes. "The Mother says that if the volunteers gain more than they give, that is fine," she explained in lilting, formal English. "It is beneficial simply to be a witness to the work, even for a single day. Then you can use it in your own home, can you not?"

She waited for me to answer.

"Yes," I said. It felt like a commitment.

"There is nothing wrong with gaining spiritually because this kind of gaining does not take from other people—but wants to give even more."

I thought of my life at home and the hoarding of things, experiences, money, and favors, as if fearing that someday there might not be enough. I seemed to assume life was a zero-sum game—wasn't it?

"The Mother is out right now but will be here on Saturday,"

Sister Dolores said. "You might be able to meet her at Mass then. You are always welcome to join us."

I wasn't Catholic or even religious, but I decided to go to that Mass. And I signed up to work at Shishu Bhavan, the orphanage for disabled, sick, and dying children.

The Missionaries of Charity also invited me to visit Titagarh, the leper colony, which proved to be the cleanest and one of the happiest places I'd seen in India. Most of Titagarh's men and women had lived ordinary lives with good jobs before leprosy struck and they were cast out. At Titagarh they wove cloth for Mother Teresa's missions and formed new families—what we might call "nontraditional families." Though they received medicines to cure their leprosy, the stigma remained, and so did they. Their gardens were filled with vegetables and flowers. The buildings were a rainbow of colors. A school on the grounds served the children of residents, or children with leprosy themselves. Everyone acted as these children's mothers and fathers.

In the evenings in my air-conditioned hotel, I read books on Mother Teresa. "Being unwanted," she said, "is the most terrible disease that human beings can experience.... Today it is the greatest disease, to be unwanted, unloved, just left alone, a throwaway of society.... In the West, there is loneliness which I call the leprosy of the West."

Leprosy eats at the body. The polio of the children in Shishu Bhavan had left them unable to move. I had embarked upon my long trip because anxiety was eating at me. I had felt paralyzed. My boyfriend didn't seem to be the right partner. I had a job I didn't care about. What was my purpose, my meaning? On my breaks from Shishu Bhavan I wandered the wrenching streets of Calcutta: pandemonium outside, just like I felt pandemonium inside.

Oh the heavy air! I swam through the city, sliding, gasping through the heat; leapt from dry spot to brick on the streets to avoid the puddles and mud; pushed through masses of people crowding narrow sidewalks lined with sizzling pots and ovens selling *pakoras*, sugarcane juice, rice, and something curried that was wrapped in giant flat leaves. I had to keep my eyes on the ground to avoid stepping in feces—from cows, dogs, humans—mingled with mud and pools of greasy frothy water. Little stinging insects flew through the air to get into my clothes.

I gave a five-rupee coin to a woman beggar with a baby on her arm then fended off others who ran to me, beseeching, flinging their silent babies in my face. A thin old man who resembled a diagram of muscles and skeleton ran like a horse as he pulled a rickshaw. The Bengalis, the intelligentsia of India, hung onto buses inching through gridlocked intersections. Slums seethed outside the city center.

The city had been called "Calcutta" thanks to a mispronunciation by the English of the city's real name: Kali-Kata, named after Kali, the fierce Hindu goddess who still demands and receives sacrifices of blood, the symbol across all cultures of the terrible power of the female, capable of menstruation and childbirth. She is worshipped by thousands who chant "Kali Ma, Kali Ma"—Mother Kali—and heap garlands of beautiful flowers over her savage face. They shower her with rice, a symbol of nourishment. Kali is the intersection of love and ferocity, the essence of a mother. She would be impatient, I knew, with my despair.

On Saturday, I walked across the city at five o'clock in the morning to attend the Mass. The Sisters filed into a room on the second floor of the Motherhouse. I had learned by now that the blue-edged saris belonged to fully ordained Sisters, while a plain white one meant that the woman was still a novice, not yet having taken her final vows. I had also heard that Mother Teresa once declined an invitation to meet the Pope when he asked that she wear a regular nun's habit instead of the sari.

I sat with the novices on the floor, my eyes searching for Mother Teresa—Nobel Prize winner, saint of the gutters, organizational genius who had built an empire of missions around the world but owned nothing. Many people, including me, disagreed with her doctrine, but that didn't seem to matter: merely the mention of her name or the sight of one of her white-clad nuns could part the chaos on a street in Calcutta like Moses parting the Red Sea.

I saw a tiny woman bent almost double walking in with some of the Sisters. She sat on the floor among them, not distinguishing herself in any way. As she lifted her head to greet the women around her, I saw that this was Teresa. Her face was carved deeply with wrinkles. It was difficult to see her expressions because the light was low and her head was bowed as the Mass began: a male priest, the only man present, leading the service.

The Sisters were murmuring, chanting, and praying: Lord, give me strength; Lord, let me see you in the poor, in everyone, everywhere. The god to whom these women prayed was male, but I closed my eyes and felt the presence of the female. India is the only country in the world where most of the people still worship goddesses, whether they come in the form of Lakshmi, the goddess of wealth in all its manifestations; Durga, the protectress who slays demons; Kali, power; Saraswati, wisdom; Parvati, beauty; or the holy river Ganges, goddess incarnate bestowing salvation—salves to our suffering. The force of the universe is called Shakti, the primal female energy as

> ───── ✸ ─────
>
> I did not always believe in God. I was not even interested in believing. But I did want with a terrible longing and restlessness, to find a meaning in life, a purpose behind it, a direction for it. I was willing to examine with unprejudiced mind every philosophy, every religion, for small hints of truth. I spent many hours reading, questioning, wondering. And one day when my soul was open and receptive, it was suddenly charged through and through by something shocking, galvanic, almost frighteningly vibrant, was suddenly flooded, irradiated by something inexplicable and beautiful and altogether overwhelming. I had not been looking for God. But to cover the impressive magnitude of my soul's experience, I found only one word—God. It was wrung from my lips and I said it aloud, "God!"
>
> —Nancy Pope Mayorga,
> *The Hunger of the Soul: A
> Spiritual Diary*

expressed in a woman's potential to give birth—the gift of life, the world itself. All of India is a Motherhouse.

So what does it mean to be a mother? On my last day in Calcutta, as I'm feeding the dying child, a single grain of rice falls off my spoon to the floor. I don't notice, but the boy does. His hand seizes the grain and thrusts it into his mouth.

That second, my heart breaks open. I ask: Am I worthy of the trust of a starving child who notices when a single grain of rice falls? Do we, both women and men, dare open our hearts to all human beings? There is no greater aspiration, no better journey.

Cherilyn Parsons started writing when she was five and traveling alone when she was nineteen. She has a Masters in Professional Writing from USC and has ghostwritten books, written and edited a variety of articles, and taught at universities—all to support the habit of hopping a plane to travel for months at a time. She is also active in human rights work and holds a long-running conversation "salon" from her home in Santa Monica, California.

SUSANA HERRERA

⋆ ⋆ ⋆

Jam Bah Doo Nah?

A Peace Corps volunteer learns
to be "in her skin."

I STARE OUT THE WINDOW, ACROSS THE DIRT ROAD, AND BEYOND the field to where a circle of women are washing clothes at the well. I watch, but they can't see me. I hide here alone. I am dressed in their traditional clothes—a sarong of green, blue, and bright yellow with a top cut from the same cloth. I feel as if I'm made up for a costume ball. Even my expression is a cleverly designed mask so they can't see my longing, so they won't be able to tell that I'm terrified they'll reject me or make me feel like I don't belong.

I hear the women laughing, and they don't hold anything back. Their shoulders rise and fall like wings of birds. One woman playfully whacks another on the shoulder with a wet, twisted cloth, and they burst out laughing. They are the most beautiful and graceful women I have ever seen. In their sarongs and matching blouses, their lovely skin is the darkest black, and my hand aches to touch their velvet cheeks.

I yearn to sit with the women upon a decorated stool cut from a tree trunk and made for women's work. I'd like to sit beside them finely dressed in a bright Cameroonian cloth while my hair is combed and braided by the young girls whose lightning fingers whip and tie strands of African hair. I long to understand their native tongue, to laugh with them, to throw my head back in surrender to their joy.

It's been so long since I've laughed with someone until my cheeks hurt. Although I haven't spoken to anyone in English for five days, it feels like years. Time in the desert is endless, without bounds. I have so much to say to anyone who will listen about what I'm witnessing out here in the bush.

The women scrub fervently, creating more suds than any washing machine. At the opposite end of the circle, a woman finishes her bucket of laundry and pushes it aside. She scoots her stool closer to the woman sitting next to her and eagerly dives in to help her finish. Another woman finishes and gathers her own bucket and a few of those of her friends and gets in line at the well to fill them for rinsing.

The women go back to their laundry but continue to tease each other. Another woman throws a wet garment at a friend, who shrieks with delight and throws it back. Their playful voices make their language sound like a sun-drenched song.

What are they so happy about?

Here I am, dying of thirst, and I dread going out there among them. I've been using water sparingly, afraid of looking like a *nasara* fool at the well in front of the women. I've never pumped water before, and I certainly don't know anything about carrying a bucket on my head. What I wouldn't give for a Peace Corps post with a water faucet, a toilet, and shower.

The lizard is here again, crawling toward my windowsill.

"I'm going to die out here," I say to him. (He's the only friend I've made so far.) The lizard nods and returns to his push-ups, seeming to agree that I'd better do something.

I watch the women and children across the way doing their daily routine so easily, washing clothes and dishes, pumping water, and carrying buckets effortlessly back home on their heads.

I can't do that. There's no way I can do that!

They've been balancing water buckets on their heads since they were children, and suddenly, at twenty-three years old, I'm going to attempt it? I really don't think I can do any of this. How do I mount the water pump and pressurize it so that water will pour out? What if I slip off the pedal and look like an idiot trying?

They have old metal buckets for a specific reason I don't yet understand. What will they think of my new blue plastic buckets that no one else has?

They'll laugh at my buckets. They'll laugh at me.

What did I really imagine the Peace Corps would be like? Not like this. Nothing like this.

I feel white. Naked. A foreigner without the skill to survive out here in their desert, their millet fields, their world without water, their world that I know nothing about. I am supposed to be a teacher here? I don't even know how to take care of myself, to fulfill my basic need for water and food. Where do I begin to learn how to live their way?

I stare out the window again. My neighbor Clotilde has arrived at the well. She has the warmest eyes in Cameroon, like chocolate melting in the sun. From the jungle, she stands out as different from the others. With her high cheekbones and a longer forehead, she seems almost white. Clotilde is diminutive, much shorter and more slender than Tapouri women. Her husband, Yves, a science teacher, will be my colleague for two years. Clotilde has made peace with the women and has become a part of their daily lives. From them, she has learned to survive in the desert. She knows she cannot do it alone.

Clotilde greets every woman in the circle by raising both hands open-palmed in front of her chest and asking, "*Jam bah doo nah?*"

It means, "Are you in your skin?" Or a better translation would be, "Is your soul in your body?" The Tapouri women all say, "Yes. Oh, yes, we are alive," they say.

They receive her greeting by offering their right wrists for her to shake instead of their wet hands and exclaim, "*Jam core doo may!*" I am in my skin!

I watch their exchange and repeat to myself, "*Jam bah doo nah? Jam core doo may!*"

The circle opens up, with the women pushing their buckets and stools back so Clotilde can sit among them. Clotilde first helps the woman sitting next to her with her laundry. Another woman brings a fresh bucket for Clotilde to wash her clothes.

Now would be the time to go, I say to myself, because someone I know is there and can help me. I pick up my buckets, and move across the room in a hurry before I change my mind. I didn't come all the way to Africa to die.

I am alive.

I am in my skin!

"*Jam core doo may!*" I say to myself as I take the first step out my door. Now everyone can see me. Everyone is curious. Everyone stares at the white woman coming out of her house like Lazarus from the tomb. The children stop playing to look. The students living in the hut next door stand up from their washing and stop to watch me. The neighbors, bending over in their peanut fields, hands deep in soil, wave, and wipe away the sweat from their foreheads and necks. I wave back as I head toward the well.

As soon as the women see me, they stop laughing.

They stop playing, and they stop washing. They don't do anything. They just stare at me.

I stare back. I have suddenly forgotten all the greetings I know in their language.

It would be easy to run, to give up right here, to call this a mistake, to take the first bush taxi out of Guidiguis tomorrow morning and go straight to Peace Corps headquarters, a three days' journey away. It would be easy to race back to the land of indoor plumbing, bottled water, and pizza deliveries.

After a long, still, and silent moment, Clotilde jumps off her stool and wipes her hand on the back of her skirt. She offers her wrist for me to shake, and I do. "*Jam bah doo nah?*" she asks.

"*Jam core doo may!*" I say.

I am in my skin like never before. I am in my skin like I hadn't thought possible. I am aware that my soul is in my body. I am here, fully present—and frightened to death.

I want to hug Clotilde tight and to tell her that she's just saved my life, to say that, without her, I had wanted to die of thirst all alone in my house. Even if I had the words, I'm not sure she'd understand if I was joking or serious. So I remain motionless, like an animal crouched in between the moment of hiding and discovery.

Clotilde takes one of my buckets and smiles at me. I relax and smile back. The women begin to wash again, and I follow Clotilde to the water pump. I know the women are speaking about me. I hear "*nasara*," but it doesn't bother me this time. I understand that it's not so much my skin color that they are referring to by using "*nasara*" but everything about me that's different or other or doesn't fit in. It's the quick steps I take, how my long hair sways when I move, my tentative smile, my nervous hands, the way I don't know how to survive in the desert. Everything says that I don't belong.

But I'm here to try.

Clotilde heads straight to the front of the line and replaces the bucket underneath the water pump with my blue one. The young girl who is pumping nods at Clotilde. Then she smiles at me, melting away my fears with the compassion revealed in her steady gaze.

I'm afraid that cutting in front of everyone is rude, and I search the eyes of those in line—but Clotilde, by reaching out and touching my arm, assures me that everything is fine. The girl pumps the pedal twice, then pulls it up high with her foot. Next she jumps on the pedal, riding it up and down. With one hand, she wipes her forehead and the front of her neck while, with the other hand, she holds on tightly to

> As she spoke, I thought of how funny it was that two lives meeting for only a moment could connect and inspire. A year and a half relationship with one person or five minutes with another could alter a life. Her free spirit embraced me and she left a spark on my recently dimmed surface.
>
> —Jean Bucaria,
> "The Encounter"

the pump handlebars. It doesn't look so hard. It's like riding a bike standing up and with only one pedal. I can do this!

When the bucket is full, Clotilde replaces it with my other one. The girl finishes pumping that bucket, and then the next in line puts hers underneath the spout and the girl continues pumping.

"*Oh say ko, oh say ko jour,*" thank you very much, I say to the girl.

"*Mon amie, c'est le temps d'apprendre comment tu vas porter l'eau,*" Clotilde says. My friend, it's time to learn how you're going to carry water.

I nod and agree. But how?

Clotilde tells me that it's in the hips that one balances, it's in the center of the body that we find our balance. It's not the head that does the work but a place in our belly that knows where to take the next step. Clotilde demonstrates. She bends her knees, lifts the bucket, and places it perfectly on her head. She smiles, then sets the bucket back on the ground.

I can feel everyone watching. "I can do this," I say to myself.

I am in my skin.

I bend my knees. My hands grab each side of the bucket while Clotilde holds the handle.

"*Un, deux, trois,*" she says, and we lift together. As I lift the bucket, I stand up straight. She doesn't let go, and I'm glad because I don't yet have a sense of balance. I try to find it in my hips, in my center, but I'm not sure if I have it or not. Clotilde lets go, and I hold the bucket up on my head with two hands. Clotilde puts her hand on my hips and looks into my eyes.

"You need to find your center here," she says. I close my eyes and concentrate. I remember the first time I learned to ride a bicycle. My father kept telling me to find my balance, and I didn't know what balance was until somehow I just felt it. I try to find it now—to remember what it felt like to find it for the first time as a child on my bike.

And there it is. I can feel it. Balance is a focused pulse in my belly that frees me to move my body with ease. The bucket rests perfectly on my head. I open my eyes. Clotilde is looking directly at me. So are the women. So are the children. I take another step.

The water laps against the sides of the bucket and spills over. Still no one moves. I take another step and drop one hand to my side. I take a few more steps. I relax. More water spills over the side. I can hear rustling behind me as the women resume their work.

I'm walking slowly now, feeling proud of myself, still not daring to release the other hand from the bucket. I look toward my little cement house and smile; I'm almost there. And then my foot slips, and my ankle twists. I try to maintain the balance, but the bucket is tilting too far. I try to keep up with little, quick steps; water splashes over me.

My ankle gives way. I see the sand swirling around me as the bucket topples. I fall hard and land sprawled in the middle of the dirt road. For a moment, there is silence. And then the women laugh like wild hyenas.

I can't get up. I'm caught in my sarong.

I wipe my face and brush back my wet hair. The laughter stings, and I can hear my ankle screaming for attention. I finally find the opening of my sarong, untangle the long cloth from my legs, and retie it. As I stand up, I'm surprised to hear my own voice cry out.

I fall again, and the women laugh even harder. How can they keep laughing like that?

Clotilde approaches and squats next to me. She gently turns my ankle. I clench my jaw so as not to show weakness. Clotilde pushes further, and I cry out. She shakes her head and reaches out to help me up.

The young girl comes and picks up my bucket and returns to the well to fill it. Clotilde puts her hand around my waist, and I put an arm around her shoulder. We walk to my house. The young girl soon arrives carrying a bucket full of water.

When we get to my door, she opens it for me and helps me inside. She asks again, as if reminding me of what's really important, "*Jam bah doo nah*, Suzanne?"

"*Oho*," I say. "*Jam core doo may!*"

The experience didn't kill me.

I am in my skin.

I am alive!

Susana Herrera is the author of Mango Elephants in the Sun: How Life in an African Village Let Me Be in My Skin, *a book that chronicles her spiritual journey as a Peace Corps teacher in Cameroon. She now teaches in a high school in Santa Cruz, California, and is writing a book about four generations of her Navajo/Spanish family history.*

EMILY HIESTAND

✦ ✦ ✦

Renewing the Sun

A pagan ritual entices a traveler
during the summer solstice.

NEAR DUSK ONE NIGHT ON LÉSVOS I AM HEADING BACK TO Afrodite's Rooms-to-Let through a small woods. Rounding a bend in the path, I come upon a group of women and children lighting three large brush bonfires on a scruff of beach at the outer edge of the village. As the women touch matches to the three piles of brush, the sun is just setting, and for half an hour—until the bonfires somewhat burn down—four orange-red shapes flare against the evening sky. As the sun slips into the sea and the flames diminish, the women and their children turn into silhouettes against the sky and sea. One skinny boy, about nine, suddenly bolts from the cluster and leaps over all the fires, one after another, whooping. His small, wiry boy-body, at apogee over the low flames, looks like a twisting shape the fire has thrown up. Now a girl runs forward and jumps over the fires, and then all the children do, sometimes several times, like kids shooting down slides then running around to do it again. The mothers stand talking along the seawall, their plump bodies, black skirts, and olive skins glowing in the heat. When the fires burn still lower, the children gather stones from the beach and begin hurling them into the embers. It is the twenty-first of June, Saint John's Eve on the Christian calendar, a quasi-advent that foreshadows the winter arrival of the Savior. And on the pagan calendar tonight is the summer solstice, one of the two great turning points in the year. These hours exactly mark the time that shorter, colder days begin. In the old culture, tonight was the night of bonfires, lit all over Europe to signal, or perhaps ritually renew, the sun's waning energy.

Along the wall, one of the mothers recognizes me from the English lessons; she waves and I join her near the fires, which are still giving off a great wall of heat. She says that the girls and boys are jumping over the fires so that they will be fertile, and she encourages me to jump too. The children are excited that an adult might join them. The fires are mostly crackling-hot stones by now, with only low flames and rogue licks leaping up; still, there is a moment of thrilled fear, sailing over the heat. Afterward, a boy named Alekos gives me two stones and tells me to throw them in the fire. When I do, he shrieks the Greek child's unparalleled shriek. The matronly women (who are probably ten years younger than I) giggle and look pleased with themselves. We stay until the stones grow cold and the light fails, and the women, who leapt over fires themselves not so long ago, round up their happy, spent children and go home. Unaware of their beauty, the uncountable leaves of the surrounding olive trees darken into the concentrate of all color.

Emily Hiestand's most recent work is Angela, the Upside Down Girl, *a book of essays. This story was excerpted from her book* The Very Rich Hours: Travels in Orkney, Belize, the Everglades, and Greece.

The Way Back

*A prodigal daughter returns
to reclaim her birthright.*

FLYING TO NEW YORK, I FEEL LIKE A TIME TRAVELER. I LOOK around at the other passengers, going or returning for pleasure, perhaps a few for business. We are fellow travelers in body only.

Not for me the New York of the theatre, or of the long sleek avenues, or of museums or even shopping. The New York I visit, while not Chasidic, is its own kind of *shtetl*. A section of Brooklyn in which one enters a time warp. A distillation to one way of living, to a world where one encounters only one's kind. Its inhabitants stroll up and down the main avenue on their errands like in a small village, greeting each other on either side of the Korean fruit stands, or in line at Chiffon's bakery. The women pull the hands of their pale, dawdling children. They don't see the others—the Korean shopkeepers, the African American children with their mother, the Puerto Rican couple, the Italian teenagers passing in a boisterous group. They are thinking about what they will cook for Shabbos. When they return home, the light is gone and many of their husbands are home from work and are silently facing east, praying *Ma'ariv*, the evening prayer.

"It must have taken a lot of courage," friends have said, "to crawl out of that world." "That world," two innocent words that contain, cupped like two small hands, the whole of my childhood. The magnificent moments, the difficult moments, the slowly growing certainty that I was not of their world. That difficult as it might be, I had to leave and find my own place. How to explain the lack of air? A world that circled in on itself, wove its own logic, built its own fences? How to explain, too, what I lost when I left?

The short flight from Boston to New York is like a flight into the eye of a hurricane. My lovely, worldly, wildly diverse neighborhood and community in Cambridge, Massachusetts, dissolves like a chimera, as if it had no substance.

The plane descends into a thick cluster of clouds, begins to rumble and shake, the sky invisible on either side. Just a soft whiteness blotting out the world. I find myself holding my breath as that whiteness outside the window pulls me slowly backward into memory. In the memory that rises, I am surrounded on all sides by the white folds of my father's tallit. I am around seven or eight, young enough to still be allowed into the province of men in an orthodox synagogue. My father, the Rabbi, summons me to him as he always does when the Cantor announces Birchat Kohanim, and I run, released from the women's section, to the storm of men gathering in the center of the sanctuary.

Under the cover of my father's tallit, his hands on my head, I rock as he rocks, enter the trance of his prayer. I know that from the outside, all that is visible is a sea of tallitim swaying, the white, uncertain motion of ghosts. But within, as was whispered about the ancient Holy of Holies, I can feel the rumble of the earth beneath us, know the urgency of the sky opening briefly and the tendrils of my father's prayers curling upward in a reverse gravity.

In the white cave of my father's tallit, I can imagine clearly what I had just learned in school: that on Yom Kippur, the high priest—having prepared himself for weeks—entered, terrified, the holy sanctuary where no man could accompany or save him. With great care, he would let the tip of his sash trail under the large door so that the public, forbidden from entering this room, would be able to retrieve his body should he not survive this encounter. Then he would face a reckoning with more than his senses could muster,

his white robes shivering in anticipation as he asked for absolution
for the sins of his tribe, the large squares of his *Urim vetumim* almost
electrocuting him with the light they were refracting.

The memory stops there as if it had encountered a wall. It drops
off into an abyss, disconnected from whatever followed.

Instead, what I remember next is how at thirteen or fourteen,
watching my father take his place among the men, I had understood—as my mother silently placed a siddur in my lap, pointed to
the words as if they could substitute—that I would no longer be
able to know certain truths from within. That instead of coming
into an age of privilege, leaving girlhood, I had had to relinquish
my passkey.

I was no longer welcome under the tallit, and the rituals, once
these pulsing enigmatic entities, alive in and of themselves, were
just a collection of motions
and prayers that turned to me
their impenetrable shell—
that never again let me
glimpse the soft belly of their
life, the fever of their pulse. I
saw men bowing, the Torah
scrolls held high in pride, the
palm fronds bending wist-
fully in every direction, the
ark of the covenant closing
with a snap.

We are already over New
York. It sprawls out for miles
beneath us as we begin our
slow and gentle descent. I
can no longer avoid thinking about why I am here,
about the ritual I am about
to attend. The wedding of
my sister whom I have not

It's winter and there is smoke
from the fires. The square,
lighted windows of houses are
fogging over. It is a world of
elemental attention, of all things
working together, listening to
what speaks in the blood.
Whichever road I follow, I walk
in the land of many gods, and
they love and eat one another.
Walking, I am listening to a
deeper way. Suddenly all my
ancestors are behind me. Be
still, they say. Watch and listen.
You are the result of the love of
thousands.
　　　　—Linda Hogan, *Dwellings:*
　　　　　　　A Spiritual History of
　　　　　　　　　the Living World

seen in five years, who has stopped speaking to me because my life choices have so departed from what was proscribed by our upbringing. Because the man I married was not Jewish, the stepchild I have parented is not Jewish, my own son is, but is still so foreign to them with his lack of tribal fears and hatreds.

I wonder who I will see, what I will feel. How I will protect myself from the stares and accusations. From the vortex of emotions sure to arise. Because I have insisted on remaining with my uncertainty—my palms open to the world—my life more than once knocked and thrown against the rocks. Still I have refused to climb back into the walled fortress of this world. How will I mingle, for even an evening, among all of these people who choose to see me as lost—who don't understand that I accept the bruises and uncertainty to have the richness and complexity that is the world?

The plane dips its left wing and I feel as if it is bowing respectfully to the powerful city below us. I can feel the old fears beginning to rise. The memories of all the other visits. Of all the times I'd needed to censor stories, censor my language, my very existence. Of all the times I'd struggled to hold on to the conviction that my choices were valid and real, despite my family's refusal to look at them. Even now my husband and son are not invited, their existence denied in public by my parents so that I had debated whether to even come to the wedding without them. The members of my family, I decide, are magicians. They have spent their lives rendering the invisible, visible; and years rendering the concrete and vital lives of my husband and son, vapor, an illusion, a secret just between us.

The plane lowers itself like a graceful heron into this large and complicated city. I step into a cab that, after a few minutes, begins speeding unambivalently toward Brooklyn. The cab flies down the Grand Central Parkway, then the BQE, then turns onto the Prospect Expressway. Before I know it, the walls of the Prospect Expressway are receding and the cab is slowing for the familiar lights of Ocean Parkway. As we crawl forward, light by light, I am surrounded by the visual palette of my childhood—men in dark frock coats and black hats hurrying to or from synagogue, their gaze cast downward, lest it accidentally graze the form of a woman. Some old couples strolling slowly, some modern Orthodox young men talking all at once, their knitted yamulkahs identifying their credo of living in both the religious and secular worlds. A few women, their hair modestly covered, are pushing baby carriages overflowing with kids.

In the midst of all this, as we are stopped at a red light, I see a young girl swerve through this tableau on an orange skateboard. Her long braids fly in the wind, her clothes are bright pink, a shock of exuberance. And I begin to laugh to myself thinking, *Who is to say that the others have a monopoly on joy, on God, on how to live in this world?* And what I realize then, like a gift from this wonderful girl, is that all along I have been accepting their premise—that because of the choices I had made, I had lost my right to the bounty of my childhood, renounced what had been my birthright. That without taking on the lifestyle, the shared norms and practices, I could never again touch the magic.

Who said that needed to be true?

The cab turns off of Ocean Parkway and moves past red brick private homes with white doors and small tended lawns from which large trees swoon and reach practically across the street. As we move softly through the shaded streets, past the homes of people I had once known, past the doors I had once entered and exited smoothly, I am beginning to know what I want to do. I want to return this time as if it is my right. To stop contracting or camouflaging myself, or agreeing to be even partly invisible. I want to say "You can't do this—sever a child without severing a part of yourself. You can't remove someone's oxygen and call it love. You can't tell a person you love that their choices will bring them misery. That you will guard over that misery day and night until their spirit is broken."

I want to say "Enough. Am I or am I not a part of you? You have said all these years that the choice is mine, but really you are the ones who whispered 'exile.' You are the ones who murmured '*shiva*.' You are the ones who look past me as if I've already dissolved."

And then I want to turn this trip into a retrieval mission, an archaeological dig for some of what got lost, for some memories from when I'd understood the magic, when I'd been allowed, briefly, close to the mystery. To close my eyes and as I once had entered the billowing tent of the tallit, enter now the shimmering temple of the wedding ritual. Disappear into the milling crowd, close my eyes to better hear the undulations of the ceremony's seven blessings, take in the seven revolutions of the bride.

I want to grow aware—not of the chatter around me, or of the prayers being chanted or sung—but of two souls yearning toward each other after an infinite separation. I want to look up and for the briefest moment, see above the bride and groom, an archway, half Jerusalem stone, half light. I want to sieve through the crowd until I can sense, as I did as a child, an anonymous and mysterious presence among the dancers encircling the bride and groom, a frenzy of potential trying to squeeze itself into a vessel of limbs. I want to take myself back. Before I could imagine the cruelty of the tribe, before the threats of excommunication, the silences, and the treachery. I want—and the words catch in my throat—to finally forgive myself. Forgive myself my wounds, the places that were amputated, the places that still bleed. Forgive myself for not having taken an easier path. For having grown foreign to those who loved me, for having loved so hard, for having wanted more than what people could give. For still wanting.

Then a silence. Complete. Profound. Only the sound of my breath.

The rabbis were right, I think, about the power of naming. Name something and it rises into itself, full bodied, strong. Name something correctly and its weapons fall clanging to the floor, its danger transformed. Name something and its taste comes to your mouth. Blood. Forgiveness. God.

The taxi slows, then pulls up in front of the wedding hall where a man is weaving flowers around the pillars at the entrance. Through the half-open door, I glimpse my father and a handful of men in the lobby rocking silently back and forth as they pray the afternoon prayer.

I step out of the taxi and walk up the path. As I do, I see my sister in her long white dress approaching my father who is concluding his prayers. He turns toward her and lays his hands on her head and quietly, privately blesses her with what I imagine are all of his gathered hopes and prayers. I wait until they are done and she turns without seeing me and disappears down a long hallway. My father looks up and sees me in the doorway, and despite everything, his eyes light up with an earlier joy as I step forward to receive my blessing.

Tehila Lieberman's work has appeared in Salamander, the Colorado Review, Salon Magazine, Literary Latté, Sideshow, *and* Travelers' Tales Women in the Wild. *She is a winner of the Colorado Review's Stanley Elkin Memorial Prize for fiction and has served on the board of directors of the Writer's Room of Boston. She lives in Cambridge, Massachusetts.*

⋆ ⋆ ⋆

Return to Keta

Some kinds of connection defy time and space.

NANA NKETSIA WAS TRAVELING TO LAGOS BY CAR AND WHEN HE invited me and his two oldest daughters to accompany him as far as the Togo border, I accepted gratefully. Now that I had decided to leave Africa, I realized I had not seen eastern Ghana.

Araba rode with me and Adae got into her father's car. Three hours after we left Accra we arrived at the small but busy town of Aflao. Nana beckoned me to follow and led me to a large, two-story stone house at the end of a quiet lane.

"We will stay here for the night, and at dawn my driver and I will continue to Lagos. Come inside, I want you to meet our host, Adadevo, the customs officer." A servant responded to Nana's knock, and his daughters, Nana, and I were shown into a daintily furnished sitting room. Before we could choose seats a young girl around Araba's age entered through a side door. She smiled and extended her hands and made a little curtsy to Nana.

"Nana, welcome. I am Freida, Adadevo's daughter. He is still at the office. I will make you comfortable."

Nana introduced Araba, Adae, and me, and Freida bobbed prettily, accepting the introduction. She supposed we would be weary after such a long journey and offered to show us to our rooms.

Nana was put on the ground floor, and I was given a second-floor guest room. Araba and Adae were to share a room near Freida.

Although I was used to the dignity of African girls, I was taken aback by Freida's grown-up composure at sixteen. She was a practiced hostess. I surmised that she was an only child of a single parent, and circumstances had forced her to grow up quickly and very well. Nana carried his shortwave radio to his quarters and I retired to my room.

For the next hours as the girls giggled down the hall, I thought of my impending departure and the Organization of Afro American Unity. There has been no mention of salary or responsibilities. I knew that I would be paid minimum wage and would be asked to raise money, organize files, recruit members, stuff envelopes, draft news releases, type, file, and answer the telephone. Those were the usual chores that go begging in understaffed and underfinanced civil rights organizations.

It would be good to see my family and old friends. Suddenly I was excited at the prospect of being back in New York City, and back in the fray.

Araba broke into my thoughts. "Auntie Maya, Mr. Adadevo is here, and dinner is served." I prepared myself and joined the group in the dining room.

Mr. Adadevo was a tall, dark brown man of pleasing appearance, and when he spoke his voice sang with the melodic Ewe accent. The girls sat together at dinner, using English to talk across their language barrier while Nana and Mr. Adadevo spoke of portentous matters of state. The hours of assessment in the guest room had drained my energy, and I was glad there was no general conversation which could command my participation.

At an early hour, I asked to be excused, honestly claiming exhaustion.

The bed, sleep, and I met together, and I rose at dawn to go downstairs and bid Nana a safe journey. He promised that he would return to Ghana before my departure.

When Mr. Adadevo entered the kitchen the day was bright and I was having yet another cup of instant coffee. He ate quartered oranges and asked me why I was only then visiting his area. I made a courteous reply, then he asked if I would like to see the nearby town of Keta only thirty miles away. Without any real interest I again answered courteously.

"That would be nice. We should start back to Accra by early afternoon." He assured me that we would have plenty of time and left to rouse the still-sleeping girls.

It was decided that we would take his large car. Araba, Adae, and Freida sat in the back, and Mr. Adadevo, his driver, and I occupied the front seat.

The countryside was beautiful, but not unusually so. My eyes had become accustomed to coconut trees and palms, and bougainvillea growing freely on country roads and city streets. A quiet murmur reached me from the back seat and since neither Mr. Adadevo nor his driver spoke, I was lulled by the car motor and the moist warm air into a near torpor.

Suddenly, I jerked alert and looked ahead. We were approaching a sturdy and graceful bridge. My heart began to race and I was struggling for breath. I gasped, "Stop, stop the car. Stop the car." The driver consented. I was sitting next to the window, so I opened the door and quickly stepped to the ground. I spoke through the back window.

"Get out, girls. Come. You, too, Freida. We are going to walk across this bridge." Although they were stunned by my behavior, they obeyed, and I said to the startled Adadevo, "We will join the car on the other side." I walked briskly apart from my charges who were unsettled by my actions and tittering nervously. My pretended concern over the waterscape and the overgrown riverbanks caused me to turn my head often, as if looking for a particular object or view. In fact, I was more jittery than the teenagers. I could not explain my behavior. I only knew that the possibility of riding across that bridge so terrified me that had the driver refused to stop, I would have jumped from the still-moving car.

Mr. Adadevo was standing at the end of the bridge, and after he saw the passengers safely in the back seat, he took my arm and drew me aside.

"Why were you afraid? I have rarely seen such terror. Do you know anything about this bridge?" I shook my head.

"Have you ever heard of the Keta bridge?" I shook my head again. I had never heard the area mentioned. "The old bridge, I should say bridges," his face was solemn, "were infamous for being so poorly constructed that in any flood they would crumble and wash away. People in conveyances of any kind lost their lives, so a century ago passengers in palanquins used to stop and get down in order to walk across. In a crisis, only people on foot could hope to reach the other side." I felt a quick chill. He asked, "Are you sure someone didn't tell you that story?" I said, "I must have read it somewhere." I apologized for startling him and knew without question that I had no inkling of the bridge's history.

After my inexplicable outburst, there was a new tension in the car. No sounds came from the back seat, but Mr. Adadevo began speaking immediately after the bridge episode and didn't stop until we reached Keta.

He talked about Accra, of Ghana's growth, of the wisdom of Kwame Nkrumah. He said he admired the American Negro athletes and Dr. Martin Luther King. He spoke of his region, describing it in detail, its fishing and copra industries, its markets and major towns, and its religion.

I half heard his crooned chant as I was more engrossed in examining my actions at the bridge.

"There is a lagoon behind Keta and, of course, the ocean before it, and that has caused the people of the town a great problem. For after the work of enlarging the ports of Tema and Sekondi-Takowadi, the ocean has reacted by backing up onto Keta. They have already lost over two miles of the town. The people are being squeezed by two forces of water. The town will disappear in time and the people have nowhere to go."

When I heard the dire story, I again surprised myself. I felt as if I had just been told a beloved relative was dying. Tears came to my eyes and threatened to run down my face. I dreaded the possibility of crying before strangers, but even more awful was the prospect of allowing Nana's daughters to see me out of control. The motto of their family was "royalty does not weep in the street," and I had spent a great effort showing them that although I was born from slaves, I was descended from kings.

I took a handkerchief and faked a cough.

Araba leaned forward, "Auntie, are you all right?"

I told her I thought I was reacting to the dust, and she was satisfied.

Adae, asserting her intelligence and explaining me to her new friend, said "Auntie is very sensitive. She has allergies." I was grateful for their presence, for without them I might have bent over my lap and let the emotion of loss drain out of me in rivers of tears. I swallowed the knots in my throat over and over and wondered if I was losing my mind. What did that bridge and the sea's encroachment of Keta have to do with me?

Adadevo was still talking as the car turned through the narrow streets of the old town. Although we could not see the ocean, suddenly I knew or felt that the next turn would give us a panoramic view of the surf. I held onto myself and hoped that the presentiment would prove false.

Mr. Adadevo said, "Now here is the sea. You call it the Atlantic Ocean. We have another name for it in Ewe."

The driver parked at the side of Keta's market and Mr. Adadevo asked me to come and meet his sister, who had a stall on the market's periphery. We walked in file with Freida and the driver carrying large empty straw baskets.

Mr. Adadevo's sister was tall and thin.... When we were introduced, I found that she spoke very scanty English, and I expected that she would speak French.

The Ewe tribe which occupied Togo and the eastern area of Ghana had been a German colony in the nineteenth century, but after Germany's loss of World War I, the allied victors took away Germany's mandate and gave the area to France. French became the province's official language in 1920, so I offered to speak French with my host's sister, but her French was only a little better than her English. We smiled at each other and shook our heads in exasperation. She spoke rapid Ewe with her brother and niece, while Araba and Adae looked on.

I waved good-bye, anxious to climb into the raised market which was issuing sounds of trade and merriment.

The narrow stairs were bounded by wooden walls, making the entrance dim. I was looking down, making certain of my footfall, when a voice above me drew my attention. I looked up to see an older woman, unusually tall, blotting out the light behind her. She spoke again and in a voice somewhat similar to my own, but I was unable to understand her.

I smiled and, using Fanti, said regretfully, "I am sorry, Auntie, but I don't speak Ewe." She put her hands on her wide hips, reared back and let loose into the dim close air around us a tirade of angry words. When she stopped, I offered, in French and in a self-deprecating tone, "I am sorry, Auntie, but I don't speak Ewe."

She clapped her hands close enough to my face for me to feel the rush of air, then she raised her voice. My ignorance of the meaning of her words did not prevent me from knowing that I was being denounced in the strongest possible language.

When I could wedge myself into her explosion, I spoke in English nearly whining, "Auntie, I am sorry, but I do not speak Ewe."

It seemed the walls would collapse. The big woman took a step down to me, and I backed down two steps. There was no room on the stairs for me to pass her, and I wouldn't have had the nerve to try to force my way beyond that now enraged giant frame. Her invective was coming faster and louder. I knew that my luck had to have totally deserted me to allow me to meet a mad woman on darkened stairs whom I could neither placate nor threaten.

Mr. Adadevo spoke behind me, and I turned only slightly, afraid to leave my back unprotected.

"Mr. Adadevo, would you please talk to this Auntie. I can't make her understand."

The woman fired another salvo, and Mr. Adadevo stepped up and placed himself between me and my assailant. He spoke softly in Ewe. I heard the word "American" while I was watching the woman's face. She shook her head in denial. My protector spoke again, still softly. I heard "American Negro." Still the woman's face showed disbelief.

Mr. Adadevo looked at me and said, "Sister, she thinks you are someone else. Do you have your American passport with you?"

I hadn't seen my passport in two years, but I remembered having an old California driver's license, which had its identifying photograph. I took the wrinkled, but still slick paper from my wallet and gave it to Mr. Adadevo. He handed the document to the woman who strained to see in the darkness. She turned and walked up the stairs into the light. Mr. Adadevo followed and I followed him.

There, the woman, who was over six feet tall, stood peering at the flimsy piece of paper in her dark hand. When she raised her head, I nearly fell back down the steps: she had the wide face and slanted eyes of my grandmother. Her lips were large and beautifully shaped like my grandmother's, and her cheekbones were high like those of my grandmother. The woman solemnly returned the license to Mr. Adadevo who gave it back to me, then the woman reached out and touched my shoulder hesitantly. She softly patted my cheek a few times. Her

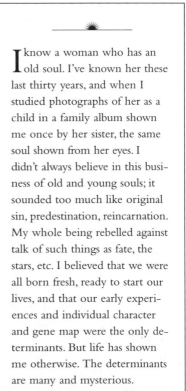

I know a woman who has an old soul. I've known her these last thirty years, and when I studied photographs of her as a child in a family album shown me once by her sister, the same soul shown from her eyes. I didn't always believe in this business of old and young souls; it sounded too much like original sin, predestination, reincarnation. My whole being rebelled against talk of such things as fate, the stars, etc. I believed that we were all born fresh, ready to start our lives, and that our early experiences and individual character and gene map were the only determinants. But life has shown me otherwise. The determinants are many and mysterious.

—Sharon Balentine, "Eyes, the Soul, Knowing"

face had changed. Outrage had given way to melancholia. After a few seconds of studying me, the woman lifted both arms and lacing her fingers together clasped her hands and put them on the top of her head. She rocked a little from side to side and issued a pitiful little moan.

In Arkansas, when I was a child, if my brother or I put our hands on our heads as the woman before me was doing, my grandmother would stop in her work and come to remove our hands and warn us that the gesture brought bad luck.

Mr. Adadevo spoke to me quietly, "That's the way we mourn."

The woman let her arms fall and stepping up to me, spoke and took my hand, pulling me gently away. Mr. Adadevo said, "She wants you to go with her. We will follow." The girls and the driver had climbed the stairs, and we entered the crowded market. I allowed myself to be tugged forward by the big woman who was a little taller than I and twice my size.

She stopped at the first stall and addressed a woman who must have been the proprietor. In the spate of words, I heard "American Negro." The woman looked at me disbelieving and came around the corner of her counter to have a better look. She shook her head and, lifting her arms, placed her hands on her head, rocking from side to side.

My companions were standing just behind me as the vendor leaned over the shelf where tomatoes, onions, and peppers were arranged in an artistic display. She began speaking, and raking the produce toward the edge.

Mr. Adadevo said something to the driver who came forward and placed each vegetable carefully into his basket. My host said, "She is giving this to you. She says she has more if you want it."

I went to the woman to thank her, but as I approached she looked at me and groaned, and cried, and put her hands on her head. The big woman was crying too. Their distress was contagious, and my lack of understanding made it especially so. I wanted to apologize, but I didn't know what I would ask pardon for.

I turned to Mr. Adadevo and asked if they thought I looked like someone who had died.

He answered and his voice was sad, "The first woman thought you were the daughter of a friend. But now you remind them of someone, but not anyone they knew personally."

My guide now pulled me through a press of bodies until we came to a stall where the owner sold yams, cassava, and other tubers. Her wares were stacked on the ground in front of the stall and rose in piles around the stool she occupied. My escort began her litany to the saleswoman. Somewhere in the ritual she said "American Negro," and the woman repeated the first stall owner's behavior. Freida began putting yams and cocoa yams and cassava into her basket. The two women were rocking and moaning.

I said, "Mr. Adadevo, you must tell me what's happening."

He said, "This is a very sad story and I can't tell it all or tell it well." I waited while he looked around. He began again, "During the slavery period Keta was a good-sized village. It was hit very hard by the slave trade. Very hard. In fact, at one point every inhabitant was either killed or taken. The only escapees were children who ran away and hid in the bush. Many of them watched from their hiding places as their parents were beaten and put into chains. They saw the slaves set fire to the village. They saw mothers and fathers take infants by their feet and bash their head against tree trunks rather than see them sold into slavery. What they saw they remembered, and all that they remembered they told over and over.

"The children were taken in by nearby villagers and grew to maturity. They married and had children and rebuilt Keta. They told the tale to offspring. These women are the descendants of those orphaned children. They have heard the stories often, and the deeds are still as fresh as if they happened during their lifetimes. And you, Sister, you look so much like them, even the tone of your voice is like theirs. They are sure you are descended from those stolen mothers and fathers. That is why they mourn. Not for you but for their lost people."

A sadness descended on me, simultaneously somber and wonderful. I had not consciously come to Ghana to find roots of my beginnings, but I had continually and accidentally tripped over them or fallen upon them in my everyday life. Once I had been taken for Bambara, and cared for by other Africans as they would care for a Bambara woman. Nana's family of Ahantas claimed me, crediting my resemblance to a relative as proof of my Ahanta background. And here in my last days in Africa, descendants of a pillaged past saw their history in my face and heard their ancestors speak through my voice.

> A woman's path need not always take her many miles from home. It will, however, always invite her to let go of where she's already been, and to be open to the Mystery of where she's going. Grace will be her guide and will ask her to trust in her own wisdom. In this way, a woman's path will invariably lead her back to her true self, and no path is ever more valuable than this.
>
> —Sally Lowe Whitehead,
> "Path of Grace"

The first woman continued leading me from stall to stall, introducing me. Each time the merchant would disbelieve the statement that I was an American Negro, and each time she would gasp and mourn, moan and offer me her goods. The women wept and I wept. I too cried for the lost people, their ancestors and mine. But I was also weeping with curious joy. Despite the murders, rapes, and suicides, we had survived. The middle passage and the auction block had not erased us. Not humiliations nor lynchings, individual cruelties nor collective oppression had been able to eradicate us from the Earth. We had come through despite our own ignorance and gullibility, and the ignorance and rapacious greed of our assailants.

There was much to cry for, much to mourn, but in my heart I felt exalted knowing there was much to celebrate. Although separated from our languages, our families and customs, we had dared to continue to live. We had crossed the unknowable oceans in chains and had written its mystery into "Deep River, my home is over Jordan." Through the centuries of despair and dislocation, we had been creative, because we faced down death by daring to hope.

Maya Angelou is an author, historian, playwright, actor, singer, songwriter, conductor, film director, and civil rights activist. She has written numerous books, including I Know Why the Caged Bird Sings, The Heart of a Woman, Wouldn't Take Nothing for My Journey Now, Phenomenal Women: Four Poems Celebrating Women, *and* All God's Children Need Traveling Shoes, *from which this story was excerpted.*

✶ ✶ ✶

No Shit! There I Was...

Tackling the river's rapids was only one
of her death-defying feats.

IT IS, AND I AM, COLD AND DAMP. GRAY SKY. WIND. DON'T KNOW
if it's raining, don't care. So much river water coming over my head,
what's a little more wet? I could be in a warm, dry office in New
York City, not crouched in a rubber boat (OK, raft), ankle-deep in
forty-eight-degree water, watching a bearded stranger row us down
the Colorado River. We round a bend. Lees Ferry, our starting point
for this journey, disappears. Two weeks? I am miserable.

"Bail," says the bearded stranger.

Twenty-four and one-half chilly miles later, we make first camp.
As soon as I set up my tent, it blows up and away and might now
be half the distance to Canada but for a big man who jumps into
the air and catches it. George is from Covington, Georgia. Quit the
Navy at thirty-eight and figures if he lives frugally he won't need
to look for a job until 2001. Meantime, George is seeing the country, having recently hiked all 2,162 miles of the Appalachian Trail.
Now he's doing the Canyon. Doing the river thing. I ask George
if he's scared of the rapids. I am.

"Nah. You only live once."

Trite, but no less true for it. What is it I say when I talk about
having had cancer? "Smell the flowers." "Take chances." "Live as

if…" I wonder: Do people know I might be lying? Right after I was diagnosed, right after I lost both my breasts and all my hair (my hair grew back), I did make time for flowers and chances. It was then I discovered the woods. Soon I came to believe this was a gift that had been waiting years for me, a Gulf Coast gal with a centrally air-conditioned past, washed ashore in the Northeast. I was nearly fifty when I began hiking and, later, backpacking, and whenever I would get to the top of something I thought I couldn't climb, I'd swell with pride and ask myself what other hills in my life might I now take on?

I am drawn to the woods by this challenge, and by solitude, but most of all by beauty. Every year, beauty becomes more important, some magic vitamin, a necessary tonic without which body and soul might wither. This is what the woods and, possibly, cancer have given me. But it's been five years. Life speeds up. Flowers are passed, unsmelled. Chances go untaken. That's partly why this trip appealed. Two hundred twenty-six miles of river. No telephone. No computer. Nothing but flowers and chances. I come to the Canyon thinking of it as woods with no trees.

Yet I am frightened of the rapids, even before I see one.

Today there was plenty of white water, although the rapids were not, I'm told, large ones. Rummaging in my gear, sorting through the too many things I've brought, trying (uselessly) to brush sand off my stuff, I remember the guy sitting across from me on the plane to Flagstaff. The back of his t-shirt read, "Face your fears. Live your dreams." Couldn't tell what was printed on the front; at the time, he was bent over, throwing up.

Make this rain stop. My shin is bandaged; I pulled a piece of the Cambrian Period down on it. Hurts, but I won't let on. I'm facing my fears, *OK*? All this talk about rock? Spectacular, but a little geology goes a long way. I'm more of a scenery junkie and the scenery is definitely being rained on. What did the boatman say? "The first day is the worst day."

I am not supposed to be here.

Two mornings later, someone asks if I would like to try the paddleboat. There are five boats. In four, the boatman rows while passengers, uncomfortably seated front and back, ride, talk, look about and hang on for dear life. In the fifth boat, six people paddle to the commands of a seventh, the paddle captain. Trouble with the paddleboat is there's nothing to hang on to, and you couldn't hang on anyway, because you have to paddle. You have to go through big hungry water, actually leaning out and shoving a stick into it at regular intervals. Counterintuitive, says someone. Suicidal, think I.

"Sure," I say. "I would like to try the paddleboat." (Checked the map; there are no giant rapids today.) Soon I'm reminded how much I like paddling, although until now the experience has been limited to canoes on quiet rivers and quieter lakes. We come to a small rapid. I manage to stay in the boat and keep my paddle in the water. I like the rush, want a bigger rapid. And then we are blessed. The rain stops. By noon, yellow sun dances on green water, bounces off red canyon walls, and shoots back up into blue sky. A crayon day. Feels like falling in love.

Takes a while for the river and canyon to grab hold. But they do. I wake in the night to catch the Big Dipper grinning like a Cheshire cat six feet above my head. *Gotcha.* Hours later, warm in my sleeping bag, the predawn air cool on my face, I say goodbye to the morning star.

On the fifth day, we hike up a side canyon, something

Days tumbled over each other. On some days I had no understanding of why I had taken flight with a madman across my country. Other days I knew exactly why. It was for those rare moments when we would rub through small passages of life along the road that could never be encountered the same way again, when I knew the only place on Earth to be was on the back seat of a motorcycle, when that conflux of place and time and joy and godliness would lift that piece of the world, that piece of life, into something magnificent, something golden.

—Laurie Gough, *Kite Strings of the Southern Cross*

we do every day, but this time I hallucinate. I hear Verdi. Another twist of the canyon and there, seated on bailing buckets, are four men, three with violins, one with cello, playing Verdi. Don't know who they are or how they got here. *Play on.* Verdi becomes Dvořák. Without warning, something inside is released. I begin to cry. So much beauty. So little time. *Canyon, fill me up.*

Our travels are not always the voyages of discovery we say we seek. Often they are rituals of reassurance. This was different. This required one to take physical and emotional chances. Not just the river. The people. *All these strangers? I'm supposed to get to know all these strangers?* But isn't one of the gifts of travel the discovery of oneself through other people?

At seventy-three, Wini is a retired professor and genuinely beautiful woman, smart and prickly. Does not suffer fools, period. This is her fourth trip down this river. One day, on a hike, Wini gets sick. Too much sun? Too little water? John, the trip leader, asks if she needs to be lifted out of the canyon by helicopter.

"No," says Wini. "I don't."

The subject is closed.

Next day, tired from being around too many people, I remain by the river when the others go hiking. Wini has also stayed behind. She stops by my camp, says she's come to realize this is the last time; she will never make this trip again. Since Wini is twenty-one years farther down the road, and because I very much want to know, I ask her what it is like to do something for the last time. I want to cry for Wini. For me, too. No matter what anyone tells you, there's nothing good about getting old.

At the moment, however, I've other worries. *Horn. Granite. Hermit, Crystal.* Bigger rapids. Bigger fears. "You can do it," says Julie, paddle captain and hero. You should see Julie. No matter where we sleep, she sleeps higher, curled up there somewhere, on some rock or another. Mornings, Julie comes down lightly, leaping from boulder to boulder, boat to boat, surefooted as any other wild creature. On the water, her voice is gentle, teaching us to paddle together, turning a group of inadequate paddlers into a team able to pass through a big rapid and come out thinking they've done it all themselves.

By now, I know the paddleboat is where I want to be. I love the thrill, love the paddling, and find it less frightening if I'm actually involved in my fate, rather than watching someone else row while I hang on and try not to notice a twelve-foot wall of water coming straight at me. But when we climb ahead to scout a big rapid and I look down into this bodacious breaking stuff, my stomach falls away like the rapid itself. *Oh, dear God, don't make me paddle this! I can't. I will panic. Fall out. Die. Worse, I will chicken out. Drop my paddle and cling, sniveling, to the boat. I can't…*

Julie says I can.

I pray a secret prayer and, in case God can't hear me for the water, pray it again, louder. Thus begin the days of the big rapids. One boat flips, tossing its occupants into the current. They're pulled out downstream, shivering, teeth chattering, humbled. But our paddle raft shoots through the beautiful white water as though it were greased. We are triumphant. There are no words. Only the song inside me. I am my own band. And I am very much in tune. I, Linda Jane, have successfully paddled the biggest rapids of the grandest canyon of the Colorado River. I feel strong and competent and nineteen. No. I feel strong and competent and fifty-two.

I am supposed to be here.

Can't wait to tell people back home about this. Julie asks if we know the difference between a fairy tale and a river story. We don't. "Well," she says, "a fairy tale begins, 'Once upon a time,' and a river story begins, 'No shit! There I was…'"

Days of long play. Of water fights and waterfalls. Of skinny dipping, alone, in a turquoise pool, then napping in soft grass next to it. Of sun and sunrises. And sunsets. Of climbing boulders I once thought too tall. Of walking ledges I once thought too narrow. Of crude drawings on canyon walls, very old graffiti, left by ancient ones who disappeared. Nights littered with stars. Do the stars know where the people went?

One hot afternoon near the end of the trip, drifting toward more rapids, Julie tells us the reason we're a good paddle team is that we do what she says, when she says it. We nod in pompous agreement. Teacher's pets. "And that is why," says Julie, softly, "I want you to put down your paddles, jump in the river, and swim the next rapid."

"Excuse me? Have we not spent the better part of two weeks doing our best *not* to fall into this rock 'n' roll river with its cold, cold heart? Now you want us to go in *on purpose*?" But nobody says that. We're too busy putting down our paddles and jumping into the river.

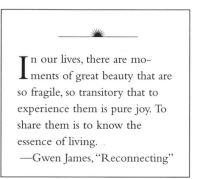

In our lives, there are moments of great beauty that are so fragile, so transitory that to experience them is pure joy. To share them is to know the essence of living. .

—Gwen James, "Reconnecting"

Whooooosh. Breath knocked right out of me. *Whooooosh.* Don't forget to breathe out. That's what John said. Breathe in at the bottom of the trough. That's what Julie said. Swallowing green and swallowed by green. The world tumbles up and over. I see sky, water, sky, water, sky, water and then it's all one thing: skywater.

The waves end. The ride is over. Julie hauls us into the raft. We are wet and slithery and loud: We are invincible. Soaked in beauty. We are alive.

Overcome with the pure joy of experience, I start thinking how great it would be to be a boatman (even women guides are called boatmen). How fine to live each day, mindful of the world immediately around you, focused on the river, the boat, the passengers, wet and dry, food and drink, sun and sand and sleep. Life 101. I'm about ready to quit my day job when Eric, a real boatman, points out a reality I've not considered. "Every year," says Eric, "I make less money. I'm sort of working toward a cash-free existence." Mmmm. Even that has a certain appeal. It is a life. A good one. But it is not my life. Not this time around.

Weeks later, back in New York City, a phone rings. A woman, someone I wrote a story about, has died from breast cancer. It was the treatment that killed her. I celebrate her courage, mourn her death, and, sorry to say, am relieved it wasn't me. The fear is always there. Although I try to live as if the cancer were never coming back, I know all the nasty little numbers; half the women who get this disease are dead in ten years. I put down the phone, tuck away the fear, and go back to work.

But at night, lying in bed, troubled by death and overwhelmed by life, I find I can shut my eyes and whisper. That's all I have to do.

"Take me there," I whisper.

The magic begins. Gold light slides down a red canyon wall. A green river sings. I am a shining thing in a shining place, far from here.

Linda Ellerbee is a noted journalist, best-selling author, breast-cancer survivor, mother, and television producer recognized for her outstanding achievement in children's programming. She has received all of television's highest honors, including Emmy, Peabody, CableACE, and duPont-Columbia awards. She is the author of And So It Goes *and* Move On: Adventures in the Real World. *This story was excerpted from* Writing Down the River: Into the Heart of the Grand Canyon, *edited by Kathleen Jo Ryan.*

PART TWO

WAYS OF JOURNEYING

LINDA   WATANABE   McFERRIN

$*$ $*$ $*$

The Masseur

Sometimes balancing the spirit
requires a helping hand.

I STILL HADN'T RECOVERED FROM THE TURNING OF THE DECADE and already I was climbing through it, about to become thirty-something and not happy about it. I was on the other side of the end of the world, the place where people drop off and die, at least that's what I'd believed for twenty-something years. Lawrence and I were in Stockholm, having left Europe, a trail of restaurants and bars strung out behind us.

I was on *tierra horroroso*, terrifying terrain, a time in my life more unfamiliar and hostile than the most far-flung and extreme of environments. My own body had become a strange place to dwell. It felt foreign, heavy, like something I was dragging along.

"It's a mood," Lawrence said. "It will pass."

"Yes," I agreed half-heartedly. "Maybe it's the weather."

Or, one too many nightcaps, one too many multicourse meals. Or, maybe the upcoming birthday.

Earlier in the day, after an enormous Scandanavian breakfast, we had crossed the Riksbron to Gamla Stan, the Old Town, squirming through the knots of tourists that jammed the Västerlanggaten, Stockholm's first pedestrian street. The multipaned windows of the old guild halls seemed to grimace down on the crowds.

A poor place in the thirteenth century when the "City between the Bridges," where the Baltic and Lake Mälaren meet, began to mushroom into a nautical trading center, this part of Stockholm still retains a tight-lipped, taciturn aspect.

We inched along steep, crampy streets and wriggled into small shops crammed with books, antiques, and nautical goods. The sun would not show its face, though the wind did an excellent job of making its presence known. It was chilly. Gray clouds scudded across a porridge-gray sky. No rain. Just cold gusts. It was a sailor's kind of day.

Deflated by travel, but determined to give Stockholm a chance, we explored the stores and boutiques on Österlanggatan. Then we walked along the Skeppsbron and crossed the Strömbron to visit the National Museum, amble along the quay and watch the slipper-shaped, steam-powered white Waxholm boats leave on their daily excursions to the Stockholm archipelago.

Crossing the bridge to Skeppsholmen, another small island in the Saltsjon, we lurked about for a while in the Modern Museum under the surveillance of several large modern installations. My somber mood deepened in direct proportion to the whimsical inferences of the art, to the children who tore about outdoors on the museum grounds, filling the air with their screams of unintelligible gaiety. The frivolity seemed to mock me.

Lawrence, as usual, moved through these landscapes, unperturbed and without second thoughts. I felt Neolithic, thinking of all those fat fertility goddesses grinning at me on my slow crawl through my third decade, beckoning toward their ample breasts, the fleshy folds, and thick mounds of torso and thigh. Where, I wondered, had my freedom gone?

"Look at that boat," Lawrence directed, trying to rekindle my usually insatiable curiosity. "Let's check it out."

Af Chapman, a tall clipper ship docked full-sail on the Strömmon, turned out to be a hostel of some sort. Students came and went up and down the gangplank. Lawrence and I were observed, it seemed to me, with the kind of suspicion reserved for alien elders encroaching upon the sacred precincts of youth. Not long ago I'd have numbered myself as one of them—careless relationships, casual trysts. Here they slept, dormitory style, on bunks. I slept in a suite at the Sheraton Stockholm, on ironed linens the color of North Sea salmon, with room service and marble-appointed baths where the perfectly packaged sundries—bath gels, mending kits, and shower bonnets—were arranged on the countertops with a great sense of purpose.

There's a certain price that one pays for these things, a heaviness of body and spirit that, at first, before one has given up and resigned oneself to it, weighs the body down. If one lets this feeling pass, it moves on to the soul.

"Let's go, Lawrence," I said grumpily. "I'm not comfortable here. I want to go back to the hotel."

On the way back, the sun was trying to push through the mealy gray of the sky, trying to thread it with blue. I sank into silence, burrowed into my coat. Lawrence took my arm.

"You're unhappy," he said.

"My birthday," I mumbled.

"That should be exciting."

"Not at this point in life," I replied.

"We'll cheer you up," he said pulling me close. "I'm taking you out for your birthday."

That night we returned to the Gamla Stan, to a restaurant called Five Small Houses, Fem Sma Hus. Nine small rooms that converged in the basements of five small houses facing the Österlanggatan, the restaurant began as a forbidden tavern in the seventeenth century under the austere reign of Charles XI. Illegality has a certain attraction. The tavern blossomed and prospered through the centuries.

We climbed down creaky stairs through vaulted, brick chambers lit with candles. Amber and ruby wines glinted like bouquets of lilies and roses on the tables in the warren of curtained, firelit rooms. I wasn't hungry at all. The world was too much for me. I wanted a salad of crisp greens and a large glass of water.

Lawrence began with an appetizer. He ordered a bottle of wine. The waiter brought back a tray that held five tremendous bowls of

various types of fish. There was herring in sour cream, pickled herring, halibut with horseradish and dill, gravlax (salmon), and mar-
inated mackerel. Lawrence sampled them all. As I watched him eat,
I could feel the good life rising up inside me in a nauseous heave.
I could feel my stomach convulse.

"So much food," I said in amazement.

"Would you like some?" Lawrence asked in response.

"I'll stick to my salad," I said.

The waiter was pleased with Lawrence's appetite and clearly
disgusted with mine.

Lawrence had sole and morels smothered in a rich cream sauce,
buttery Swedish potatoes, consommé, and homemade bread. He
had pheasant in a wine sauce and King William potatoes.

I needed sleep and a simple diet—pale green walls, white sheets,
seven days in a sanitarium. That, I thought, would fix me right up—
a brief respite, a haven from excess.

Lawrence was considering chocolate cake for dessert. The
waiter conspired with him to draw out the meal, add courses. He
suggested dark chocolate and port.

"Lawrence," I said when the waiter left, "we've had so many
courses. I can't sit through dessert."

"You don't like this restaurant, do you?" asked Lawrence ab-
jectly, his good humor falling away. "I picked it because it's your
birthday."

"It's too extravagant, Lawrence," I responded. "I am full—full to
the brim. I can't take any more."

"Look, I'll call back the waiter," he offered. "I'll cancel dessert."

We walked back to the hotel in the piss-lit evening light, and I
sat in the armchair in the suite's far corner staring into the yellow
night while a procession of frenetic performers cavorted on MTV.

Lawrence, surfeited, happy, and of iron constitution, slept like
a lamb.

Dawn didn't break. It wormed its way into the poorly lit, lean
side of night and grew like a boil until it took over. Another year
of my life swang into motion.

Lawrence woke up bright and well rested.

"Honey," he said. "You didn't sleep."

"I can't," I said miserably, knowing that he'd read the unhappiness in my voice.

"Well," he said gently, getting out of bed, stepping behind my chair and placing warm palms on my shoulders. "I have one more present for you."

What? I wondered. Diamonds? Travel? Nothing seemed worth getting excited about.

"We are in Sweden," he said, stating the obvious. "I've arranged for a Swedish massage. The masseur will come here, to the hotel. There's a massage room next to the sauna. What do you think? Would you like that?"

"It sounds fine," I consented reluctantly. I was not feeling "at one" with my body.

"Good," Lawrence said. "Your appointment's at one o'clock."

I met the masseur with the enthusiasm of a condemned person meeting an executioner. Lawrence, who among his many accomplishments has somehow managed to become a licensed masseur, came with me.

The sauna was on the eighteenth floor, constructed of blue tile and pine. There were mountains of fluffy, salmon-pink towels.

My masseur had already arrived. He was a blond young man with a flour-

To walk into a Swedish sauna was to unravel the layers of myself that I had constructed over time. The walls I had built around me were gently melted away by the casual comfort of foreign friends, the sense of adventure being in a new country, the freedom I found alone on the road, and the intense heat of the sauna. I discovered that if I simply let myself be, I had no fear at all and I was at home with my body and me.
—Lisa Bach, "A Path of One's Own"

white face. His eyes were forget-me-not blue. His hair looked like corn silk, lank, drained of color.

I had wrapped myself in one of the hotel's white terrycloth robes.

"Please take a towel, lie down, and relax," my masseur said, motioning toward the massage room.

As I undressed in the small blue-tiled room, I heard him speaking with Lawrence.

"She seems very tense," the masseur was saying. "She has trouble relaxing."

"Old injuries," Lawrence confirmed.

I'd climbed up onto the narrow table and wrapped myself, like a crepe, in a shellfish-colored towel.

The conversation on the other side of the wall ended. The masseur entered. He spoke softly.

"Relax," he said.

I closed my eyes and attempted to do as he instructed. I felt his hands on my neck and my shoulders. I felt his hands on my shins and ankles. He parted the towel. I felt his hands on my breasts and my stomach, his hands on my hips and thighs. It was an introduction—his hands, my body. His hands moved over my body, brushing my skin, a couple of dragonflies lighting here and there, like feeling a face to meet a person, identity defined by a browline, a nose. I could hear his slow breathing in the silent room. I could also hear mine.

"Turn over," he whispered.

I did this without opening my eyes. Now, he would meet the back of my head with a stroke of my hair. Now, he would meet my back. His fingertips traced the particular, very personalized curve of my spine. He cupped his hands at the base of my buttocks, to familiarize them with his touch, palms wide, fingers spread slightly, eager to move in, hard-put to resist the urge to begin. His hands moved quickly down my legs, fluttering monarchs migrating south. At the soles of my feet his fingers tapped messages, secret codes for unwinding.

Then his hands moved back up to my neck and shoulders, pressing hard, digging into the knots of tendon and muscle, untangling them like a spinner working with yarn. His smell rose up around me. He probed his way around my shoulder blades, lifting and separating them like a pair of delicate wings from the tight slabs of muscle in which they were embedded. His palms pressed into my shoulders, shoulders not yet scarred as they would be in a few short weeks from a bicycle accident, the long downhill slide on a country road over gravel and rock.

"Lawrence is a masseur," I announced.

"Yes, he told me," the masseur said.

His thumbs pressed into the tight hinge of my jaw, a jaw full of stress, popping and creaking with TMJ (temporal mandibular syndrome). That TMJ would be permanently cured in Switzerland when I ripped my jaw open flying over the handlebars of my bike, landing, chin first, in the same bicycle accident that scarred my shoulder and arm.

His fingertips applied gentle pressure just under my ears. I felt like a fist unclenching.

"You are like a flower, opening up," he said.

"That's beautiful," I mumbled into the table. "You're a poet."

"Only with my hands," he laughed.

"With your hands," I repeated. "Lawrence is a masseur."

"You told me," he said.

Moving down my back, he massaged my spine, seemed to lift each vertebrae and hold it in his palm, a separate piece to be examined, twisted this way and that, explored like a rock or some artifact at an archaeological dig.

"Did you fall?" he asked seeing the historical record written in the units of bone.

"Yes."

I told him about my accident on skates, how my spine was curved incorrectly.

"I see," he whispered.

"But, you're in pretty good shape," he added, hands grabbing my butt.

His accent was strong.

"I feel awful," I whined into the table.

"You're retaining fluids. You are drinking a lot. You are tense."

"Uh, huh, tense," I confirmed.

I began to perspire as he kneaded my haunches.

"God, I'm sweating," I laughed embarrassed.

"So am I," he said softly. "It's OK, let it go."

I let it go.

"Turn over," he said.

I turned over.

The corn-silk hair hung limply over his ears, on either side of his jaw. The blue of his eyes had deepened, looked violet. When his hands moved onto my chest and my breasts I felt laughter collect deep inside me. A couple of chuckles escaped.

"You speak very good English," I said trying to distract him from the ridiculous behavior of my nipples. They were making a spectacle of themselves.

"Thank you," he said.

"*Taak. Taak sa meuget*," I offered. "That's my only Swedish."

"It means, 'Thank you,'" he said.

"Yes," I responded. "It's a good phrase to learn."

Thank you, I thought, feeling better, feeling gratitude swell up inside me. *Thank you for the massage. Thank you for reminding me that my body and I are one.* We lapsed into silence, my masseur working intently. Few words. Much communication. It reminded me of Texas, of cowboys, of two-steps, of little black dresses and pearls. I closed my eyes, drifting into the physical trance inspired by the massage.

Then his fingers danced over my body in a quick *tapotment*, a furious flamenco of digits flying over my flesh. It was brisk and refreshing.

"How are you feeling now?" he asked.

"Much better," I said with a smile.

"Next time you feel like this, you must get a massage."

"Not with you," I said. "You are too far away. You're in Sweden."

"Lawrence is a masseur," he said with a quiet smile.

"Yes, he is," I affirmed.

Lawrence had returned. He was waiting outside the room when we emerged.

"All better?" he asked hopefully.

"Yes," I said beaming. "*Taak*," I said to my masseur. "*Taak sa meuget.*"

"You will use that phrase often," he laughed.

"Yes, I think so," I answered.

Lawrence said, "Let's take a sauna. You can see the Karlbergsjon from the sauna."

"OK," I said, all compliance.

He was right. Standing side by side in the dry heat of the sauna we could see Stockholm's copper roofs and sparkling waterways framed in the room's picture window. The years had been kneaded out of my body, the anxieties untwisted and thrown out with the towels and the sheets.

It was like starting over, the flush over our sauna-warmed bodies bespeaking a rosy new future. I was rested and happy and whole once again.

"Did you like your present?" Lawrence asked circling my waist with his arm.

"Yes, Lawrence, I loved it."

"And do you promise to take care of yourself?"

"Yes, I promise." At that moment, I really meant it.

"And to love yourself?" he asked gently.

"Yes," I promised. After all, anything was possible. "Yes, I'll promise to do that, too."

Linda Watanabe McFerrin is a poet, novelist, and travel writer. Her work has appeared in journals, newspapers, and magazines throughout the United States, and in such anthologies as Wild Place, American Fiction, *and several Travelers' Tales titles. She is the author of two poetry collections, the novel* Namako: Sea Cucumber, *and the short story collection* The Hand of Buddha. *She is a winner of the Katherine Anne Porter Prize for Fiction, and lives in Northern California.*

JILL JEPSON

* ✷ ✷

Cave Temple of the Goddess

In India, a skeptical pilgrim
encounters the divine.

BEFORE I SAW THE TEMPLE OF THE GODDESS, I CALLED IT THE
Holy Hole, though not in front of Kathy. It was her idea to go
there. All I wanted to do was get to Kashmir, float around the waterways, and shake off the clamor of the North Indian plains. But
Kathy was a student of religion, and as soon as we started talking
about a trip together, she pulled out an obscure map and a pile of
esoteric books on the goddess known as Vaishno Devi.

We were both students in those days. Kathy was studying Hindi
in New Delhi, and I was doing the same down the Ganges at
Varanasi. One day, Kathy would be a professor of religions and
write a book about the Goddess. But that warm Indian autumn, I
had no idea why she wanted to take an arduous trip to a distant
cave, when Kashmir's lakes awaited. And until I got there, I didn't
know why I agreed to go with her.

It was October when we left for the mountains. The monsoon
had ended, leaving the plains lush and the days clear and warm.
From our second-class train window, we watched the flat land rise
into hills as we headed north from Delhi. Hours later, we arrived
at the city of Jammu, and, after a noisy, restless night in a crowded
inn, we embarked the next morning on a harrowing bus ride

studded with astonishing turns and vistas. We finally arrived, bone-jarred and weary, at the base of a mountain, and found our journey had just begun.

No one knows how Vaishno Devi came to have a temple in a cave, but her name is known throughout India, and people flock to see her. To reach the cave, the pilgrims must wend their way up a steep path by foot, in a line so long the end disappears at a point in the distance, and so slow moving that starting the trek at dawn will barely get the visitor to the temple by late afternoon.

I was still dazed and fatigued from our journey as we joined the queue, and Kathy and I inched our way up the path in silence. Above us loomed the western Himalayas and the keen blue of a mountain sky, but the smells were human—the scent of spices and hope. I peered up the path at the line of worshippers disappearing around a bend then reappearing at a higher point up the slope, and I tried to figure how many hours it would take to reach the temple, and how many steps.

But Indians are patient people, and the Goddess was apparently worth the wait. The pilgrims chatted, got to know each other, and shared stories about politics and movies, careers and families—and also about their journeys here, and their reasons for coming. All the while, they stared at us two fair foreign women dressed, like the Indian ladies, in cotton saris and tennis shoes. The cave temple of Vaishno Devi was not a tourist destination in 1977, and Kathy and I, the only foreign faces in the crowd, apparently made a more interesting sight than the mountain vistas.

To someone unfamiliar with India, these pilgrims might have looked similar—the women swathed in color and glass bangles, the men dressed in brown polyester—but I had been here long enough to know that they had traveled from very different places. Amid the odd strains of Indian-style English, I could hear a half dozen other tongues—Gujarati from the vermilion deserts of western India, Bengali and Bhojpuri from the lush Gangetic floodplains, Malayalam from the shimmering beaches of Kerala, and many dialects and subdialects.

The pilgrims had come here for different reasons as well. They were childless couples, men without work or hope for work, parents of sick and dying children. Women came to pray for the long lives of their husbands; men, to ask the Goddess for success. A few were deaf or blind or otherwise afflicted, come to pray for a cure; many were mourners seeking respite from grief. I wondered if I was the only pilgrim who had come with no request.

"What are you going to pray for?" Kathy asked. She was a sturdy, fresh-faced young woman, with waist-length hair and a matronly way for someone not yet thirty. The queue had come to a complete halt for the sixth or seventh time that morning, and knowing it might be a half hour before it moved again, we had sat down on the path, leaning our backs against the mountain. I looked at Kathy blankly.

"That's what it's for," she said, her voice tinged with impatience. "You don't make a pilgrimage to see the sights. You come to ask for something."

"*You* come to ask for something." I closed my eyes and shielded my face from the sun. "I left off praying long ago."

Kathy sighed the kind of irritated sigh normally reserved for children. She fussed with the edge of my red and white sari, until it lay in neat folds on my shoulder. "You're wasting an opportunity, then. So you don't believe! So what? Hindu deities don't demand faith the way Jehovah does. You don't have to believe in them to get a boon, you just have to ask."

I shrugged. The thin air and fatigue were lulling me into an unpleasant stupor, and I wondered again why I wasn't floating in a boat on a shimmering Kashmiri lake. "I'm only a tourist at the temple," I said, trying to shrug off Kathy's insistence. "I didn't come here to worship. I came to catch others in the act." But even as I said the words, I realized they weren't true, and I was surprised to feel an old need arise.

I have always had a love for blessed spots: sacred groves and wayside shrines, cathedrals, and holy springs. I lost my faith in my family's religion at a young age and spent many years searching for a place to hang my soul. It was a long pilgrimage, through prayer meetings and meditation groups, Bible readings and Zen. Too many revivals later, too many regrets, I had given up the search. But I had never lost the need to find a place to rest. And opening my eyes to the mountain sky, I realized why I had come to see this temple in a cave: because I longed to stand in a sacred place.

"Get up! Let's get going." The line had begun to move again, and Kathy was jostling my shoulder like a mother waking her child for school. "We've only got a mile or so to go, but we'll lose our spot if we don't keep up." I struggled to my feet and began to walk again, keeping my eyes on the sky so I wouldn't think of how far I had to go.

It was late afternoon by the time Kathy and I reached the mouth of the cave. The crowd quieted as we approached, more from fatigue, I thought, than awe. But as we neared the entrance, an uneasy murmur moved among the pilgrims. And when the crowd parted slightly, and I saw the opening to the cave, I stopped in my tracks and stared. A black hole opened into the rock. It was barely wide enough for even a small person to enter, and six inches into its mouth, it was dark as a tomb. One by one the pilgrims were stepping into the crevice and disappearing into nothingness.

"We're going to be buried," I said.

"Stop complaining. Pilgrimages aren't supposed to be easy," Kathy said. But then her tone became comforting. "There's another opening, where the line comes back out. You'll be fine." But I had not expected this: I had imagined a shaded grotto, flowers, incense, prettiness, not this gaping maw. An ancient fear burned inside my belly.

As we drew near to the opening, the crowd melded together into a single file. Kathy was behind me; in front, a man with an ancient face and eyes so full of fire that they seemed to be lighted from behind. I wondered if I could change my mind, step aside, allow the others to pass, and wait for them to emerge from the other side. But I swallowed my fear down and did not step from the queue. The movement of the crowd propelled us forward inch by inch until the mouth of the cave was immediately before us.

The ancient man moved ahead of me. He stepped between the walls of rock and appeared to become part of the earth itself. It was too late for me to back out now. I was pressed up so closely against the man in front of me and Kathy behind, that I could feel the movement of their sinews and bones. With my first step, the jagged walls scraped my arms on each side. With my second, I was engulfed in darkness so dense I could not see the old man's head, though it was only a few inches from my face.

I wondered where the passageway led. How far would it take me into the earth, and what would await me at the end? How long would I be trapped inside the cave? I choked down panic. I was desperate to break free. We edged forward, blind as worms, and I

> I ndividually and collectively we need to integrate the dark side. The setting of the Black Madonna in the woods is a place of growth and life, but also of death and decay. Her darkness answers our need for wholeness.
>
> Without words I stayed there in the chapel in the middle of the dark woods. Now a grandmother, I felt rooted both physically and spiritually in her darkness, reaching down into the earth back through the centuries to earlier times and to unknown Mother Goddesses.
>
> Here is the mystery of the Black Virgin. Her darkness welcomes our darkness. All embracing, she waits for us, there at the end of the trail.
> —Susan Tiberghien, "The Black Madonna of Mont Voirons"

tried to breathe the dead, unmoving air. I thought, I am going to be trapped in the stone. I am going to die here. I swallowed and prayed for air and for light. I prayed to Vaishno Devi or any other deity who might be listening to bring me to safety.

I do not know how much time passed in the darkness. Time seemed not to move at all inside the mountain. I remember this—the sound of my pulse in my ears, murmurs of people that seemed to come from deep within the soul of the earth, thoughts of being buried alive.

Then, quite suddenly, the narrow passage opened into a small, lighted cavern. Three pilgrims moved into the cavern together: the motherly woman who was my friend, the ancient stranger who had somehow become our companion, and I. Together, we stepped inside the chamber of the Goddess.

Vaishno Devi, the Goddess in the form of a stalagmite, stood before us, dabbed with the red paint of Hindu worship and bedecked with blossoms. The faint fragrance of sandalwood incense wafted in the dense air of the cavern. From some hidden crack, a shaft of light pierced the darkness. A priest, who seemed to have lived within this cavern as long as the Goddess herself, sat cross-legged next to Her, staring at us with blank curiosity. Then, apparently deciding we were no more interesting than any of the endless stream of worshippers he faced in his long hours at Vaishno Devi's side, he chanted a blessing. We had a moment to ask the Goddess for her boon. My companions prayed: the man in silence and Kathy aloud, asking for the whole world to be at peace. But I could think of nothing to say, and too soon, the priest was dismissing us so the next group of pilgrims could enter the chamber.

We exited the tiny cavern into a second dark, narrow passage opposite the first. Again, we were swallowed by darkness, and again I thought I might become entombed in stone. But we had seen the Goddess, and we were going not into the earth, but toward the light. I could feel fresh air waft against my face, and I knew I was being released by the earth. A moment later, I stepped into brilliant sunlight and the air full of the scent of the mountains.

To my surprise, the old man turned and looked at me with his fire-lit eyes. "What did you request of Vaishno Devi?" he asked. I had no answer: I had asked nothing of Her.

But I had found what I did not know I was seeking: the calm place at the heart of my fear; a space in the darkness where divinity resides.

Jill Jepson is a writer and linguistic anthropologist living in the Central Valley of California. Her work has appeared in many newspapers and magazines, including Sky & Telescope, Arizona Highways, *and the* San Francisco Chronicle. *She is the editor of* No Walls of Stone: An Anthology of Literature by Deaf and Hard of Hearing Writers.

EMILY ZUZIK

✦ ✦ ✦

Going Without at Ramadan

During the Muslim fast in Morocco, a traveler
finds sustenance from within.

I AM NOT A PIOUS WOMAN. I DIDN'T GO INTO RAMADAN WITH A long history of restraint. In fact, the most I knew about fasting was from my Catholic childhood during Lent, where you went without some chosen item for forty days. There were also meatless Fridays, but you still got a good fish sandwich from the church that night.

No one expected me to fast in Marrakesh, not even my traveling companion, who had chosen to do so to practice self-discipline. But we had decided to swear off Western extravagances on this trip—no E-mail, no expensive indulgences, and with luck, no expat communications—and hey, when in Rome...Besides, I thought, if I couldn't go without food during daylight hours, what kind of weak human was I?

I spent the night before the first day of fast with many other Moroccans and tourists in the Place Djemaa el Fna, a large open market area jammed with food stalls, snake charmers, musicians, and general business. There was a continual procession of cars, buses, motorized bikes, bicycles, scooters, horse-drawn carriages, and every other conceivable form of transportation. Exhaust hung gray-blue against the road. I saw two parents and three children crammed on one bike. Motion was in every direction.

I was eating what would be my last large meal until tomorrow sundown. I wasn't praying or analyzing the challenge ahead of me; in fact, I wasn't really thinking about it. I was simply absorbing the general commotion that extended late into the night and drinking mint tea, which was affectionately called the "whiskey of Morocco."

Ramadan is practiced by Muslims to develop an Allah-consciousness in the practitioner's heart and soul. But it's not merely a fast from food; it also includes drinking, smoking, and sexual relations. It is mandatory for all sane adult Muslims with exceptions for pregnant women, the elderly, the ill, and those responsible for heavy machines, like pilots. The fast begins every day at the Salatul Fajr call to prayer, or break of dawn, and

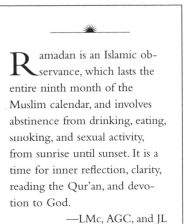

Ramadan is an Islamic observance, which lasts the entire ninth month of the Muslim calendar, and involves abstinence from drinking, eating, smoking, and sexual activity, from sunrise until sunset. It is a time for inner reflection, clarity, reading the Qur'an, and devotion to God.

—LMc, AGC, and JL

ends at the Salatul Maghrib call, or sunset. I knew with my low blood sugar that if I were Muslim, I could be exempt from the fast, but I had decided to tempt fate and the peaceful rapport with my traveling companion by fasting anyway.

The morning of the first day of Ramadan I awoke to the cry of my empty, aching belly—and figured it would be best for both of us if I had something small to keep my head together. I decided to eat. This added an extra challenge to the morning: There was no food at our hotel, and we had to find one of the few hotel-cafes in town that catered to Western tourists, where you pay for the privilege of eating during the fast. In this setting, I could partake of my few guilty bites without pressing my Western weakness upon those fasting and still respect the public restraint. We stopped at the Hotel Ali. Ironically, I ended up feeding more of my bread to a scruffy street cat who was begging at my feet than to myself. I resolved to make a go of it for the rest of the day.

With the decision to fast, whether to prove self-restraint or to respect the prevailing culture, came a contempt that I didn't expect. I found myself sneering at Western tourists who didn't know it was Ramadan, except that they couldn't get an espresso because most cafes were closed. Members of large French tour groups puffed away on cigarettes while being led through the markets. I watched one scene where an older Moroccan woman stared in disbelief while a camcorder-toting tourist ate a large pastry beside her. He seemed to have no clue about how rude this was. I raged over his ignorance. I was embarrassed for Western culture and its postcolonial insecurities. It was as if his action was screaming out: your country may no longer be ours, but we don't care about your culture and it will never rival our own.

The sun burned from above, drinking all moisture from my body, and I found myself dehydrated by 2 P.M. My friend had gone without food, but decided to splurge on water. Since thirst hadn't consumed my mind outright, we decided to push on. Temptation was everywhere. At least five orange-juice stands stood near the edge of the plaza. Each owner called to us, outbidding his neighboring competitor. I smiled and answered, "No thanks. Ramadan." This reply elicited some odd looks from them. I can only imagine what they were thinking: she's white, she's Western; why would she be fasting?

After a while, I took my shaking hands as a sign that I should probably have something to drink. This situation led to another challenge—where would we be able to drink water out of sight? There was the Hotel Ali or our hotel deeper in the medina. We were closer to the Hotel Ali, so we entered the closed cafe, found a shadowy corner and drank from a bottle of Sidi Harazem, one of two national bottled-water brands.

After the drink, I felt a renewed sense of possibility, and we set back out into the fray. It was as if that little break had healed all the weakness that was beginning to show. Despite my determined spirit, I had begun to feel faint before the water. This is another problem with the Ramadan fast. I was told later in my trip that the mental resolve to fast often has health repercussions. One man told me how his mother, who took shots for diabetes, went against doctor's orders and refused to take her insulin in order to keep the fast. She was hospitalized the next day. Both he and his uncle shook their heads and said this was quite normal in Morocco.

About an hour or two later, I felt the next pang of general restraint—illogically fluctuating mood swings. My generally calm demeanor spiraled to deeply agitated, bordering on volatile. My traveling companion was experiencing a similar strain. We started to bicker over which streets to take, what we were seeing, almost anything. And we began to see this happening all around. In the afternoon hours, we witnessed two scuffles between groups of men and three men being escorted into the police station. It's another irony of the fast—you go without to better yourself, and as a result of the hunger, you get really nasty to one another.

I found it to be a decided advantage to accept what I had and feel grateful for it rather than wish I had more. Wishing only made me feel even more hungry and thirsty, whereas acceptance and gratitude for what I did have allowed me to deal with the problem and channel my energy into moving ahead at a good pace.

—Helen Thayer, *Polar Dream*

Agitation hung jaggedly in the diesel-laden air. Listening to the shop owner hawking his wares became a hardship. My friend and I walked through long lanes in the souks, some winding around back to where we had started. I became frustrated by my inability to see that I was walking in circles. The shop owners would see me come by for the second or third time and pick up their haggling where they left off. I didn't want to deal with shopping. I didn't want to haggle. I was tired of people staring at me. I hated the crowd pushing in every direction. I marveled at how much patience these people had for all the delays, the random loaded mules lumbering down the narrow passage, the noise and air pollution from scooters passing on the same route. Even a sign for Coca-Cola in Arabic script bothered me. I wanted out.

We decided to leave the enclosed markets and return to our hotel.

The lack of food, walking, and the generally unpleasant atmosphere had worn both of us into exhaustion. We passed through a side street on the way to the hotel, and when a young man offered us hashish, my friend yelled, "No!" and shoved past him. The man returned with, "Fuck your wife!" My companion turned with rage, "Hey, fuck you, motherfucker!"

By then, the guy had disappeared, but my friend just snapped. He broke from my side and tore off in the direction of the man. Panic rushed over me as I saw him dash off. I didn't know what would happen. I was suddenly alone and surrounded by possibly pissed-off friends of the dealer, but even though I felt like a target, I couldn't help shaking my head and laughing at the lunacy of situation.

I waited in the passage with only people's stares to keep me company until my friend returned. He was breathless and expressed disbelief with how he had lost control. He said he didn't know what he would have done had he caught the guy. It was crazy and yet somehow appropriate. That's what happens when you have a city filled with people starving themselves for the first time in eleven months.

We headed to our room at the Hotel Smara, where we planned to rest until the Salatul Maghrib. When we arrived, Mustafa, a young man who had just finished school and started working at the hotel, smiled and greeted us. My first impression of him had been when we were pricing rooms upon arrival. He was listening to an English-language instructional tape that cut between bits of Lionel Ritchie's ballad "Hello" and British English speakers reciting the lyrics to teach usage. We were his first American guests, Mustafa had told us.

Now he greeted us and asked us how our day had passed. We explained our agitation and exhaustion from the day of fasting. But why are you fasting? he asked. We wanted to try it out, my friend explained. And out of respect, I added. He smiled. We retired to our room. It must have been around 4:30 or 5:00 P.M.

I lay on the bed and felt an immense weight lift from me. The room's cool air fell like a blanket over my weary frame. It was as if all the muscles in my body clung to the stuffed futonlike mattress and refused to let me move. I barely spoke. After a few minutes, I fell asleep.

About an hour later, I woke to the sound of the shrill, amplified voice singing the call to prayer. It is a strange noise that lingers below the hum of the city. You wonder if you're hearing anything at all. Then you listen more closely, concentrating on the softer drone until it slowly rises to where it becomes the siren of sunset. Next you begin to hear other calls rising out of the distance from mosques all over the city. It is a cacophony of religious outpouring, and becomes a way of marking time throughout the day. At that moment, it was a celebration that my day without food had finally ended. I didn't remember my vow to fast or my reasons behind it, I only rejoiced in the fact that food was on the way.

Elation set in. I fantasized about the day's "breakfast," a term most Moroccans use to describe the meal taken at sundown during Ramadan. It included a bowl of *harira*—a traditional Moroccan soup—plus brochettes, pita, rice, fries, and mint tea. I could almost taste the first bite. I smiled at my friend, who now seemed like the perfect person to celebrate my first meal with. He understood my sentiment and seemed to return it. We left the hotel and meandered through the thin streets of the medina toward the plaza. All the surfaces shone orange-red from the setting sun. It cast a surreal glow over the place that earlier had felt like a prison to me. On that pilgrimage to the *harira* stand, I decided to fast again the next day. If this was the high for all the "suffering" throughout the day, I wanted more.

Upon arriving at the stand, the young man who had so cordially wooed us into eating there the night before greeted us and guided us to benches among other hungry Moroccan men who had just locked up their shops and come for their first meal of the day. The young man gave my friend and me each a bowl of soup. I asked a man beside me in French to pass the salt and gestured my thanks. My shoulders slumped forward. I let my body fall limp and lifted the soup bowl near my face. Its sweet aroma pierced the dirty air around us and sent a wave of delight through my entire body. I slipped into a slow trance of spooning the hot broth into my mouth. I was without thought, like a robot mechanically maneuvering the utensil.

For some reason, I glanced up between bites and shuddered. I saw my reflection. My traveling companion, all the men eating beside me, and I were all slumped over, all spooning in silence as the sun ran slowly over the plaza like golden syrup. Some invisible force held me, and for the first time I didn't feel like an outsider. We had all fasted that day for the first time in a long while. We had all faced the mean-spirited ambience that comes with physical resistance. And now, we were together eating a family meal.

In the days that followed on my journey through Morocco, I spoke to many people about fasting and my reasons for doing it. Those people seemed impressed that I should want to respect the measures that they took for what they believed as well as to subject myself to such restraint. In doing so, I found a place that I never knew existed. Before going to Morocco, I believed that people had forgotten the idea of fasting and the inner strength that comes when you eliminate extravagance. I went to Marrakesh to see—and left having lived.

Emily Zuzik is film editor for Siren Magazine. *She has also written for* Feed, PAPER, Maxi, San Francisco Weekly, *and* Salon.

KELLY BOOTH

* * *

El Maestro's Magic Water

A witch doctor's rituals offer "spring cleaning" for the soul.

ON MY FIRST NIGHT IN PERU, THE PROPRIETOR OF A PIZZA JOINT gave me a free pizza dinner, complete with a yellow, bubble gum-flavored Inca Kola. I insisted on paying, but she wouldn't have it. Outlined against the electric, bare-bulbed night, she swooshed a glossy nailed hand at a halo of hovering insects and said it was her treat, "Because I want you to end up with at least one good memory of your night in Tumbes."

And that's what I have—one good memory.

Sometimes omens, like bugs on a bicycle ride, just seem to hit you in the face every time you look up.

Other times, they cross your path like an oncoming truck.

When my backpack had nearly been stolen from a bus in Colombia, it had become quite apparent that the only things I was really afraid of losing were my diary, my photos, and my sketchbook. With that realization, I'd begun to worry about them, a lot. So to assuage my growing unease, I'd sent the precious items and loads of gifts home, through a reliable mail agency I found in Ecuador.

Unburdened, I'd continued on my journey south and had finally crossed over the border into Peru.

Early the next morning I phoned my parents and was relieved to hear that my parcel had arrived as planned; everybody liked their presents; every last thing was accounted for.

Except my photos.

And my diary.

And my sketchbook.

I was devastated. The sudden loss of all that hard work—the only tangible evidence from my entire journey through Mexico, Central America, and Colombia—sent me reeling.

My carefully plotted route south vaporized and before I knew it, I'd veered well off course to make a pilgrimage high into the mountains, where I'd been told I could bathe in the lucky waters of some magic lakes.

I wasn't convinced it would help, but it wasn't going to hurt either.

After eight hours of altitude- and motion-sick switchbacks, the bus pulled into the village. I found a hotel and started trying to arrange the next leg of the journey. It wasn't easy. Whenever I asked about transport from there to the magic lakes, people looked at me strangely and said they weren't sure which lakes I meant. For some reason, it seemed as if nobody trusted me.

Eventually, a woman who ran her own makeshift, all-night snack stand in the alley behind my hotel explained that bathing in the lakes wasn't really enough.

"You must spend the night in the home of a witch doctor, a *curandero*," she told me.

She went on to explain, "The most famous *curanderos* in all of Peru live near here, and people come from as far away as Lima—

> Sometimes the true victory is to let go.... The well-balanced person strives not only for a goal but lives fully in the flow of life, because every expression in the process is equally important.
>
> —Lene Gammelgaard,
> *Climbing High*

even Ecuador—to visit them. Each *curandero* has a specialty. Some are best with matters of the heart, and they can mix up love potions no person can resist. Others can cure diseases of the body with magic and medicines that only they know how to make. Still others, like Juan Manuel, can do everything. Juan Manuel…*El Maestro*…you must visit him, I think. He is very famous; very powerful."

Right on cue, a man sitting at the other end of the bench piped up and declared that he was a personal friend of El Maestro's, and would be happy take me to his house.

Hours later I was introduced to Juan Manuel and his friends. It was 7:00 A.M. and they were drinking some kind of foamy-green alcoholic concoction. They were already three sheets to the wind. I joined them briefly, but couldn't keep up.

I excused myself and set out looking for somebody to explain what was to be expected from a guest at a witch doctor's house. I found a group of women in the kitchen but as soon as they saw me, they stopped speaking. I was an outsider, and had no right to interfere with their conversation.

Feeling displaced and misunderstood, I went to seek refuge in my room. Thankfully, it was private and stocked with a pile of fragrant, fresh-smelling, woolen blankets. I was glad something was clean, because I also found a pan of somebody's excrement congealing on the dirt floor. And it was apparently up to me to remove it.

I took the pan to the outhouse and passed through a room—halfway indoors, halfway out—which housed all manner of jungle beasts; killed, skinned, and hanging from the rafters. After disposing of the offending pan, I rinsed my hands off and walked into the village.

Almost everyone I encountered stared at me motionless from beneath brightly colored witch hats that were missing the pointy tips. Some say that part of Peru retains the purest form of the old religion. If Catholicism hadn't invaded the lives of the local people, luckily for me, Spanish had. Because the few men who did venture into conversation warmed considerably when they realized I spoke their language.

I finally found one woman who wasn't afraid of me, and I was so relieved, I gave her almost every piece of jewelry I had on. I'd lost everything that mattered to me, what did it matter if I gave everything else away? She was so pleased that I proceeded to hand over my scarf, my hat, and the rest of my jewelry, which we both agreed suited her little daughter perfectly.

I wandered aimlessly for hours and went to bed early to escape the odd silence. I laid my sleeping bag on top of the straw mattress and climbed in, still wondering if there was some place I was supposed to be, or something I was expected to be doing. It was freezing, so I piled on heaps of those sweet-smelling blankets, and finally fell asleep lulled by the faraway giggles of a young girl. She was explaining to someone that due to El Maestro's unfortunate drunkenness, everyone would have to return the next night.

A rooster's crow yanked me back into consciousness, and I noticed that sometime during the night, three more people had fallen asleep in my room. Outside in the new blue light, the homestead was crawling with donkeys and a slew of city folks who had come up on a predawn bus. Everyone was preparing for the ceremony, the *misa*, including El Maestro, who showed no signs of being hung over.

I studied the situation carefully and tried to rent a donkey, because it seemed like that's what everyone was doing. But I must have done something wrong, because an incomprehensible fiasco ensued. I couldn't to do anything right. El Maestro was called in to settle everyone down. He showed me which donkey I was supposed to rent and gave me a tiny glass bottle stuffed with green herbs. I paid the creature's owner and climbed aboard, joining about thirty people on a trek up through rutted mud tracks.

After a few hours of climbing, we left our donkeys tied to moss-covered trees and trudged down through spongy bogs to a small alpine lake. It was one of the lakes I had come to dip in, which suddenly struck me as entirely absurd. It was freezing up there.

Teary-eyed women were filling plastic containers with lucky water while the tiny beach at the edge of the lake was prepared for the *misa*. El Maestro's helpers planted several brass and wooden sticks in the ground which the hopeful crowd then surrounded with photos of loved ones, lucky charms, and bottles of perfume. With a ceremonious flourish, I added the vial of lucky herbs the witch doctor had given to me that morning.

In the center of the arrangement stood a large, ornate wooden staff. It had a cup carved into the top, into which the maestro's helpers poured lake water. Then the crowd became silent.

Abruptly, El Maestro pulled the staff from the ground and began chanting. He took a few sips of water from the staff's cup and spit them in each of the four cardinal directions. He did the same with some perfume, then proceeded to drink the rest of the water from the staff.

Through his nose.

Gulp after gulp, he downed every last drop, through his nostrils.

El Maestro's entourage eventually joined him. Loud burps and vulgar gurgling noises proved that it is not an easy thing to drink liquid through one's nose. Not even for a witch doctor who makes his livelihood doing just that. As I watched them swallow noseful after noseful, I grew ever more thankful that as a member of the congregation, all I had to do was stand there and watch.

A few minutes later, El Maestro's helpers lined each of us up at the edge of the lake and passed out palm-sized silver dishes with indentations in their rims. One of the men filled our little dishes with a familiar smelling liquid that we were instructed to swallow.

Through our noses.

Nobody escaped the nose drinking. It's hard to control the gag reflex while gulping liquid through the nose, and most everyone spit at least some of it back up. It would have been disgusting had it not been for the lovely fragrance of whatever we were regurgitating. I recognized that smell, too, just like my blankets back at the maestro's house.

All day we stayed there, spitting perfume into the breeze, being shaken, stretched, and rubbed with magic sticks. And all through the day, sometimes from the special silver dishes, other times from cow's horns, we downed nose brew after nose brew. The effort of plunging naked into the icy water for our ceremonial baths turned out to be mild by comparison.

Eventually we returned to the maestro's house, where the crowd thinned. I wandered around for hours trying to process the ordeal I'd just been through. For a while I wondered when the bus would come, and then I began to question the arrival of any bus ever again. Had I misunderstood? Did I need to find another way down the mountain? Just then, I realized I'd left my favorite sweater somewhere near the lake, and felt the pang of loss welling up inside. But I was too tired to dwell on it, so I simply let go of the anxiety. As my belongings continued to slip away, it felt like I was being forced to surrender to a plan I was not making, and I finally just gave in and let everything go.

No bus came that evening and I was almost relieved, because more than anything, what I desired was sleep.

But I would never get another chance to curl up under those mysterious covers, because the second half of the ceremony was just about to begin.

It took place throughout the longest night of my life, in the room full of splayed animals.

We nose drank some more, spat more perfume, shimmied in the starlight, and tried—every now and then—to sneak half-lucid naps on straw mattresses arranged on the floor.

At one point, we were each given a cupful of liquid to drink orally. I wondered why, after so many nose drinks, we were switching to something so mundane. Shoot, any schmuck could drink through their mouth.

But what we were all drinking that time was no mere fragrant water. What we all drank—little old ladies, little old men, bankers, lawyers, and homemakers; good church people and upstanding citizens—was the mescaline-laced juice of a local cactus called San Pedro. And we all began to hallucinate.

Motionless in the darkness, nobody spoke. A cough punctured the stillness. Sinuous light began to swirl in from just beyond reality; imaginary metallic jungle shrieks spun delicate threads of color through our minds.

I pulled the wool poncho over my head to escape the raw air. Sitting there, I may have dreamed, or it may have only felt like a dream: there was an instant of palpable awareness; an unearthly shriek pierced the silence. Against a flash of white, an enormous silhouetted hawk soared above me.

Hawk, who inhabits the dry place close to the sun, sees the larger picture, sees things that would be invisible from below. He glided on El Maestro's whispers: "You lost what you thought you needed…because you were too attached,. and they were nothing more than words and lines which have served their purpose. All that you learned from making them is still with you."

I nestled deeper under the poncho and for the first time in days, I felt safe.

Sweet comfort was stolen when we were awakened for one more dance out under the frozen stars. Only there weren't many stars anymore. It was morning, and the only visible heavenly body was a smiling crescent moon.

Without sleeping, we packed our bags and caught buses back to earth.

Strangely, I felt elated. I was physically more exhausted than ever, but I was no longer worn out. I felt free; free of unnecessary material objects and free of worry. All those mentally, emotionally, and physically draining feats I'd been through had turned into being a spring-cleaning for the soul. And outside of the bus, off to the right, I noticed a hawk sweep by on invisible currents of air. I knew once again that I was exactly where I was supposed to be, and my spirits were soaring, too.

Kelly Booth has worked as a fine artist and as a graphic designer in a variety of industries since graduating from art school several years ago. She lives in San Francisco and works in Silicon Valley.

* * *

Sweat Lodge

Some truths can be seen only in darkness.

I AM A "FEAR TYPE" WHO DOESN'T LOOK AFRAID.

In the past, my strategy has been to avoid fear or other strong feelings that make me uncomfortable, using whatever strategy I can think of. Usually I just try to keep busy.

I was about to leave Berkeley for a month, when a friend asked if I wanted to come to a sweat lodge that Saturday. The timing wasn't good and I didn't know much about the ceremony, but I had a romantic image of heat, American Indian wisdom, wholeness—and a chance to bless my journey.

My friend, who had participated in the sweat lodge ceremony many times, assured me the people were sympathetic. The rural Sonoma County setting had the spare vastness of a New Mexico landscape. The ceremony would be conducted by a Lakota Sioux woman.

One at a time, the twelve of us crouched to get through a small flap in the canvas door and entered a tepeelike structure. I sat cross-legged on the earthen floor, my head practically touching the ceiling of the tent. The twelve of us formed a circle around a large fire pit. Very slowly a woman began carrying in lava rocks on something that looked like an elongated pizza carrier, placing each one of them carefully in the center of the fire pit.

While she was doing this there was a bit of chanting and a few instructions, and then the leader told us that if we chose to leave at any point in the ceremony, we would not be allowed to return.

Feeling rather pleased with myself that at sixty I was willing, even eager, to take on an unexpected adventure, something quite foreign to anything I had ever done, I sat there, calm, anticipating an interesting "event." When the last of the twenty-eight coals was placed in the pit, the woman left, closing the flap of the door behind her.

Total darkness.

Water poured on the rocks created a whoosh of furious steam heat. Heat permeating every air space. I love steam baths, so I had looked forward to this part of the ritual. It took only four minutes for me to be afraid.

Very afraid.

My friend had suggested that if it got too hot, I could lie down on the earthen floor. I tried that but it made no difference. I tried poking my fingers under a tiny opening at the bottom of the tent, hoping that would relieve my growing anxiety, but nothing worked.

> Each of us originated in the darkness of our mother's womb.... My twenty-five years of work in holistic health care makes me a firm believer in body memories and cellular consciousness. On an individual and collective level, the body *remembers* the darkness as the source and the beginning.
>
> —Deborah Rose,
> "The Black Madonna:
> Primordial Ancestress"

This fear wasn't attached to any thoughts except *how* I was going to survive.

The last thought I had was that *if* I managed to get out I wouldn't be hard on myself. I had done the best I could. Then no thought. Only fear. Raw, palpable, free-floating fear in every cell—and darkness.

Too paralyzed, or too civilized, to yell "let me out," I was half aware of people talking with great feeling, telling what had brought them here. Each asked for guidance and a blessing from the leader, and the power she represented.

My own civilized notion of why I was here was gone. I had thought it was to ask for a blessing for my journey and for the book I was writing, but now, lying on the ground, my heart pounding so hard I thought it might explode, I didn't think I was even in a condition to speak. My friend, sitting next to me, spoke in a firm voice I had never heard her use before.

When it was my turn I heard myself, in a quiet, slow, tiny, soft voice say, "*I am very afraid.* I'm not sure I can stay. I am very, very frightened."

"Come and sit next to me," said the leader, who was sitting next to the exit door. She spoke some wise words, none of which I can remember now, as I crawled halfway around the circle to where she was, feeling at the time it was the most natural of things to be doing. I lay down very still, still needing the security of the cooler ground for support.

Someone put a steady hand on my leg—and that hand stayed there, not moving, for the rest of the ritual. In the darkness I never saw who that person was. That steady hand, of a man or a woman, I never learned who it was, was a great help.

Time passed.

The enormity of the fear began to diminish.

More chanting, a long wooden pipe handed from person to person, prayers, and the ceremony was over. The fear began to be bearable. I stepped outside and the night air was cool and welcoming.

I felt calm.

Having no place to hide, I had felt my fear and the "fear cracked open."

A giant weight had lifted off my shoulders. A huge chunk of fear I had carried just below the surface for a long time had been dislodged. Whether this fear had anything to do with my harsh judge, I didn't know, but suddenly I felt like I was traveling through life with a lighter knapsack.

Recently I read a description of a sweat lodge: "You will probably die during the ceremony," an Indian leader had said. "And today is, after all, a good day to die." That did not sound overly dramatic to me. If anyone had warned me about what might happen during the sweat lodge ceremony, I wouldn't have taken the risk.

I saw a curious relationship; the more I was able to stay with, not move away from, uncomfortable feelings, the more I was also able to feel happy and alive.

Remembering how calm I felt when I stepped out into the night air after being in the sweat lodge, I now know I don't have to wait for an exotic ceremony to turn toward, rather than away from, difficult feeling.

I have a chance almost any day.

Sue Bender is an artist, author, and lecturer. Her books include Plain and Simple: A Woman's Journey to the Amish *and* Everyday Sacred: A Woman's Journey Home, *from which this story was excerpted. She lives in Berkeley, California*

AMY G. CARLSON

✶ ✶ ✶

The Way of Tea

In Japan, the essence of an ancient
ritual is finally touched.

"SIMPLY GATHER WOOD, BOIL WATER, AND DRINK TEA," EXHORTS
the sixteenth-century Sen Rikyu, master of all masters of the
Japanese tea ceremony, *chanoyu,* The Way of Tea. "Yeah, sure!" I
groaned, feeling universes away from understanding that spirit of
Zen-like simplicity as I sat, cramp-legged, at my first tea ceremony,
attempting to follow an incredibly complex set of rules: Turn the
bowl, bow to him, bow to her, admire that, slurp, don't blow your
nose, thank the hostess, sit straight...Except for an exhilarating high
from the tempera-paint-green tea, I felt nothing remotely resem-
bling the *wa, kei, sei,* or *jaku*—harmony, respect, purity, or tranquility—which the tradition espoused.

I was just twenty-two, living in Japan for a few years. Although
I was considered a small person by home standards, in Japan I felt
big, bumbling; a monster with many elbows—especially at the tea
ceremony that day. As the powdered tea was prepared, bowl by
bowl, and individually served, all eyes rested on me, the American
giant. Self-consciousness flooded in. I expanded under their gaze,
knocking over my bowl; whacking my neighbors with elbows as I
tried to bow; uncrimping my legs, jutting them out into sacred
space; turning my bowl the wrong way as I set it down; bowing to

the wrong person at the wrong time; taking too many sips, way beyond what was proscribed. Harmony and tranquility scattered in fear from the sight of the buffoon. I sat defeated, longing to enter the timelessness and grace many friends had told me this ceremony entertained. But it remained beyond comprehension. I returned to the States still a mystified, frustrated *chanoyu* virgin.

Now twenty years have past, and I have come back to Japan, here to reconnect with the people and place I have so dearly missed—and perhaps to get another chance at glimpsing The Way. It has been a long time since the disastrous first attempt.

I arrive one evening at the home of Noriko, my landlady from two decades ago. Noriko had always been lovingly protective of her *gaijin*—foreigner—on the fourth floor, often leaving me hot custard at my front door, which I would discover upon return from a long day of teaching. Now she has become a teacher of *chanoyu*, and she has invited me here tonight to guide me through its magic ritual of wood, water, and tea.

I hesitate before I knock on her door, the memory of my young self stumbling through the tea ceremony all too clear. Still, here I stand, filled with hope that with Noriko's gentle guidance, this time things will be different.

Noriko greets me in her stone foyer with a bow and graciously leads me, slipper-clad, into her home. She serves me a sumptuous repast of homemade sushi and daikon, all of which looks more like art than food. With dictionaries in hand, we giggle in our linguistic stumblings, but somehow we understand each other. Then, after dinner, she asks me to wait while she prepares.

Minutes later she reappears and leads me into her inner sanctum of tatami, a room whose simplicity immediately grounds me—just grass mats, hues of gold and brown, rice paper, and bare wood. My shoulders drop away from my ears where they had been roosting. My pulse slows. My breath deepens. I feel at rest here.

With grace-filled movements and grand pauses that saturate my spirit, Noriko begins the dance of Tea, moving fluidly through ancient ritual. Generations of tea masters gather in the stillness of the air, guiding her, unseen. The smooth sliding of a hand down a bamboo handle; the sound of water being poured slowly from a great height; the swirling of the steam; the careful turning of the whisk; the frothy bright green thickness of the powdered tea. I sit mesmerized, shedding my worries and my harried, vain wanderings. I sit full of the present, mindful of every seemingly imperceptible shift of a finger, reflection on a bowl, trace of a smile on the lips.

We bow to each other. I am ready. As I drink deeply this rich hot green liquid, I feel as if I am communing, taking part in a transformative, sacred act that will usher me into a new reality. Warmth suffuses my body as I sit with eyes closed, floating in a warm placid lake, buoyant, embryonic. I glide into pools of shining darkness, a glittering otherness, where I leave my old bumbling self onshore. This gentle darkness washes away my self-consciousness, the thing that had tripped me up in that *chanoyu* twenty years ago and made The Way so elusive.

I float through this timeless state effortlessly into harmony's cove, tranquility seeping into my bones. Gently, in hushed tones, Noriko calls me back. I reluctantly open my eyes, pulling myself back into the room. She is bowing yet again and inviting me to enjoy a second cup.

I cannot speak; I do not want to destroy this enveloping sense of calm. I slowly shake my head "no." I want to hold the stillness inside of me forever, or at least its possibility. My skin tingles. My breath expands to my toes, stretching sinews like a cat waking up from a nap in the sun. I feel more at peace than I ever have before.

After a while, I reluctantly bid Noriko good-bye and gather myself together for the ride back to my lodging on the bike I've borrowed. Yet as the night air pushes me home, The Way remains, shrouding me in calm. I feel impervious to the rush of frenzied traffic, the barks of jailed dogs, the brash glare of streetlights. I climb into bed, the feeling of being Noriko's honored guest still blankets me with tranquility. Gone is the restless American beast, the monster with many elbows.

Still, as I drift off to sleep, I think of how I must soon head back to the land of the Big, back to the speed, the double espresso, just-do-it culture where stillness is a historical event, from the time before cars. How will I keep the spirit of *chanoyu*—that graceful silence—within me? How will I return to the placid lake I so briefly entered; that opening of sparkling timelessness I had momentarily touched?

Days later, with visions of my teacher's hand whisking the steaming tea still fresh in my heart, I board the plane. Noriko will help me. She will guide me in The Way as I attempt to bring this Japanese blessing home with me. It seems so simple: just gather wood, boil water, and drink tea. But I am an American in a hurry. Will I have time? I only hope so. Be with me, Noriko-san.

Amy G. Carlson is a teacher, editor, and gardener who lives in Leavenworth, Washington, with her husband Reed, juggling many projects including building a house.

✦ ✦ ✦

Initiation

A skeptic touches the hem
of the Goddess's skirt.

IN 1971 I WENT TO ISRAEL TO LIVE ON A KIBBUTZ. I WAS LONGING for regeneration through humble work. I connected this desire with *eretz Isroel*. The earth, the soil. Since I had first walked into the valley of black sheep at the Powerscourt Estate, I had longed to kick back the dead leaf and uncover the true ground of myself. But with every step I took, the skeptic in me had something to say.

This skeptic, hard-edged, never innocent, born knowing, rather bitter, not likely to take the risk of believing in anything, narrowing its eyes, puffing out its chest, smiling scornfully at my "female exaggerations," had been driven against the wall and was fighting back for all it was worth. It directed its sharpest thrusts against my "mysticism, and related rot," trying to reason me out of my growing fascination with the subtle, extremely potent, as yet unnamed something I found in nature.

Every time I walked off the kibbutz, into the fields and hills that surrounded it, I responded to the landscape with a growing rapture, as if I were returning home after thousands of years of absence. The black goats grazing on the white rocks in a rust-red earth, the wild river valleys where dark-skinned women from neighboring villages tended their flocks, the purple mountains covered in mist, drawing away into the distance, all called to me from an old knowledge, demanding my surrender.

But how could I surrender?

The gossip. The woman raving. The witch. The woman who mutters beneath her breath. The woman who can't think without weeping. The woman who gathers herbs by moonlight and dries them in secret beneath her bed. The woman who claims to see what isn't there. The woman who knows the future before it happens. The woman who doesn't read the newspaper, hasn't a clue what is going on in the world, but insists that her daughter, ten thousand miles from her, is in danger. This creature, for whom we have been taught so much contempt—is she what I was becoming?

I had left my daughter in California with her father. It was painful to think of the time that would pass before I was settled enough to send for her. In fact, I never did get settled enough. I returned home ten months later. I was a different person when I got back. An arrow, spinning in circles all my life, had now pointed.

On the kibbutz I became an expert pruner of trees. I made a few friends. They came over to have tea with me in the late afternoons. But the nights were difficult; the wild mountain setting, a few yards from the Lebanese border, where the Israeli army was building a security road, did little to give me peace of mind. I was not frightened by the sound of shelling or the sudden arrival of Israeli soldiers on the track of terrorists hidden in the neighboring caves. It was, rather, the wildness of the place calling to the kindred wildness in me that unsettled my efforts to become a hardworking farmer, hands hardened by toil. In the early evenings I would climb up into the guard towers that looked down over the valley.

One day a bird swept out over the landscape. I watched it soaring and wheeling against the darkening sky. Then I noticed something remarkable. For that brief instant the world was suspended in a perfect balance. In everything there was an equal light and darkness. In the grass below me, in the purple mountains, in the piercing blue of the Mediterranean, in the taut wings of the bird. A poise. A stillness. All things divided equally between day and night, the light and the dark, the expectation and the fulfillment. It was a universe held in perfect balance, its opposites contained and reconciled. I sensed, in that image, the sudden, rapturous possibility of bringing about a state of accord between the warring parts of myself.

By the time I got back to my room I saw a lot in this idea. Reason had its place, without doubt, in what I was experiencing. Its categories had helped me give shape over the years to a highly irrational, often chaotic experience. But there were times when these categories had to be set aside so that a new perception of life could emerge. If this experience upset the neat labels that had been put upon things then it would be the work of reason to reorder its ordering principles and make them serve the exposition of intuitive truth. I would never cease to think about my experience. But I could not use reason as a way of warding off the power of rapture. That was like being forced to choose between day and night, light and darkness, the known and the unknown, as if only one of these polar opposites were real.

> We are dark creatures feeding on light. We need light to balance our dark. The mystery of our knowing is a dance, a spinning, an exchange between dark and light, and among all the things those two worlds hold. We are struck, always, by those times at the threshold—dawn, dusk—by the mystery of light dying and being born. We watch the light rising, sinking, changing, striking the dust and clouds of the atmosphere, painting such marvels of color and form, and we know then something of the deeper mystery and beauty of ourselves.
> —Sharon Balentine, "Eyes, the Soul, Knowing"

I lit the heater and got under the covers. That was it? As simple as that? Here, finally, was the next step I had been trying to take? Where I had previously perceived irreconcilable opposition between reason and worship, I now grasped the possibility of bringing them together. This was the lesson I had been trying to learn.... I was capable of logic, discipline, and self-control. I was capable of wild, exuberant, visionary dreaming.

A few days later I was in my room after a day of strenuous labor in the orchards. Lying in bed, I heard a voice. It said: "For it is possible to rise by joy, through those same stages of initiation suffering required."

I sat up and folded my arms around my knees. "Voices? Now she's hearing voices?" the undying skeptic in me immediately brought out. But this time instead of mocking and dismissing the voice, why not listen to it?

I went to look out the window; I opened it wide and leaned over the valley. Later, if I wanted to, I could work out some theory about subvocal, mental voices. For now, this voice had named what until then had been nameless. From the moment I had knelt down before the tree in the mountains above Dublin, I had been involved in a process of initiation.

What could I say about this experience? To begin with, it was not separate from my body. Usually it arose as my menstrual blood dropped down. Although spiritual, it did not require a mortification of the body. Furthermore, it made me capable of a particular type of thought. Since that day in Dublin I had been fascinated by questions about the nature of reality, which had not really interested me before that time. Evidently, this type of initiation asked me to overcome the conflict I had always perceived between thinking and feeling.

And then there was nature: In my early twenties I had felt myself to be outside of nature. Now I participated in it. The flow of my blood was connected to the cycles of moons and tides; a bird in flight called me into its flying. Working in the orchards I felt in need of strong roots, seasons of change. When the afternoons were hot we lay down under the apple trees to rest and I grew back into the earth, into a second body.

Moreover, over the years the initiation process had irreversibly changed my mode of perception. Now, every stone and tree I looked at seemed to have a soul, to feel and bleed, rejoice and suffer. All this I had come to understand not through reading holy books that instructed me in religious doctrine, but through my own immediate, intensely felt relationship to the universe, which I had come to know not by taking it as an object of study but through a process of identification and participation that overcame all sense of separation between what I looked at and what I became in the process of looking.

Consequently, the organizational categories I had always taken for granted had also changed over the years. One day, observing the tiny, blue-star-shaped flower that grew from a weed out of the cracked earth on the path behind the kibbutz, I had wondered why people categorized some plants as desirable and some as weeds—everything I looked at seemed to have, in that moment, the same quality of a majestic beauty. It must have been that day I first noticed the exquisite purple color of cow dung drying on the path. It, too, although it embarrassed me to think it, seemed to hold the same quality of a revealed divinity, a sense that the deepest possible meaningfulness and presence were woven into the humblest, most insignificant bits of matter. Cow dung and weeds, apple trees and black goats, the Arab boys wandering after their flocks in the dry river valley, the hawks soaring overhead, the woman crouched down on the ruins in a state of ecstatic observation—all told the same story of a divinity embedded in the human body, rising from the earth, dropping down from the sky, weaving together thinking and feeling, perceiving and being in a linked participation that gave order, meaning, and direction of life. If this experience shattered the idea of the divine as male and unknowable, if it called into question the idea of spirit as an elusive essence that hovered unattainably outside of human reach, then it was time to give up these ideas and place myself at risk in a new relationship to the universe. Whatever I might someday become, for now this is what it meant to be a woman.

The value of such thinking was immediately apparent. It shifted the focus of my preoccupation from theories about experience to the experience itself. It brought to mind an event that had occurred almost two months earlier, a few days after I had arrived in Israel.

I had been wandering about by myself in a small village of Moroccan Jews visible, below in the valley, from our kibbutz. We had driven down in the late afternoon and parked the truck discreetly out of sight, knowing that we should not be driving. It was the evening of Yom Kippur. Most of us had eaten a small meal in the dining room and would not eat again until nightfall of the next day. When we reached the village on foot the others went ahead, walking in a purposeful stride toward the synagogue. I came along more slowly. The village was interesting to me. It reminded me of the small town in Russia where my mother had been born. The same dusty streets, dilapidated houses, dogs and chickens wandering in and out. A sense, too, of something ancient and enduring that had managed to survive the poverty and dirt.

I lost track of my companions. The village girls, who had not gone to temple on the holiest night of the year, came to walk with me. At first there were only a few of them. We walked on, the little girls trailing after me. Soon we were joined by others, who came running toward us, delighted by this opportunity for diversion. I provided plenty. There I was, in a long, brightly colored dress, a shawl over my shoulders. I looked as if I belonged somewhere ethnic but I was unable to speak a word to them. My only Hebrew was the absurd phrase that I could not speak Hebrew. This set them off into wild laughter; after all, there I was, speaking it.

They tried again and again, chattering at me, pointing to themselves, pointing to the kibbutz on the mountain, running around me in circles. I would listen intently to what they were saying, hesitate for a moment when they had finished talking. Then, as they waited with great anticipation, standing up on their tiptoes, their eyes wide, mouths open, sucking in their breath, I did it again. No, nothing had changed: I still had only my one phrase. I could not speak Hebrew.

Eventually they must have decided that I was not playing a game. They began to look at me with a serious compassion. Finally, overcoming their shyness, they drew close and took charge of me. They crowded around me, grabbed my skirt; they went on chattering at me in Hebrew and kept right on laughing when I couldn't chatter back. Then I had an inspiration. I knelt down in the dust. I put my arms around them and told them my name. That much at least I had learned in Hebrew class. "*Ani Kim,*" I whispered. "I am Kim."

It exhausted my eloquence, but they no longer cared. They grabbed me by the hand, pushed each other aside, threw their arms around my neck, kissed me, dragged me to my feet. I had a fleeting thought about my companions in the synagogue. Would I have learned more about God if I had joined them there? And then I heard, as we walked on together about the village, echoing from the whitewashed buildings and the dirt streets, at nightfall in this ancient homeland that did not cherish its girls, "Keem, Keem, Keem, Keem." My name had become an incantation.

I thought of those girls while I stood at my window, looking down past the village all the way to the Mediterranean—the sea that had carried those of my people who survived away from their homeland after Bar Kochba, the great legendary hero, had failed in his uprising against the Roman legions during the first century of the Christian Era. I thought about those girls and wondered when I would see them again, with their dark eyes of old knowledge. I told myself it had been no commonplace event, that wandering in the dusty streets while my companions sat indoors, the women excluded from the service upstairs behind the scene in the synagogue. Initiation, was it?

Through the doorway of a crumbling house I had seen an old woman, wrapped in a fraying shawl, crouch down to place cow dung on a fire. She beckoned me in when she saw me looking, hobbled over on bare feet, drew me inside. The little room was filled with smoke; it smelled of too many lives and too much poverty. I drew back when she placed in my hand a cup of mint tea. The little girls, who had trooped in after me, were watching my face apprehensively, afraid I might refuse this hospitality. I wanted to. There were circles of grease floating in the pale green liquid, the glass was smudged, and I knew, nevertheless, I was going to drink it. The old lady watched me as I sipped. Sweet, hot, fresh as the night sky. I had to wonder whether wine sipped from a ceremonial goblet on Shabbos was any more holy than this smudged glass offered, from the fullness of poverty, to a stranger.

I held the glass between my hands when I had finished, bowed my head over it to thank the old woman, pressed the glass to my chest. That pleased her; she came up close to me, took me by the elbow, shook me lightly. Then she began to talk and chatter with the same urgency the little girls had shown when they began to love me. She pointed to her heart, to each of her breasts, and then drew me to the threshold and pointed to the mountains, just then taking on their purple shadow beneath the sky. I strained toward her with my entire attention, but I could not figure out what she was trying to say. Finally she gave up, took me by the shoulders, drew me down, fixed me with a penetrating gaze, released me.

A short time later I caught sight of my companions from the kibbutz winding back toward the truck parked on the outskirts of the village. It was dark by then; the moon was not yet up. The girls came along with me, looking pleased with themselves, very secretive. They wouldn't let me join my companions, a few streets ahead. They pressed close against me, led me on a route of their own so that I arrived at the truck a good while before the others. And then, in twos and threes, they took themselves off, waving good-bye to me. A tall girl remained with me, holding my hand until everyone else had climbed into the truck. Then she pressed my hand against her heart, whispered my name to me in a meaningful way, and said: "You don forghet uz…"

I had thought back to the night of Yom Kippur before now. But always I had been involved in my usual conflict, insisting the event had been "more than ordinary, very significant, guided by some nonrational force," while at the same time I hollered with derision. Distracted by this inability to determine "the true nature of the event," I had not paid attention to my desire to return to the village to see the girls again, or to the fantasy set loose in me when I wondered what the old woman had told me. Could she have asked

me why that night was more holy than any other? For the first
time, at my window looking down over the valley, I asked myself
whether the girls had led me to her deliberately.

The answer to these questions did not come to me for many
years. When it arrived finally I did not link it to the little girls, the
old woman, the mint tea, the waking rapture at the window. But I
had decided to write a story about a sect of women that secretly
worshipped the Goddess within traditional Judaism and had done
so for the thousands of years since the Hebrew conquest of
Canaan, handing the tradition down from mother to daughter.

The idea for this novel, *The Flame Bearers,* came to me in 1978,
seven years after I left Israel and returned to California. But I no
longer doubt that fiery seed was cast deep into my imagination
during that night walk through the small village in the darkening
valley. Not a single man had been visible in the streets. For those
hours of sunset we walked and wandered in a women's world,
making up incantations, finding ceremonial forms and our own
sense of the sacred in the dusty streets, outside the synagogue.

The Goddess was with us that night, even if the little girls knew
nothing of her. She was there when the small fire was kindled from
cow droppings by an old crone stooping over the flames. It was she
who helped me put the dirty glass of tea to my lips. I had no need
to think of her as an objective reality hidden somewhere in the
universe keeping an eye on the world as God is said to do. She was
fully present long before I learned to name her. Already then, she
had risen from the dark soil, to lend a more than ordinary significance to my encounter with the girls. In darkness she had been
born to my imagination, in darkness over the next seven years she
continued to ask me questions.

I had gone far when I walked away from my companions and
went out wandering with the girls. But I continued to fuss about
whether one should trust to irrational events and what their true
nature might be and whether the girls' coming upon me in the
streets was simply coincidence or some other kind of guidance.
And if guidance, on what authority? And if authority, from what
source? I had glimpsed the possibility of bringing peace between

the skeptic and believer who continued to war within me, but that brief glimpse was all I could achieve.

I stayed awake with these thoughts. I woke wrestling with them as if they were a mighty angel that surely would bless me if only I could get the upper hand. And meanwhile I did not go back to the village, although I lived in Israel for many months. I did not go back although I continued to gaze down longingly at it from my window. Within a few months I no longer thought about the old woman and what she had been trying to tell me. Even today I do not know.

But I had touched the hem of the long skirts of the Goddess, there in the streets on the holiest night of the year. I had tasted her in the cup of tea, looked into her eyes, failed to understand her. To figure out what she had told me I would have to unearth the reasons I fought so militantly against my imagination. Why is this night more holy than any other night? To answer that question I would have to go on following the little girls.

Kim Chernin also contributed "Awakening the Stone" to Part One.

LUCY McCAULEY

* * *

In Ronda

She found what she was looking for—
although not in the way she expected.

THERE IS SOMETHING ELUSIVE ABOUT THE SPANISH, AN ASPECT of their spirit that defies definition. It has to do with their almost pagan instinct for pleasure—all of that exuberant dancing and hand clapping—but also with a kind of melancholy, an innate understanding of tragedy that Spaniards possess. In all my years of visiting Spain I had never been able to wholly understand that paradox. Even as a college junior, when I lived in Andalusia and believed that my sheer affection for the country would allow me to know what it meant to be "Spanish," I still could not grasp it.

That hope for some kind of understanding—or some tenuous reconciliation with my inability to understand—is why I found myself not long ago on Spain's southern Costa del Sol, boarding an early-morning bus for Ronda. From what I had heard, Ronda embodied the enigma of Spain: a place at once romantic and sorrowful, a fortressed village whose views from craggy cliffs were both lovely and sad, carrying the weight of the town's shadowed history.

I had also read somewhere that Rainer Maria Rilke, the German poet, had lived in Ronda for a few months, when he was in his mid-thirties. I planned to visit the hotel where he had lived and to read the poetry that he'd written there. I thought that he'd probably grappled with similar questions about the Spanish that I had.

The bus from Málaga to Ronda wound up mountainsides, past white clusters of towns. With each curve of the road, I felt myself curling backward through the years as we left the crowds of the Costa del Sol farther behind. I thought of what I knew about Ronda: a town perched at the edge of a mountain range and divided in two by the Tajo gorge. The Tajo drops 500 feet into a river whose roar, after the rains, can be heard from the streets above. Ronda is the perfect place, Hemingway wrote in *Death in the Afternoon,* "if you ever go to Spain on a honeymoon or if you ever bolt with anyone."

But I had also heard about Ronda's less-romantic side. There are many dark stories of this place, and here is one: Pedro Romero, Ronda's renowned eighteenth-century bullfighter, discovered his wife, Elena, with a lover. He stabbed the man then carried his wife through the streets to the Tajo gorge, where he threw her into the void. (Prosper Mérimée would later base his *Carmen* on this story.)

As the bus approached Ronda, the town rose out of the morning fog like a Brigadoon that had slept for a hundred years and was about to awaken. We snaked through narrow streets and curtains of mist until we stopped at a small depot, and I stepped out. Obligations I had for the next evening left me only twenty-four hours to spend in the city.

The Hotel Reina Victoria, where Rilke stayed, is a white turn-of-the-century manse at the top of Calle Jerez. I'd read that Rilke's room was open to visitors and set up just as he'd left it: a bed, a chair, a little desk, a few books he'd left behind. But when I inquired, the receptionist brushed me off.

"The key isn't here just now," she said. "Come back tomorrow." When I told her I was leaving in the morning, she shrugged: "Come back later, then."

Disappointed, and determined to gain entry to that room later, I went in search of other clues to the enigma of the Spanish sensibility. I headed for the Tajo gorge.

The gorge drew me, I confess, because of its gruesome history of suicides and murders, rather than for its dramatic views. Besides the story of Elena and Pedro Romero, there was another episode in the gorge's history that intrigued me. Although the town was not named, Ronda is said to be the setting for the event, described in Hemingway's *For Whom the Bell Tolls*, in which townspeople loyal to Franco during the Spanish Civil War were forced to run down the main street toward the gorge. They stumbled through lines of peasants armed with flails, before being thrown over the cliff. No one has proven that story true, but it is known that hundreds of Nationalists were murdered in Ronda.

I walked down the main avenue toward the gorge, the same street where Hemingway's doomed Franquistas ran. I reached the Puente Nuevo, the eighteenth-century bridge that overlooks the Tajo. But there I was again disappointed, this time by an enormous crowd, thronging to see the view.

I crossed the bridge into the Old Quarter, where simple, white-washed homes stand beside mansions with wrought-iron balconies. I found the ramparts, the city's fortification that is still partly standing. I walked along them, though the height scared me. Ronda had been quite a protected place, settled first by the Celts, who called it Arunda, then by the Romans, and later by the Arabs, whose capture there opened the way to the final conquest of the Moors, at Granada's Alhambra palace.

I headed back over the bridge to the setting of another of Ronda's dramas: La Maestranza, one of Spain's oldest and most famous bullrings, built in 1785. When there is no bullfight, a small entrance fee gets you into both the ring and its bullfighting museum, several long rooms built into the curve of the ring. The museum features displays of brilliant *trajes de luces*—matadors' "suits of lights," heavy and compact, which add bulk to the diminutive frames of Spanish men. High on the walls hang stuffed heads of the most noble fighting bulls, most without ears, which were taken as trophies for the matador. Torn and bloodstained ruffled shirts of gored bullfighters lie in glass cases. Other cases hold photographs and newspaper articles immortalizing the best-loved matadors who have died in the ring, including Manuel Rodríguez, known as "Manolete," who died in 1947; a photo shows him lying on his funeral bed.

Outside the museum, I climbed up a dark stairwell to reach the spectator stand for a better view. The ring is graceful, with curved benches and wooden beams overhead, a red-tiled awning hanging over double arches and more than 175 columns. I climbed down to the ring and stood behind the *barrera*, painted the red-yellow-red of the Spanish flag, where the matadors wait before they enter the ring—and where they run behind, sometimes, when the bull starts to charge.

I walked into the ring and thought of bullfights I'd been to in Sevilla, years before: the sound of tinny horns and snare drums, the scent of wine and black tobacco infusing the spectator stands. The "suits of lights" in glimmering gold and black, or electric blue and pink. The matador's white smile and flushed cheek. But also, the bull, sprung from its pen onto that ring of orange sand, facing certain death.

There in the Ronda ring, I remembered the contradiction of that morbid Spanish ritual: that during the season of the *corrida*—the bullfight—there is no end of celebration. The *corrida* is the reason for the fiestas, and the fiestas define, somehow, the death in the afternoon at the *corrida*. It is a paradox echoed as well in flamenco, in the insistent swirl of the dancer's skirt against the music's mournful key.

Early evening, I returned to the Hotel Reina Victoria. A stout uniformed doorman, who'd observed my earlier encounter with the receptionist, took me aside and explained that the key to Rilke's room was actually lost: another tourist had walked off with it a few days before.

"Come back tomorrow afternoon," he said. "Perhaps the tourist will return it, or we will have found a locksmith."

I shook my head. "I have to leave early in the morning."

"You should stay," he said, frowning. "One should always have one more day in Ronda." Then he added lightly: *"A vivir que son dos días."* Live it up: Life lasts just a couple of days.

That old Spanish saying caught me off guard, made me hesitate for a moment and think about changing my carefully planned itin-erary. But I quickly brushed the thought aside: A change would inconvenience the friends I planned to connect with the next day in Málaga.

> A journey makes such a particular shape; up or down; hills or valleys; busy, peopled, modern buildings; or empty, calm, ancient stone spaces. But the shape doesn't feel like a line outwards. Strangely, it feels like a series of circles; smoke rings. Perhaps it is because all the experience is rooted in you, the choice and manner of the journey must be yours.
>
> —Jennifer Lash, *On Pilgrimage: A Time to Seek*

Later I sat at a table in a bar whose doors were open to the night and to the sound of guitars strumming in the plaza. I drank chilled, dry sherry, ate a tapa of grilled tuna, a flan for dessert. I watched a small group of Spaniards standing up at the bar, clearly all old friends. I thought back to my college days in Spain and how, when the hour would grow late, my Spanish friends wouldn't think of going home. Instead they would linger at a favorite bar then move to another, insisting that I come too. They would drink red wine from glass tumblers, eat with their fingers from small shared plates of grilled mushrooms or garlic shrimp. And if an *alegría* played from a radio at the bar, they would clap and stomp their heels. And if a *soleá* played, someone at the bar might begin to undulate above the talking, sing in a voice mournful and slow, until everyone was silent. And no one thought it strange.

That is what the Spanish intuitively understand, what they acknowledge in the way that they live and in their rituals around the bullfight and in flamenco: that the line between laughter and despair is fluid, each informing the other. That life lasts "just a cou-ple of days," as the doorman had said; one may as well enjoy it.

In Ronda the next morning, I awoke early and made my way

to the bus station. The station doors were locked, and the lights were off. A cab driver out front told me that I must have misread the schedule: my bus to Málaga wasn't due for several hours. So much for my careful itinerary. But I was grateful: I had time to return to the Hotel Reina Victoria and one last try at Rilke's room. I would place a call to the people I was to meet in Málaga and tell them I'd be late.

The doorman didn't seem surprised to see me. "One should always have one more day in Ronda," he said again. Still, he shook his head. "No key, *señorita*."

I started to turn away when the doorman spoke again: "But have you seen the garden?"

I followed his pointing finger through the back door. There, a garden of palms and century plants grew thick, overlooking the Tajo gorge and river, which ran full and brown that day. Unlike the night before at the Puente Nuevo, there were no other tourists; I had the view to myself. I sat on a bench, enveloped by the scent of pine and of the garden wall's brick, wet with dew. Then, something in the corner of my eye made me turn.

There was Rilke; it was a life-size bronzed statue of the poet. He stood with a small book in one hand, his eyes looking out to the gorge and beyond, sharing the view with me: the groves of olive trees, the earth parsed into plots, the misty blue sierras. Birds chattered around us—while from the gorge, the river roared in an ominous undertone.

Since that trip to Ronda, I have heard various things about Rilke's fabled room. One disappointed visitor I spoke with was told that the room was under renovation and could not be viewed; another told me he'd heard that, in fact, the room didn't exist. I've encountered no one who has actually seen it. And although I too failed to glimpse the quarters where Rilke stayed, I did not leave Ronda disappointed.

As with the best journeys, I didn't find what I expected, but I did happen upon what I was looking for. The key for unlocking the mysteries of the Spanish, it turned out, was not to be found in the portal to Rilke's room or even at the Tajo gorge. Rather, I glimpsed it by opening myself, just a little, to the words of a wise doorman: *A vivir que son dos días.*

Boarding my bus for Málaga that afternoon, I hoped to keep the essence of Ronda with me. Rilke, who after a few short months in Ronda moved on to Paris, apparently shared my wish. I settled into my seat and read these lines from his "Spanish Trilogy":

> Let me, though, having once more the thronging of towns
> and tangled skein of sounds and chaos
> of vehicles round me, uncompanioned,—
> let me, above the enveloping whirl,
> remember sky and that earthy brim of the vale
> where the homeward-faring flock emerged from beyond.

And as the bus wound down the mountain toward the thronging of the Costa del Sol, I recalled that "earthy brim" of the Tajo: that moment in the garden, listening to the rapturous song of the birds—and to the minor chord of the river ringing from the gorge below.

Lucy McCauley is the editor of Travelers' Tales Spain *and* Women in the Wild. *Her writing has appeared in such publications as the* Atlantic Monthly, Los Angeles Times, Harvard Review, Fast Company, *and several Travelers' Tales books. She lives in Dallas, Texas.*

DIANE ACKERMAN

* * *

Encounter in the Sea

Wild creatures have lessons to teach
about trust and play.

HUMANS LOVE PLAYING WITH OTHER ANIMALS, AND SOMETIMES this leads to a purity of exchange almost magical in its intensity, deep play at its best. For instance, I once heard about a friendly group of spotted dolphins that are drawn to music played underwater and readily swim with divers in the warm currents of the Bahamas. Research teams visit yearly to chronicle their history and habits. Villagers in the sea, the dolphins form a community that changes as couples mate, young are born, the aged die, and new alliances are forged. There is nothing like the indelible thrill of meeting a wild animal on its own terms in its own element, so I decided to join a week-long trip. One morning I flew to Grand Bahama, took a cab to the West End, and boarded a two-masted schooner along with eight other researchers. We were hoping to encounter spotted dolphins often enough during the week at sea to be able to identify and catalog individuals.

At 6:30 the following morning, we left the West End behind and cruised toward the Little Bahama Bank, a shallow area that spotted dolphins seem to prefer. After a few minutes, we hoisted the mainsail, from which two rows of short ties hung like fringe. Then we sat on benches or low deck chairs, finding shade under a large blue canopy stretched over the center of the boat and attached by a web of ropes over the boom. The ocean poured blue-black all around us with rose-gold shimmers from the sun. Gradually, the water mellowed to navy blue, then indigo, and finally azure, as we drew closer to the shallows. Clumps of turtle grass looked like cloud shadows on the floor. After three hours, a pale-blue ribbon appeared on the horizon and we headed toward it. Flying fish leaped near the bow and hurled themselves through the air a dozen yards at a time, like rocks skipping over the water.

Soon we entered the dreamtime of the aqua shallows. This area rises like a stage or platform in the ocean, without coral or large schools of fish. It appears to be a desert, a barren pan; but there are few places on earth without life of some sort. Here there is a bustling plant community, from simple blue-green algae to more complicated plants with stems and leaves. Plankton, the first step of the food chain, thrives on the banks, even though the waters look quite empty to the casual observer.

A bottlenosed dolphin leaped near the boat, then zoomed in and lined up with the bow, swinging back and forth like a surfer finding the sweetest spot of a wave. Soon it was joined by a second. Hobos hitching a ride, the dolphins weren't moving

---

I went for a swim and allowed the salty antidote of the lagoon to wash over my hot skin. And my brain, dizzied by the endless panorama of blue, finally understood why poets and painters and Crayola had been unable to settle on a single, perfect word to describe it. Azure. Sapphire. Turquoise. Cerulean. All are the colors of this paradise....

I don't think I actually spoke to a soul that Sunday on Aitutaki, except perhaps my own. But what memorable talks I had. The ocean, the sand, the sun, the stars, the rain, the roosters, the geckos are quite wonderful conversationalists if you simply allow yourself the time to listen.

—Donna Heiderstadt,
"A Symphony of Solitude"

their tails at all, but were carried along at speed by the bow wave. They seemed to relish the sport. Beautiful as these dolphins were, we were on the lookout for their cousins, the spotted ones.

A Concorde sailed overhead, making a double *boom!* as it passed. What is speed to the passengers on that supersonic, I wondered, or to the dolphins surfing on the bow wave?

"More dolphins!" the captain cried, pointing west.

As seven spotted dolphins homed in on the boat, we donned snorkeling gear and jumped into the water with them. A mother and baby accompanied by another female arrived first, swam straight up to us and started playing. A dolphin went close to one woman, waited for her to follow, then started turning tight circles with her. Like dervishes, dolphin and human spun together. Meanwhile, two other dolphins dived down to the bottom, about forty feet below, and made fast passes at me. I turned to follow them. Slowing, they allowed me to swim with them in formation, only inches away. By now the dolphins were all over us, swirling and diving, coasting close and wiggling away to see if we'd follow. If I dived, they dived, and they often accompanied me back to the surface, eye to eye. At first it was startling how close they came. We have an invisible no-man's-land around our bodies that others don't enter unless they mean to romance or harm us. To have a wild animal enter that dangerous realm, knowing that you could hurt it or it could hurt you, but that neither of you will, produces instantaneous trust. After it happens once, all fear vanishes. Somehow, they managed to keep their slender distance—as little as two or three inches—without actually making physical contact.

But they were touching in another sense, with their X-ray-like sonar, patting our skin, reaching deep inside us to our bones and soft tissues. At times, I could feel their streaming clicks. They seemed especially interested in one woman's belly. Could they tell she was pregnant? Probably. I wonder how the fetus showed up on their sonar. Could they echolocate our stomachs and know what we ate for lunch? Could they detect broken bones and tumors? Could they diagnose some diseases in us and in themselves? Hard to say. Because we couldn't touch them, they seemed aloof. But

they were touching us constantly. For them, the contact was intimate, sensuous, if one-sided. What do dolphins feel when they
echolocate one another?

At least we know *how* dolphins echolocate: they produce narrow streams of clicks (intermittent bursts of sound that last less
than a thousandth of a second each) by blowing air back and forth
through nasal passages. When the sound enters a fat-filled cavity
in the head, it's focused into a single beam that can be directed
wherever the dolphin wishes. First the dolphin sends out a general
click, then it refines the signal to identify the object, which usually takes about six clicks, each one adjusting the picture so subtly
that only chaos theory can explain it. At lightning speed, the dolphin sends out a signal, waits for the echo, decides what pulse to
send next, waits for that one's echo, and so on, until it detects the
object and classifies it. Some likely categories are: edible, dangerous, sexy, inanimate, useful, human, never-before-encountered,
none of the above.

For an hour, the dolphins played exhausting, puppyish chase-
and-tumble games. Meanwhile, we tried to study their markings.
Each had a distinctive pattern of spots, tail notches, blazes. Often
they darted to the sandy bottom and found silvery sand dabs that
they chased and ate. They were like hyperactive children, easily
bored, full of swerve and spunk. And we were their big bathtub
toys. Taking a striped, pink-and-purple ribbon from the end of my
long braid, I let it float within eyeshot of a dolphin. In a flash, the
dolphin grabbed the ribbon, then tossed it up, caught it with a
flipper, tossed it backward, kicked it with its tail, caught it with the
other flipper, spun around, slid it over its nose, swam away with it,
then returned a moment later and let it fall through the water like
a cast-off toy. A clear invitation. Taking a lungful of air, I dived
after the ribbon, grabbed it with one hand, tossed it back to my
fins and flicked it with a clumsy kick. By this time I needed to
resurface to breathe, so I let the ribbon drift down, undulating like
a piece of kelp. The dolphin collected it at speed over the pyramid
of one flipper, let it slide back to the tail, whisked it up and tossed
it with the other flipper. I knew the rules of the game, but I didn't

have the breath to play it. Even if I were a pearl diver and could hold my breath for over five minutes, I would still have been out of my league. After a few more of my clumsy lunges for the ribbon, the dolphin swam away, turning its attention to a human who could stay underwater longer, a man taking still photographs with a flash camera.

When at last they veered off toward the horizon, we gathered under the blue canopy to fill in sketch sheets and record the details of each animal. These rough sketches would be compared to photos of known animals, and become part of the researchers' catalog. You'd think nine observers might supply the same facts, but we didn't all agree on what we saw. Indeed, we sounded like people comparing different versions of an accident. As I filled out sketch sheets, I scanned my memory for head, tail, and flank markings. Living mainly in the tropics, spotted dolphins have long, narrow beaks, and can be heavily freckled. Like reverse fawns, the young begin life solid colored, usually gray, and only develop white spots as they age. By the time they're elderly, they're covered in swirls of spots and splotches. They grow to about eight feet long, have teeth, and are gregarious. They love to play, which they do with endless ingenuity and zest. Athletic, acrobatic swimmers, they leap into aerial pirouettes, cartwheels, and what seem like attempts to see how long they can hover in the air.

Over the next week, we encountered spotted dolphins every day, the longest session lasting three hours, so long in fact that we were the first to give up out of exhaustion, only to find the dolphins racing after us and trying to tempt us back to romp. Mother dolphins often brought the sleek little surprise of their babies, which appeared perfect and unmarked by life. Sometimes a baby would swim tucked underneath its mother, making a crescent shape, so that it looked as if the baby were still being carried inside. We grew to know them as individuals, a rare privilege. In our travels across the banks, we played with dolphins nine times. The most frequent visitor was a particularly rambunctious five-year-old female called "Nicky," and she became a special favorite. Often, the dolphins arrived like a visitation. Long hours of waiting, in a slow-motion of heat, glare, and water, were suddenly broken by the wild and delicious turmoil of incoming dolphins. When they left, everything fell calm again and we waited once more, at a low ebb, under the harrowing sun.

On our last day, after a particularly exhausting afternoon with Nicky and her friends, we gathered on the deck to watch the sunset. These were some of the most dramatic moments in each day, when the soft aqua of the water fanned through rainbow blues and was washed away in the molten lava of the setting sun. Night fell heavily, in thick black drapes. Retreating to the galley downstairs, we sat and talked about the week. Despite the mild discomforts of ocean sailing, everyone was sad the voyage was over, and all felt nourished by a week of such intimate play with wild animals. I was especially surprised by how eager the dolphins were to make eye contact. Their wildness disappears on one level and is enhanced on another when you stare straight into their eyes, realizing that these are wild creatures and there is something special happening inside their minds. At the very least, there is a willing gentleness and an awareness that draws you in. One reason the plight of the dolphin touches us is because we fear they may be self-aware, not just meaty animals but intelligent life-forms. Suppose, like us, they have inner universes? Suppose they are not like elk or salmon, but animals with a culture of sorts, animals that can judge us?

During the night, the winds kicked up and four-foot seas rolled in from the southwest. Sleeping on deck, I awakened to find that I had slid off my air mattress and my legs were suspended over the side of the boat. Hands folded on my chest, I looked set for burial at sea. So I retreated below, wedged myself into a narrow bunk, and tried to sleep, which was nearly impossible given the lurching and shuddering of the boat. My thoughts turned frequently to the dolphins. Where were they now? What were they doing in that incomprehensible darkness of sea and greater darkness of night? I was stricken both by our kinship with them and by the huge rift between us evolution has created. They were minds in the ocean long before we were minds on the land. They abide by rhythms older than we know or can invent. We pretend we can outsmart and ignore such rhythms, but in our hearts we know we're steered by them.

Diane Ackerman is an award-winning poet and author most praised for her essays about nature and human nature. She writes regularly for The New York Times, The New Yorker, *and* National Geographic. *Her books include best-selling* A Natural History of the Senses, A Natural History of Love, *and* Deep Play, *from which this story was excerpted.*

PART THREE

Transforming the Self

NATALIE GOLDBERG

Train Ride to Wisdom

Sometimes you have to let go
and enjoy the ride.

EVERYONE IN MY FAMILY WAS BUSY, BUT BUSY DOING WHAT? MY mother was busy being on a diet. She ate thin, dried white toast, which she cut diagonally, leaving a line of brown crumbs on the white paper napkin. Then she spread lo-cal cottage cheese over it and drank black coffee. She bought things with credit cards in department stores and then returned them. My father was busy running a bar, the Aero Tavern, in downtown Farmingdale, going to the racetrack, eating T-bone steaks with lots of ketchup, and a wedge of iceberg lettuce with ranch-style dressing from the bottle. My grandfather mowed the lawn with the new power mower that automatically collected the cut grass in an attached pouch. He read the Yiddish paper, smoked stogies, and sat in a brown suit on a lawn chair in our driveway. Grandma told me stories and baked cookies. My sister, I suppose, was lost in her own activities of being the youngest. I never really got to know her, though we had slept side-by-side in the same bedroom all our lives.

This alienation is the American disease. It is our inheritance, our roots. It can be our teacher. Mother Teresa, who works with India's poorest of the poor, has said that America has a worse poverty than India's, and it's called loneliness. Mr. Cates once asked

us in class after we read *King Lear*—after Gloucester plucked out
his eyes and Lear anguished over the betrayal by his daughters—
"Which would you prefer? Physical torment, or mental and emotional suffering?" When we thought about it enough, no one in
class could honestly choose.

Tibetan Buddhists say that a person should never get rid of their
negative energy, that negative energy transformed is the energy of
enlightenment, and that the only difference between neurosis and
wisdom is struggle. If we stop struggling and open up and accept
what is, that neurotic energy naturally arises as wisdom, naturally
informs us and becomes our teacher. If this is true, why do we
struggle so much? We struggle because we're afraid to die, we're
afraid to see that we are impermanent, that nothing exists forever.
My childhood suburbs gave the impression that they would exist
forever, placid, plastic, timeless, and monotonous, but natural wisdom, the other side of neurosis, embodies the truth of transiency.

I will give you an example of this transformation of energy
from my recent life. Kate, my dear friend, and her three sons,
Raphael, age ten, Elliot, age eight, and Jordan, age three, were sub-
letting a house for a month last summer in Taos. Of course, I was
delighted; and though I do not have children of my own, I tried
hard to include them in activities and not to continually suggest,
"Hey, Kate, why don't you get a babysitter, so we can…" I found
a brochure advertising an all-day train ride on the old Cumbres
and Toltec railroad. I suggested all five of us go on a Sunday. We
left Taos by car at 7:30 A.M. for Antonito, an hour and a half away.
I had miscalculated somehow and we arrived an hour early for the
train's departure. Kate suggested we have breakfast at the cafe that
was especially for tourists. I said OK—I wanted to be a good
sport—and sat among souvenir conductor caps, postcards, flags,
and maps, eating white-flour pancakes with fake maple syrup. For
the last two months, I had been trying earnestly to cut out all sugar
and to eat well. As I poured the artificial maple sugar over my pancakes, I thought, *Oh, well, this is a special day. You have to learn to be
flexible: you're with kids.*

When we settled into our seats on the train, I looked around.

Everyone seemed to be from someplace else—Iowa, Kansas, Texas. I shrugged. I don't know why I thought the train should be full of my Taos friends. A man in front of me wore a baseball cap from Texas Instruments; a man behind me had on a GM t-shirt. These people are on their two-week vacations, I thought. In our small car, I was surprised to see five women with bleached blond hair. They're still doing that? Way back in my high school days, I had known girls who had done that. I felt like a foreigner, in the middle of America.

The train chugged along. It went surprisingly slowly. Uh-oh. This was going to be a long eight-hour ride. As soon as the train began to move, people bolted out of their seats to go to the open-air car in back and to the food car. Kate and the kids went with them. I sat almost alone for half an hour.

After a while I, too, wandered back to the last car. Kate's kids were sucking Tootsie Pops, leaning against a rail, and feeling the wind in their faces. We traveled through empty land full of sage for mile after mile. People were wildly snapping pictures. I wondered what they saw out there. Then I remembered this land was new to them. They asked other people to snap pictures of them standing with their families. Kate offered to take a picture of one family: a husband in a yellow nylon shirt, a wife wearing turquoise earrings, and, in front of them, a son entering adolescence with a rash of pimples across his forehead and a younger boy, clear faced, blond, more innocent, less disturbed. The mother's arm was around the younger boy. The father's arm was around his wife.

"Smile," said Kate. History was made in New Mexico for this Oklahoma family.

I turned to Raphael. "Have anymore of those Tootsie Pops?" I didn't want to be left out. These people seemed to be content. Maybe I could learn to be happy like them.

He eagerly offered to get me one. "What flavor? I have cherry." He held his out. "El has grape." He pointed at Elliot.

"Cherry," I said.

He ran off to the concession stand.

Kate returned with Jordan. She'd just bought him a gray-and-white-striped conductor's cap. He did look cute, with a brown curl sticking out the back.

By four in the afternoon, I'd eaten three Tootsie Pops and many Chips Ahoy. We traveled in the dazed rhythm of the train. Elliot had fallen asleep in my lap. All day a strong fear of American "normalcy" had chewed at the edge of my psyche, but I'd successfully kept it at bay, surprised at how I was quietly enjoying myself.

Then, suddenly, a terrible blues descended on me. An old desperation that probably began on nothing-happening Sundays in suburban America when I was a kid. Sunday, the Christian day of rest, was when my friends went to church. We were Jews. We didn't go to church, and in the fifties, the stores and malls that served to fill up suburban life and give the illusion of activity and accomplishment—"I finally found that blue sweater I was looking for"—were closed all day on Sunday. What was left for me, a Jewish kid in Farmingdale, Long Island? No spirit, no religion, a desert of empty shopping centers.

The feeling on the train was familiar: There was nothing for me. My life was bland, and would always be this way, and juxtaposed to this was the nagging feeling that everyone else was having fun, everyone else belonged. They were content, somehow filled up in an America that left me empty.

The feeling descended and I was about to grasp it, hold it hard, and be unhappy, all the while struggling against it. Instead, like an act of grace, I let that old Sunday feeling fall all around me and I didn't grab it. It kept falling and the space opened up—big space, the

> In my dream, the sun glinted off a small vial that my grandmother held in her hand. It was water, I thought. She stepped toward me, offering the vial. I took it. My grandmother was instantly reclaimed by the desert. As she vanished behind a tree, I knew then that it was not a vial of water, but of tears, my tears, tears which I had not been able to shed since I was a little girl.
> —Deanne Stillman, "In Sunshine and in Shadow"

space I used to be scared of, that told me I was nothing, that made me clutch at my life. Now, yes, it was true I was nothing, but not separate, not alone. I didn't struggle, so I merged with everything around me: kids, Tootsie Pops, the sage, couples in t-shirts and Reeboks. My life felt empty and jolly and open. Nothing could stop me, freeze me.

I was excited. I had physically experienced what the Tibetans talked about, the transformation from neurosis to wisdom. I sat in the train and watched my letting go, my opening into an old painful feeling, and I experienced it in a new way, felt another dimension of it—its largeness.

Natalie Goldberg is a poet, writer, artist, and teacher. Her best-selling book, Writing Down the Bones, *has inspired many writers to practice their craft and encouraged others to use writing as a form of meditation. She has written several other books, including a novel,* Banana Rose. *She lives in New Mexico. This story was excerpted from* Long Quiet Highway: Waking Up in America.

LORENA CASSADY

✳ ✳ ✳

AWOL in Aquitaine

Far outside the monastery walls,
a Buddhist nun communes
with her spirit.

AFTER THE BITTER WINDS OF WINTER ROAR THROUGH THE
landscape of Aquitaine in southwestern France, there is a great
hunger in all living things for the forgiveness of spring. By mid-
April I could contain myself no longer. I rose just before dawn one
Monday morning and decided to go AWOL from the Vietnamese
Zen Buddhist monastery where I lived as an ordained nun. It
would be one of many AWOL days, which would lead eventually
to my departure from monastic life. I had begun to recognize
within myself a certain divided loyalty between my great love for
the pristine countryside in which Zen monasteries are often
found, and the less pristine human construction of priestly hierar-
chy, rigid sex roles, repressed libido, and spiritual politics. This divided loyalty felt especially acute here, in a land sprinkled with
massive limestone plateaus and strange rounded hills carved by ter-
tiary ice, where some of the greatest vineyards in the world cling
to the undulating lowlands of the Garonne and Dordogne valleys.

This land was more than beautiful to me. It was home to one
of my distant relatives, Eleanor of Aquitaine, and by extension her
infamous son, Richard Lionheart. Between 1173 and 1183, in his
tumultuous teens and early twenties, Richard had lived at Beynac,

a castle fortress which clings to a high cliff above the Dordogne River, only forty minutes away to the northeast. Though Richard infuriated the French as an outsider, he ruled, brutally defended, and loved the land of Aquitaine to a fault. He died at Fontevraud, after a life of staggering excess and violence in the Crusades, admired by his peers as a poet and troubadour, at the middling age of forty-two. His death, caused by yet another act of pointless aggression against one of his peers, left no heirs. But through a bastard line, I eventually appeared.

In the darkness of the nuns' dormitory room, I found my daypack and coat and slipped out the door into a brisk morning. There is an almost constant wind blowing in this part of France, a meteorological borderline where two weather patterns collide to form chaotic skies and almost horrific anvil thunderheads in the summer months. On this morning, though, the sky was clear and calm. I hurried to the kitchen so I could raid the pantry before the stars faded altogether. I took a large chunk of homemade bread, goat cheese, a smear of plum butter, a few apples, a liter of water, and a small container of yogurt and hurried down the white limestone driveway into the orchard of plum trees. This was the best route to avoid discovery as I made my escape. I knew this, because only a few days earlier I had fled this way from French policemen who made an unannounced raid on the monastery looking for Buddhist nuns with expired visas.

After winding my way through the orchard, I continued down another limestone path where the nuns and monks often went for walking meditation. Beyond the end of that path was a small copse which opened into a vast plowed field. By now the sun was rising over the walled medieval town of Puy-Guillaume to the east, and the sound of a rifle shot ripped through the bone-cold air. I had forgotten that with the arrival of spring, the local hounds and their masters would be hunting on Monday and Thursday mornings. I paused on the periphery of the plowed field and gauged my chances of getting across it alive. The hunters, I knew, were in the Bois de Meyrac, a large copse which began on the opposite side of the field. About two hundred feet into the copse they had built fantastic treetop blinds, rigged with a complex system of pulleys and weights which were triggered somehow by ducks, I presume, lured there by live decoys planted by the hunters. I had examined the empty wire cages of these hapless decoys on many off-season hikes. Another shot rang out. From their high vantage points, the hunters sent their deadly metal flying in unknown trajectories. We at the monastery had survived many walking meditations through a hail of bullets. But would I be so lucky this morning? The young couple who owned the neighboring orchard had recently found two ragged holes through the wall of their baby's room—bullets meant for plump fowl, not tender newborns. Finally my passion for escaping the monastery surpassed my fear of duck hunters and I stepped boldly into the field.

Now, crossing a plowed field in Aquitaine is no easy matter in early spring, before the sun and warm rains have had a chance to soften and break down the massive clods of frozen earth. The soil here is heavy, dense, hard, black clay. With some difficulty one can break a piece off, mould it into the shape of a Buddha, and it will last for at least 900 years on a dry shelf. Used as mortar to hold the local limestone together, houses and abbeys constructed this way have been standing here solidly since the Middle Ages. To turn the soil for a garden, you need a back of steel and sturdy tools that will not snap under its weight. Cut deep and turned over by heavy tractors at the end of the growing season, the unevenly spaced clods in the farmer's fields are boulder-sized, and the dark crevices between them can be over a foot deep. It is a long, ungraceful, and treacherous way to the other side. More rifle shots exploded nearby. It was a noisy start to my stolen day.

Once across the field, I decided to leave the Bois de Meyrac to the hunters for the moment, and I struck out for Le Pey, a tiny village high on a magnificent limestone bluff to the north. From the exposed farmer's field I disappeared into thick, shoulder-high grass. Each footstep pressed down the mass of green in front of me, and I could see nothing ahead except the sky and the tips of a budding plum orchard. The grass in some places had been pressed down into a nest, and as I wondered what kind of animal made its home here, a young fawn bolted out of its hiding place and showed me the quickest way out of the marshy meadow. My memory of that place still teaches me about the color green, and some of it permanently stained the hem of my gray monastic robe.

Soon I was on the road, the sun warming my bald head. My body was strong and hard from the physical labor that is part of the monastic routine, and I was eager to stretch my legs in the long uphill climb to Le Pey. I met no one coming or going. This part of rural France has no industry, no shopping centers, nothing exciting to hold the young on the land. Only seasoned vintners and their gruff peasant workers can survive here in the silence, broken only by distant thunder and the whine of mosquitoes. I did, however, meet trotting toward me a lean, red-haired dog the size of a small pony.

It was one of those unexpected feasts of the spirit— one that can only be stumbled upon. While driving in Wales, I noticed a small sign for an unfamiliar place, Wyre Park, tilted awkwardly in the direction of a large grove of trees. Parking the car and wandering toward the grove, I realized the leaves on the ground had suddenly changed, now damp and wind-tossed about. Hearing water rushing nearby, I followed the sound and came upon a glorious waterfall. Not a large one, but one that left me in awe. Walking off to the right along a wood path, I found another world, one in which I wanted to get lost in for days and days and days.

—Lisa Bach,
"A Path of One's Own"

He turned to follow erratically behind me on my journey, occasionally bolting ahead to chase small game into the thicket. The dogs in France are nothing like their pale counterparts in other parts of the world. Here, dogs work for a living, and since the French consider it uncivilized to neuter them, their canine hormones drive them forward in perpetual motion and agile aggression. They are not pets. They are something to be reckoned with.

By the time I reached the high tabletop of Le Pey, the red dog had disappeared with a bloody rabbit hanging from his chops into the vineyards. I stopped for lunch at a small, abandoned country house where I had the habit of hiding away. Here I could sit on an old wrought-iron bench in the middle of a high, unmanicured boxwood hedge and stare at the vast, tumultuous French skies that outdo even the American Midwest in tornado season. The pungent scent of boxwood and a bellyful of bread and cheese soon had me curled up on the ground for a nap.

At two o'clock I woke with a start at the sound of the monastery bell two miles away. My brothers and sisters of the cloth had just finished their long formal lunch and meditation, and would be retiring for a one-hour nap. Had they noticed my absence? Out of the pecking order of twenty-five nuns, would they sense the blank space toward the end of the line where their junior sister should have been? Would they send out a hunting party?

Here at Le Pey I was free to choose what to do according to the rhythms of my body instead of the lockstep Zen routine, and I decided to take my meditation in the ruins of an ancient stone windmill which overlooked the Garonne Valley. I was slipping irretrievably into pantheism, possibly encouraged by my late-night studies of Thoreau, John Muir, and Krishnamurti.

Energized again from a quiet sit, I started slowly to make my way back to Meyrac, stooping to pick the occasional wildflower which I pressed in a sutra book from my backpack. The rhythm of my long downhill steps and the familiar sight of the walled town of Puy-Guillaume in the distance reminded me of my roots. Elizabethan folk tunes learned in childhood started to bubble up and roar forth from my parched lips, as if I were in a tavern in nearby Sigoulés singing for my ale. Richard Lionheart appeared before me, in all his magnificence, on horseback. When he encountered the bald Buddhist nun in her gray robes at the crossroads he bowed politely, giving no sign of recognition, though his stallion sidestepped in wariness. Eventually he faded into the endless plum orchards.

At the Bois de Meyrac I jumped the ditch between the road

and the copse and entered the quiet wood. The rifles were silent, by law, after midday. Overhead a black cloud of geese flew north, smartly avoiding carnage by scheduling their trip late in the afternoon. I was suddenly overcome by awakening desire—for what I knew not. Plunging deeper into the copse, through waist-high ferns and dense stands of alder I was pricked by thorny berries. I felt the elastic pull of invisible spider webs across my face as I moved forward through the blur of lovely green. Finally I stopped in what I imagined was the middle of the wood, as far into it as I could get without beginning to leave it from the other side. With no thought but some dim hunch of all that had passed in this wood since the cavemen of nearby Lascaux had begun the human adventure in Europe, I dropped my Zen robes on the soft moist ground and stood tall and naked with the trees. My survival at that moment, I felt, somehow depended on my nakedness. I stood and breathed in and out, feeling the filtered wind of Aquitaine on my white winter skin. I walked around in a circle to establish my temporary kingdom, squatted briefly to pee, cleaned myself with a broad-leafed fern, and reclined on a fallen tree to survey the hole of sky directly overhead. My lungs expanded with precious air. I was in love.

Gradually, in the sweet passion of homecoming, I became aware of a tiny sound, then the sharp crack of a dry twig somewhere in the wood. I rose on my elbow and squinted into the leafy shadows. My heart suddenly pounded in my ears as I recalled that the nuns occasionally walked through the Bois De Meyrac on the way

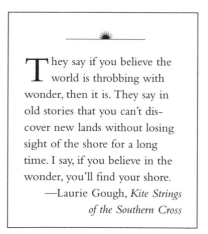

They say if you believe the world is throbbing with wonder, then it is. They say in old stories that you can't discover new lands without losing sight of the shore for a long time. I say, if you believe in the wonder, you'll find your shore.
—Laurie Gough, *Kite Strings of the Southern Cross*

to market. My eyes scanned the forest for bald heads and gray as I slipped off the log onto the forest floor and groped for my robes.

There would be at least two of them as we are not permitted to travel alone.

Another twig snapped. Gradually, as my eyes adjusted to the darkening wood I saw a hunter, his rifle slung casually over his shoulder staring at my naked body from about seventy-five feet away. His dog was loping toward me. *"Arrête!"* I screamed. The dog stopped in his tracks, looking anxiously back at his master. I crouched behind the log, locking eyes with the hunter until he called back his dog and turned slowly to leave the scene, baffled. My breath came heavy for many minutes, as I tried to regain the sweetness of solitude. I dug into the softened ground for a handful of black soil, pressed it into a small brick, and held it tightly in my fist to remind me that I was now part of the unwritten history of the Bols de Meyrac.

By seven o'clock I was back on my cushion in the dark meditation hall, number twenty-two in a line of twenty-five nuns. The bell sounded, and we lowered our eyes in the stillness to a spot on the floor approximately five feet ahead. Our backs straight, the sound of the wood fire crackling in the iron stove, we turned our minds inward to the stillness we had been trained by traditional Vietnamese discipline to find. In the dim light, no one had noticed the grass stains on my wrinkled robe or the dirt under my fingernails. My absence, if noted, was not mentioned. I think they already knew where I was headed.

Lorena Cassady is a Santa Cruz writer who has previously published an autobiographical novel, Hair Suit, *a book of poetry,* Smoker, *and various feature articles, excerpts, and poetry in newspapers and small press magazines.*

ANNE CUSHMAN

* * *

The Sadhu from Texas

There were lessons to be learned
from this peripatetic yogi.

I FIRST MET CHARAN DAS IN SANTA FE, NEW MEXICO, WHEN he knocked on the door of my adobe cabin one cold November night. The churned mud of my driveway was frozen into icy ruts, but he was barefoot; he wore only a swath of brown cotton around his waist and a brown wool shawl. A sharp wind fluttered his matted dreadlocks.

"We just met your roommate at Jemez Hot Springs," he said. "She said we could stay at your house for a few days."

I was twenty-two years old and believed in opening the door to mystery. "Of course." I peered past him into the dark. "How many of you are there?"

He gave me a radiant, gap-toothed smile. "Just this one," he said.

Over almond tea in front of the wood stove, Charan Das explained that he was a sadhu, one of India's millions of wandering yogis, who live on alms as they travel from village to village in pursuit of God-realization. In a previous incarnation, though, he had been a Texas college student who had gone to India to research Indian spiritual sects. Now he had come back to the States for the first time in ten years, to visit his somewhat alarmed family and make a pilgrimage to the sacred sites of the Southwest.

He referred to himself in the plural, he explained, as an ego-deflating spiritual practice. "Our we," he said, "includes you, too."

"Should I refer to you as 'they'?" I asked.

"They is fine with us," he said, and began to giggle.

Over the next few days, Charan Das told me stories about sadhus. They live without possessions, he told me, entirely dependent on the generosity of strangers. They never stay anywhere longer than a few days to avoid becoming attached to places and people, and to spread spiritual teachings as widely as possible. To remind themselves of life's impermanence, they meditate in cremation grounds and smear themselves with the ashes from the funeral pyres. To break their attachment to the physical body, they often vow themselves to seven-year cycles of extreme ascetic practices— such as holding one arm up in the air until it atrophies to a withered twig, or dangling upright in a sling from a tree branch instead of lying down to sleep.

"Would you like to hang a sling from our rafters?" I asked him.

"No, we'll be happy on the couch," he said.

He covered my kitchen table with snapshots of throngs of naked *babas* plunging into the Ganges to wash away their karma in the sacred river. "Come to India," he told me. "We'll be your guide."

"But how can I find you, if you're always wandering?"

"Oh, we only wander half the year," he said, cheerfully. "The other half, we have a lady friend in the holy city of Benares."

Ten years later, I finally made it to Benares (better known in the West as Varanasi). I had become an editor at *Yoga Journal;* I was researching a guidebook to ashrams, meditation centers, and pilgrimage sites in India. Synchronicity seems to be the only law that is enforced in India; so I wasn't altogether surprised, my second day in Varanasi, when I spotted Charan Das sipping *chai* in the rooftop cafe of the Hotel Ganges View. His dreadlocks had turned gray, and a new pair of wire-framed spectacles perched unsteadily on his nose.

"We knew you would get here!" he said, as if resuming a

conversation that had been interrupted a few hours ago. "Would you like some *chai*?"

From our hotel roof we had a sweeping view of the city— already ancient at the time of the Buddha—stretching downstream around an elbow-shaped bend in the silky gray Ganges. Varanasi is the hometown of Shiva, the god of destruction, and a city sacred to death. Hindus believe that dying in Varanasi ensures liberation for the soul—on your deathbed there, Shiva himself will whisper a mantra in your ear that ensures your safe passage to the other side. The banks of the Ganges are lined with hostels where people come from all over India to die. The funeral fires have not stopped burning for several thousand years.

On the dirt road below meandered an intermittent stream of traffic: a herd of water buffalo lumbering to the river to drink; a band of pilgrims with six-foot staffs on their shoulders, weighted at both ends with bundles of cooking supplies and offerings for the temples; mangy, purposefully trotting dogs; a sadhu with orange robes and a pitchfork-sized trident, his forehead striped with the three horizontal bars that mark a follower of Shiva.

I told Charan Das that I was in India researching a spiritual guidebook and would appreciate his insights.

"We were working on a spiritual guidebook, too!" he said in delight. "That's why we originally came to India twenty years ago."

Somewhat alarmed, I asked him what had happened to his project.

"Our notes were all locked up in a friend's house in Benares," he said. "A whole trunkful of them, on hundreds of ashrams all over India. But the friend died many years ago. The trunk was moved, and we're not sure where."

He began to laugh—a zany, low-pitched chortle that went on long after my own laughter had stopped—and I knew that for him, a spiritual guidebook had long since lost all relevance. My publisher would have been alarmed, I'm sure, at how uplifted that perspective made me feel.

Charan Das invited me to meet him that evening at the Hanuman Temple, where he and his guru, Kathia Baba, were stay-

ing. Hanuman is the monkey god; the temple courtyard was strewn
with peanut shells and swarming with bold-eyed, leering monkeys,
covetously eyeing my day pack. I found Charan Das and Kathia
Baba seated cross-legged on a caved-in sofa in a back room, sharing a fat, cigar-shaped *chilam* (a pipe containing a mixture of tobacco and marijuana, a plant considered by sadhus to be sacred to
Shiva) with a handful of Indian and Western devotees.

"This is Anne," Charan Das told Kathia Baba. "We stayed with
her in New Mexico ten years ago."

"For this evening, you are not Anne," Kathia Baba told me,
clasping my hands and beaming. He was a stocky Indian man with
a short-cropped beard, dressed in a white *kurta* and *mala* beads,
with an expression of almost shockingly innocent pleasure, as if
perpetually unpacking a Christmas stocking. "For this evening you
will be called Annapurna, the goddess of plenty."

"And this," said Charan Das, gesturing toward a muscular blond
woman in a green sari, "is Maya. She is from the Pleiades."

"You're a long way from home," I said.

"Earth will never seem familiar to a soul from another star system," she said in a strong German accent. "But Benares is more like home than Germany." She reached out and took the *chilam* from Kathia Baba.

"She is telling me so many things I have never heard of," said Kathia Baba reverently.

The *chilam* went round and round. Charan Das told me who really killed J.F.K. Maya told me that she was a

> However tenuous and unar-
> ticulated they may be, the
> ties between the tracker and the
> person up ahead constitute the
> very heart of tracking. Without
> fail, following someone else's
> footprints always forces me to
> walk alongside them long
> enough to rethink the most per-
> verse of my origins. As we track,
> we too are being tracked.
>
> —Hannah Nyala, *Point Last
> Seen: A Woman Tracker's Story*

"walk-in," a soul from the Pleiades who had stepped into an earth-
ling's body in midlife to help save the planet from destruction.

Kathia Baba told me about meditating in a cave in the Himalayas, where he went into a trance and lived without food or water for six months.

Charan Das told me that the FBI had genetically engineered the AIDS virus as a plot against homosexuals. Maya told me that it was possible that I was from the Pleiades, also. Kathia Baba told me that Charan Das intended to bring him to America and drive him across the country in a VW van. "He is telling me about the Rainbow Family," Kathia Baba said. "It is truly a wonderful thing."

Finally, unsteadily, I stood up to go. From a cotton pouch slung around his bare shoulder, Charan Das produced an address book, tattered as an ancient Sanskrit manuscript.

"If we ever come to California," he said, "we will give you a call."

A year and a half later, the phone rang in my room in the house I shared with three other roommates on a hilltop on the edge of a redwood forest in Marin County. I was going over my notes on yoga history, preparing to go on the radio the next morning on a live call-in talk show about the *Yoga Journal* conference on "Body, Mind, and Spirit" that was being held that weekend at the Sheraton Palace Hotel in San Francisco.

I really shouldn't have answered the phone, but I was expecting a call from a man I had just started dating. I hovered my hand over the phone for three rings, so as not to appear too eager; then answered in my most professional voice.

"We're in Portland," said a voice that was not the one I had been hoping for. "We heard there was a yoga conference happening, so we're flying to Oakland tonight. Our plane gets in at 5:30. We were hoping we could stay at your house."

Frankly, I wasn't thrilled to hear from Charan Das. I was nervous about the radio show and fretting about my love life, and the last thing I wanted was a visit from a matted-haired, barefoot Texan sadhu in a shawl and *lungi*. But it's not good karma to turn away a wandering renunciate. So I picked him up that evening at the cafe in a bookstore across from the Airporter bus stop.

He was standing near the magazine racks, his bare, bony feet sticking out from under his *lungi*, surrounded by tables of bored professional couples drinking lattes and reading the *San Francisco Chronicle*. His smile was huge under a fluff of gray dreadlocks; he looked like a dandelion on acid. Slung around his shoulder were a spare *lungi* and a cotton sack of books. "We bought these at the Bodhi Tree Bookstore in Los Angeles," he told me. "They're full of information for the revolution we're planning."

I drove Charan Das home to meet my roommates, whom I had tried to prepare for the occasion with a convoluted explanation of the ancient history of Indian asceticism. "So he's a sort of a monk?" asked John. John works at the vitamin counter at Wild Oats health food store and believes that world peace would come sooner if we all switched to the lunar calendar favored by the ancient Maya.

"Not exactly." I explained about the *chilams*, and the lady friend in Varanasi, and how Charan Das wandered through the country sleeping in temples and train stations and living off the proceeds of a small trust fund set up by his parents in Dallas. "Ah," said John, in comprehension. "An advanced Deadhead."

I made Charan Das a meal of baked potatoes with nutritional yeast, while he told me about how extraterrestrials were harvesting human embryos and raising them in huge factory farms in outer space, and how the CIA knew all about it. He offered to read the manuscript for my guidebook to spiritual India, and check it for accuracy. "We have met so many of the holy men in India," he said. "We know all of their girlfriends."

I went to bed nervous about going on the radio the next day and talking about yoga, which I had been told was a big step up the ladder of my spiritual career. I lay awake for hours, picturing myself saying, "Yoga is about inner peace," in a quaking voice. Early the next morning I tiptoed out of the house past Charan Das snoring on my sofa, wrapped in his brown wool shawl. My manuscript lay on the floor next to him, untouched.

When I got home Charan Das was waiting for me on my redwood deck, sunning his bony legs. "We heard you on the radio," he said with a big grin. "You sounded great. Would you like to be on the TV show we're going to start on public access TV? It's going to be a spiritual show, and we're going to be the anchorman."

Later, I took Charan Das with me to Whole Foods market to get lunch at the deli counter. Whole Foods always reminds me of Buddhist depictions of the Pure Land, the sort of place you'd pray to get reborn, with lotus flowers, jewels, and rainbows everywhere—a land flowing with organic BGH-free milk and raw unfiltered wildflower honey. Charan Das and I made our way past the stacks of strawberries and kiwis flown in from New Zealand, the Hawaiian pineapples and the Mexican papaya, the aromatherapy bath salts and the cruelty-free lipstick and the herbal diet pills and the books with titles like *Stop Aging Now.*

We came to the deli counter and selected our lunch: quinoa-orange salad, jerked *seitan* skewers, yam millet patties. I was pointing out the vegan rum balls for dessert when we were approached by a teenager in a Whole Foods apron.

"I'm sorry, sir, but you'll have to put on your shoes," he said to Charan Das. "It's the store regulations."

"Oh, but we don't have any shoes." Charan Das seemed slightly bewildered. "We haven't worn shoes since 1969."

"It's an insurance thing," the Whole Foods official explained. "If you were to step on glass and cut yourself, Whole Foods would be liable."

"We often walk on glass. We walk on rocks, snow, hot coals—we never hurt ourselves!"

After some debate, it was concluded that if Charan Das hadn't worn shoes for almost thirty years, the bottom of his feet probably legally qualified as shoes. Charan Das and I picked up our plates full of food—I paid for both of them—and we sat at the tables by the window and ate. "Whole Foods is the only place anyone ever asks us to wear shoes," Charan Das said. "Whole Foods and when we're getting onto an airplane. We always have to put paper slippers on our feet when we walk down the ramp. Then we take them off as soon as we reach our seat."

"The funny thing is," he added as we walked out to my car, "we were one of the original founders of the Whole Foods co-op. In Austin, Texas, back in the 1960s."

"Really? Did you keep any stock?" I asked.

He shook his furry head. "No. We don't believe in money."

That night I took Charan Das to the *Yoga Journal* conference to hear the keynote speech by Stephen Levine, the author of *Who Dies?* and *A Year to Live*. Strolling into the chandeliered lobby of the Sheraton Palace Hotel, Charan Das looked like some sort of exhibit—like he'd accidentally stepped out of a diorama on ancient yogis. A bellhop in a red jacket with gold buttons held the door for him, expressionless.

None of the other yogis looked anything like Charan Das. Clad in form-fitting work-out clothes—setting off buttocks and pectorals sculpted by Sun Salutations—they milled past the booths full of silk-screened t-shirts and buckwheat-hull meditation cushions and ginseng tonics, eager as pilgrims crowding to the Ganges to bathe.

I was grateful for my positive experience with Amma, but once again I couldn't make the guru-disciple path *my* path. Yes, Amma had given me the embracing, unconditional love that she is known to give, but I sensed her true gift to me was to help me see more clearly what I believe. In a quote I read, Amma said, "Love is a universal religion and what society really needs. Religion is just a means and once you attain that goal, you don't need the means." Perhaps I had already done my time living in the presence of a master. I felt that with that last shove away from Amma's body, the gift of the sandalwood paste on my forehead, she was sending me out on my own to love the world as best I can.

—Cathy Armer, "Visiting Gurus"

"What would Indian yogis think of this scene?" I asked Charan Das.

"You never know," he said. "Maybe everyone here is a reincarnated yogi. Every guru wants to be reborn in America."

In the Grand Ballroom, Stephen Levine gave a keynote speech on death. He led a very long meditation on softening your belly, and Charan Das fell asleep in the chair next to me, snoring gently.

The next morning, I tried to hustle Charan Das out of the house in time to hear Lilias Folan, a teacher made famous by her yoga classes on PBS, give a talk called "The Joy Is in the Journey." Charan Das—whose sadhu's sense of time was measured in lifetimes—was standing by my kitchen sink, filling a Knudsen's strawberry apple juice jar with water.

"We'll never get used to toilet paper," he said. "It makes no sense to us. Water is so much better, you can clean your whole lower intestine that way."

"Mmm," I commented noncommitally, and walked out onto the deck, looking meaningfully at my car. Charan Das followed me, brandishing his jar.

"America seems crazy to us. None of it makes any sense to us. Toilet paper, shoes, driver's license, having a job, insurance, money, the capitalist system—it's all so inhumane."

"Throw it all out," I said. "Start with the toilet paper, end with capitalism. Let's start now."

He looked at me with delight, as if I were a deaf-mute who had just spoken for the first time. "Start now! With a good shit!"

"But let my roommates keep a little toilet paper," I said.

"Oh, we don't believe in controlling people. We believe in freedom," he said. "We would never legislate no toilet paper."

"It would be difficult to get it through both the House and the Senate," I said.

He set down the juice jar on the railing and stared across the valley toward Berkeley. "People should love each other," he said. "Toilet paper just gets in the way."

Two days later, Charan Das left, heading for the Rainbow

Family Gathering in Scotland. He took a copy of my guidebook manuscript with me, promising to make comments in the margins and send it back; I haven't heard from him since.

Before he left, he enveloped me in a huge hug. His shawl smelled faintly of India—a musty blend of cow dung and diesel fumes.

"We'll see you again," he said. "Expect us."

Anne Cushman is the author of From Here to Nirvana: The Yoga Journal Guide to Spiritual India. *She lives in Northern California.*

$\star$ $\overset{\star}{}$ $\star$

Enchantment

In the mountains of Washington,
surprising visions and secret music
light upon a hiker.

DARKNESS OVERTOOK US. FORCED TO BIVOUAC OUR FIRST NIGHT in the mountains, we slept fitfully on the sloping, rocky ground. It was August of 1959, almost half my lifetime ago. I hadn't started backpacking and mountain hiking until I was forty and my husband, Bill, forty-four. But from then on it took over our lives. We fled the city and headed for the hills whenever we could.

Bill developed a passion for high mountain lakes and had "discovered" a magnificent granite basin of lakes with our daughter, Peggy, an avid climber in her own right. Father and daughter had followed directions in a fisherman's guide, bushwhacking their way up the side of slippery steep slopes, around meadows, through forests blanketed in snow. There were no maps at the time of this area of Washington State, but Hal Sylvester, head of the Wenatchee National Forest early in the century, had named it the Enchantment Lakes. Bill and Peggy had found it enchanted indeed.

And now Bill had brought me to see it too. After our uncomfortable night's sleep, we began the long climb to the rim of the granite basin. We reached the top, and I saw for the first time that other world of the Enchantment Lakes: the snowfields and lakes gleaming from below, the rugged peaks and pinnacles encircling

155

the basin in a great embrace. We knew right then that we would return here again and again. We had been called.

Over the years we became intimate with the terrain, christening many of the lakes and tarns with names from legend and mythology—Excalibur, Grail Tarn, Lake Viviane, Leprechaun—and in the austere upper basin, Norse names: Freya, Brynhild, Valhalla Cirque. Slowly more and more hikers discovered this magical country. Maps were made and trails cut, but our hearts remained true to the pristine wilderness we had first encountered.

Our favorite time to go became the first week of October, a time we called "Golden Week," when the alpine larches were ablaze. One such autumn we arrived midafternoon at Lake Viviane—at 7,000, the lowest of the Enchantment Lakes. We found our usual place under an overhanging boulder, part of a lichen-blackened pinnacle we had named Merlin's Tower, which rose above us. Like marmots in our lair, we settled in. Bill got our pads and sleeping bags out, and we lay down to nap until our hiking companions caught up to us.

Just before I fell asleep, I heard a lovely, haunting tune. It sounded like music from bagpipes.

But after a moment, I decided that no, it wasn't real bagpipes I was hearing—it couldn't be. To the east was a mountain named McClellan, a Scottish name, as it happens. Its several pinnacles rose like pipes. Below McClellan, a rounded ridge ran down and alongside of Lake Leprechaun, creating a shape almost like the bag on a set of bagpipes. The wind was the drone. The echo of a waterfall across the lake seemed to make a tune against the cliff beside us.

"Darn," I thought, addressing my now-awakened rational brain: "It wasn't bagpipes at all."

"Or was it?" came the reply from another part of me as I drifted off to sleep.

When our friends arrived, we rose in the gathering dusk to eat a meal together around our backpacking stoves, and before long were once again in our sleeping bags for the night.

Then, in the twilight between sleeping and waking, the music began again. In my half-sleep and through half-closed eyes, I saw a vision of pipers marching two abreast in kilts, playing the pipes. Down the ridge they came, past Lake Leprechaun, and then disappeared into the mists of the waterfall tumbling into Lake Viviane. I saw leprechauns on the lakeshore peeking from behind rocks and trees to watch them. From the lake, water nymphs thrust their heads up to listen.

As I slipped into sleep, elated by my vision, I knew I had been given a gift; a very special, private gift. What I had seen made no sense at all, but it was somehow holy, precious.

I didn't want to tell anyone about it at first. But soon I decided to tell Bill; it was so important a part of myself that I had to share it with him. Then, not long after, one of my brothers was visiting, and I told him about the pipes.

"You know," he said, teasingly, "they have places for people like you."

I didn't tell anyone else after that.

The next year we went again to the Enchantment Lakes basin, and this time our son, Willy, and his wife, Sandy, joined us. We hiked and camped in an incandescent light that seemed to glow from trees, ground, and sun. It was a magical time.

Back at home a week later, Sandy and I were washing dishes after dinner when she suddenly said, "You know, Willy had a strange experience in the Enchantments."

I held my breath, wondering what she'd say next. She hesitated, then: "He heard bagpipes."

Since that time, I have heard the bagpipes again.

I cannot make it happen. They go away if I start talking or if someone talks to me, or if I begin doing work of some kind.

I have never been able to summon them.

They come when they want to.

Margaret Paul Stark, born in 1916, lives in Leavenworth, Washington, with her husband Bill. Both of them have spent much of the last forty years in the mountains of Washington.

BRENDA PETERSON

✦ ✦ ✦

Stag Dance

A shamanic ceremony brings healing
and transformation through
the "power animal."

ABOVE US THE WIND SHOOK THE TALLEST TREES AND WHITE
showers fell down on us like a blessing. As Flor and I walked home
through the snow, I thought of all the snakes still hibernating un-
derground. I remembered my own early years in the woods. My
first rattle was made from a rattlesnake's tail tied to a twig with
leather thongs. As I crawled, I'd clutch that little rattle in my fist
and so startled towering adults who might mistakenly step on me.
When I was four and a half years old, we left the forest for some
years by the sea. It was thirty-eight years before I saw my forest
birthplace again. I returned to the High Sierra at the tip of
Northern California to attend a week-long women's summer solstice camp.

At first it felt odd to be back in the same woods I'd known as a
child. But after a few days, it was simple: I was playing again in my
woods. Over the week 200 of us attended open-air classes in
meadows and among the trees. We sat in circles on the ground
while we heard speakers on every subject from "Basque
Mythology" to "Eleusinian Mysteries of Ancient Greece" to
"Mayan-Hopi Wheels of Transcendence." We slept in tents or
under the stars and soon the sensible camping shorts, hiking boots,

and visors gave way to long, colorful skirts, bare feet, and bright gypsy scarves. It took surprisingly little time to forget the polite strictures of society and remember our more primitive tribal roots. In this, we had the 8,000-foot altitude as our ally.

On the last day of this gathering, I took my part in the Dance of the Tonals. It is said that when we are born, a *tonal*, or power animal, is born with us to live alongside and offer itself as messenger between Earth and spiritual worlds.

Led by a woman who'd spent her apprenticeship with a Peruvian shaman, our study group of ten women spent a day together in silence and meditation.

"You can call your tonals to come dance with you," the medicine woman said. "They will come gladly. They have never been far away from you. And once you remember them, they will always be here."

She told us that our tonals live alongside us like shadows, teaching us what animals know and humans have forgotten. "When you die," the medicine woman concluded, "the animal dies, too. And maybe next life, you trade places."

Then we did a series of exercises to call our animals home to us. Different tonals were silently summoned to take up their spiritual residence in each of the body's chakras, or power centers— from root to belly to crown of the head. In my navel center I felt the intricate circlings of a chambered nautilus; in my heart a grizzly; in my root and crown chakras two connecting serpents, coiled and patient as if they'd waited there forever for my memory to return to me.

"At first I didn't see anything," a woman said when we finally broke the silence to sit in one circle in the center of a stand of ponderosa pines. A thick blanket of dried needles cushioned us. Late-afternoon heat shimmied in the air like a mirage. "Then all of a sudden I realized I wasn't looking up," the woman marveled. "I was gazing *down* at the tops of these trees. I was looking out the eyes of an eagle as it glided."

We all told of the animals who answered our silent calls. Next to me was a large woman who did have some of the gruff, maternal grizzly about her; next to her was a dove, several snow leopards, a dark-skinned jaguar, and a flaming-haired woman whose hooded black eyes gave her the regal fierceness of a red-tailed hawk. One woman I recognized from several of my other classes chose to keep her own counsel. She asked not to participate in the ritual painting and costuming that the rest of us undertook in preparation to dance in this ritual ceremony of recognizing and claiming our animals.

I knew this woman Diana's story; she'd confided it to me earlier in the week as we sat by the lake in full sunlight. Her story was set in the shadows: Diana was a double incest survivor. When her family's secret was discovered by a relative, she'd been sent to a foster home. There Diana lapsed into a silence that lasted several years. All that would rouse the child was sitting in her rural backyard forest alone for hours at a stretch. Even when Diana began speaking again, she never talked about her parents. She told people they had died when she was very young.

Now Diana had children of her own and a loyal husband. Still her hunched-over shoulders bespoke the hunted posture of the victim. When she spoke, which she did rarely, she cringed as if the sound of her own voice were too loud. Of course, the other women let her be. Of course, none asked Diana to dance.

In preparation for our dance, we busied ourselves in the forest. Grizzly looked for pinecones to make a great necklace, the Eagle feathered fallen branches across her arms for wings, the black Jaguar crouched low in feline wariness. One woman emerged from her nearby tent with a leopard-skin mask she'd saved from her childhood. Another woman, Elephant, remembered to thud on the forest floor with her big, bare feet, pausing to listen to her own earthquakes.

At the sound of the drum's steady beat, calling us from the forest, we came back to make a circle in the pine needles. Many of us had painted our faces. I had silver zigzags running like lightning down my arms and face. Several women had elaborately painted bird faces, and one woman, Salmon, showed delicately etched blue-green scales up her bare back and legs. In the deep woods, without much clothing, with faces painted and bodies adorned by leaves and branches, anyone can become Aboriginal. Anyone can remember that this is our native land and we are all primitives. The child in us remembers.

As I finished painting my legs, I was startled by a movement in the forest. Diana stepped lightly toward me, holding out a box of brightly colored watercolor crayons.

"Will you help paint me?" she asked.

Diana was so transformed, I just stared at her. Atop her head was a branch, a stretch of bark antlers. Her nose was painted black, proud and sensitive as she seemed to sniff the air for signs of hunters. Around each bare breast was painted a phosphorescent red-black-and-yellow bull's-eye. There was a flat, heavy stone clenched in each hand—her sharpened hooves.

"Who…what are you?" I asked, though I already knew.

Diana's voice was low. "A stag," she said simply. Then she turned around, naked except for a branch encircling each ankle. "Will you paint my ass like my breasts?" She asked.

I didn't move. A fear came over me. "I can't…" I said. "It's…it's too terrible." I shook my head. "I don't want to help make you a target again."

Diana fixed me with dark, oval eyes that softened slightly. "Please," she said. "It's part of my dance." Then she laughed huskily. "I can't be my stag without it."

I nodded. As she stood at her full height, I painted two bull's-eyes on each buttock, my hands shaking.

In the circle, the drum did all the talking, like a great heartbeat in the forest. After dancing together for what seemed hours, we all sat silent. Then each woman stepped alone into the center of the woods and, in rhythm to the drum, let her animal move with her.

Grizzly never left the earth; Eagle never touched down; Snow Leopard danced only a second, then as usual eluded us in the underbrush; Elephant broke the silence with a scream and shook the ground with her stomping two-step. I did my Cobra dance low in the pine needles, swaying to the drum as the trees above me swayed. On my belly, I felt the Earth pounding against my navel.

At last it was the Stag who stepped into our center. A few women caught their breaths, hardly recognizing Diana. She had never moved like this: deliberate, forceful steps, massive head turning this way and that to watch us, eyes black like bullet holes in her impassive face. As Diana danced, a masculine sway to her wide hips, her hooves pawing the ground, I remembered a hunting scene I'd witnessed once in Colorado.

> Putting forth your best effort relieves the ego of its need to justify its existence. The strenuous push is equalled by internal effort. The uphill climb, like orgasm, leaves little energy remaining but to cry, laugh, or love everything without hesitation.
> —Janine Pommy Vega,
> *Tracking the Serpent: Journeys to Four Continents*

In a game preserve, I stood watching a herd of deer graze. Suddenly a truck pulled up and some drunken men jumped out. They were not hunters; though this was the season, they wore no orange jackets. They had no notion of tracking the stealthy forest stalk. One man rested his rifle on the barbed-wire fence of the game preserve. Before he could get his aim, a subtle change ran through the herd. As if electrically charged, they all grouped together tightly and moved slowly backward. From their center stepped a huge buck; his antlers must have been six feet across. Very deliberately, the buck stepped forward, steadily moving toward the man, his head lowered. With a curse at what he thought was the buck's challenge, the man pulled the trigger.

The shot echoed off the far ridge. Like gazelles, the herd scattered swiftly. But the buck kept coming toward the man. Another shot. The buck dropped to his knees, stared straight at the man, and toppled. With a hoot of triumph, the men jumped back into their truck and took off. There was no ceremony, no asking forgiveness of the deer for his sacrifice, no ritual to clean and dress the buck, then partake in his great spirit so he might live on in our nourished bodies.

I crawled through the wire fence and ran toward that buck. It lay alone in the meadow. But I could feel the eyes of his herd watching me from the forest. I kept my proper distance; the buck was still alive. He lay there bleeding from two wounds, panting, his eyes liquid and dilated. At last the dark eyes fixed, rolled back. With a breath like a sigh, the deer died. As my father had taught me, I put a branch in the buck's mouth—food for his journey to the spirit world's forest. Then I laid my palm on his warm flank, tracing with one finger the bloodied bull's-eye.

The same stag danced again in Diana. She was all thunder and rage as she spun around within our circle. Some women fell back from this raw display; other women leaned forward, eyes riveting on the fierce antlers adorned with dangling brass earrings. The Cobra in me swayed as the ground echoed staccato poundings of drum and fading hoofbeats.

Much later Diana rejoined our circle. She still kept her own counsel. But I never saw her cringe again, not once.

The next day when we were all leaving that forest to return to our homes, Diana approached me quietly. "Thank you," she said, her eyes steadily holding mine.

"Yours was the most beautiful dance of all," I told her.

Diana threw her head back, then said in a deep voice, "The stag in me was never wounded." She laughed. "They missed me. They'll always miss me." Diana turned to leave, calling out, "Goodbye, Cobra."

I have never since then seen a deer without thinking of Diana dancing naked in the woods, bull's-eyes all over her body.

Now when I find myself midlife walking in the dark woods, I know I am not alone. The animals are my allies; the trees are gods and goddesses who in deep stillness keep the Earth's counsel. All that is alive calls out to me to come play, to take my part in the dance.

Brenda Peterson has worked for The New Yorker, *lived on a farm near Denver, where she was a fiction editor for* Rocky Mountain Magazine, *and taught at Arizona State University in Tempe. Now an editor and environmental writer who lives in Seattle, she is the author of several books, including* Duck and Cover, Singing to the Sound: Visions of Nature, Animals, and Spirit, Build Me an Ark: A Life with Animals, Spirited Waters: Soloing South through the Inside Passage, *and* Living by Water, *from which this story was excerpted.*

IRMA ZALESKI

✦ ✦ ✦

The Door to Joy

...is the same door between
time and eternity.

IN THE LANGUAGE OF RELIGION, JOY IS NOT A MERELY HUMAN emotion but a spiritual experience. It is a "fruit of the Holy Spirit," a *grace.* Joy comes to us from a place outside of ourselves, or from so deep inside that we cannot reach it at will. This is why we are always, as C. S. Lewis has said, "surprised by joy." It may burst upon us in moments of great happiness, in a world flooded with beauty, in an ecstasy of love. We hear it, perhaps, in the sound of our children's voices playing outside, or the song of birds, or the night rumor of the sea. We recognize it in a great work of art. But joy may also come to us in the midst of unbearable suffering, at the end of our endurance, in the face of death. It breaks into the prison of our misery and pain and, for a moment we forget ourselves and are free. True joy is a form of ecstasy, a state of being out of our ordinary minds. In the words of St. Augustine (on Psalm 99:3ff), joy is a "song of the soul," a spontaneous response of the human spirit when it is able to step away beyond the confines of its own ego and find itself in the presence of God.

God is not a concept or an "article of faith." Although we give him many names, he is not a creation of the mind. We may not even believe in him, yet, he is real. Children see God quite often, I think. They see him in the essential *mysteriousness* of things, they experience him in wild joy which seems at times to possess them, in laughter and play. They also meet him, perhaps, in an abandonment to grief, in a flood of uninhibited tears. When we begin to grow up, however, we quickly lose our ability to encounter God in such direct, simple ways. Our minds are too restless, too noisy to hear the sound of his coming. We cannot believe what our hearts experience, we cannot find him among the evils which seem to rule the world. We think and worry too much and try to create our own safe gods. This is why we must relearn to see the signs of the Divine Presence and to open ourselves to it. We must find our way back to joy....

When I was little, in Poland before the war, we used to spend nearly every summer at my grandmother's house in the mountains. She lived alone, in a house built by local craftsmen on the edge of a torrent. The noise of its rushing waters was the background of every moment of our holidays, and the first sound of eternity which I learned to hear. My grandmother was the kind of grandmother that everybody should have. She was brilliant and wise, although a little bitter at times. She had lived through wars, revolutions, a bad marriage, and the death of two children. What had saved her sanity, I believe, was her love of beauty and a passionate interest in all the things of the mind. She loved literature and art, she was fascinated by science. Above all else, she loved the beauty of the mountains among which she lived and among which she eventually died.

I must have been five or six at the time. One night, I was awakened by my grandmother leaning over my bed. There was a noise of a great storm outside. Grandmother picked me up and carried me out onto a big veranda which ran all along the front of the house. "Look!" she said, and turned my face toward the mountains, "Look, this is too beautiful to sleep through." I saw black sky, torn apart every few seconds by lightning, mountains emerging out of darkness, immense, powerful, and so *real*. Thunder rolled among the peaks. I was not frightened—how could I be?—I was awed. I looked up at my grandmother's face and, in a flash of light, I saw it flooded with wonder and joy. I did not realize it then, of course, but now I do, that what I saw was *ecstasy*. My grandmother was the first to point out to me a *door to joy*.

The war years in occupied Poland were not conducive to joy. Like millions of other people, we lived on the edge of disaster, surrounded by horror and fear. There was very little beauty in our lives. We did not go to the mountains, we heard very little music (orchestras were disbanded and the radios forbidden), theaters and even schools were closed. It was hard, often impossible, to get away from the city. We dwelled in a bleak, inhuman world, in small rooms filled with all the belongings we had managed to save, always aware of the evil outside.

And yet, even during the darkest years, there were times when joy would suddenly burst out of darkness like lightning and, for a moment, all was well. It could have been on a summer night, when tossing and turning on the bed I shared with my mother, I would hear a song of a nightingale in the jasmine bushes outside, and the beauty of it would be nearly impossible to bear. Or, on an autumn evening, as

---

The stillness under stars. The sky recalls the painting I made of heaven when I was five; great blue-black swirls that I could never get dark enough.

I stand, as my grandmother once did, in the darkness by the house, the moon-shadow of a tree. Its feathery arms touch the shadow of the eaves. She was alone a lot in those early years: my grandfather traveling by horse-drawn sleigh or buckboard or Model T, making house calls in the country. "I was in good company," she always said, "worried I got, but never lonesome."

A jet passes over, blinking, on its way to cities in the East.

It is so cold it hurts to breathe. This is the side of the moon that no one sees.
—Kathleen Norris, *Dakota: A Spiritual Geography*

I was hurrying along a gray, empty street, anxious to be home before the curfew, I would look up and see the flaming glory of the setting sun and, for a split second perhaps, there would be no more darkness or war. A door would fly open at the center of my being, and I would walk through it unafraid. The darkness, of course, would soon return, and I would run home, fearful again of the curfew police.

The war finally ended, although not in the way we had hoped. In September of 1946, we—my mother, my brother, and I—escaped from communist Poland, and eventually joined my father who had spent the war years with the Polish Army in the West. Upon our arrival in Britain, my parents decided that in order to learn English as quickly as possible, I was to be sent to a boarding school in Scotland, run by Catholic nuns. I loathed it at first and made myself a nuisance, I am afraid. I was angry, rebellious, and scared. But the nuns won me over in the end. In spite of myself, I was moved by the beauty and peace of the life they had embraced, by their kindness, by the way they prayed and sang in church. I began to appreciate the beauty and the sacred order of their religious celebrations and liturgies. Sometimes, as I knelt with the other girls at evening prayers in the dimly lighted church, a faint scent of incense lingering in the air and the flickering flame of a vigil light throwing immense shadows on the high ceiling above, the horror and the chaos I had lived through receded, and I would find myself relaxing into silence and peace. Without realizing it, I think, I had begun to pray.

I also learned to love the hills among which the convent stood, the tall, dark trees which surrounded it, the pale Scottish sky, and, above all else, the walled-in garden where I often escaped to be alone. It was in that garden, when I was about fifteen, that I wrote this poem, the first one I had ever written and which, miraculously, I have kept:

> God struck a chord of purple and gold,
> behind the pine trees on the
> lawn,

and as he was very near, I said softly so that
only he could hear,
that it was good.

God smiled, the wind gently sighed and
smoothed the dark heads of
the trees.

God came where I stood and said it was very
good
then began to light the stars.

It was not a great poem, of course, but it expressed, however naively, a beginning of an insight which was to become the root of my spiritual life: that God was very beautiful and that all created beauty was a sign of his presence. I began to realize that to be touched by beauty, to search for it in all things and rejoice in it, even amid the ugliness and sorrow of life, was to be for me a path of prayer and the way to God.

Such moments of insight are very rare; they pass and one forgets. It has been so in my life at least. But I have never ceased to search for God, however childish and superficial some of the ways I looked for him were. I studied different religions and read books. I talked to priests, Zen Masters, Buddhist monks. I joined meditation groups and investigated every spiritual path I came across. But still, I was never satisfied, never at peace. A friend who knew me well used to become exasperated with what he called my "running into caves." "For heaven's sake, woman," he would shout, "do you think God is a pussycat that you can play with? God is a tiger! You'd better watch out if you ever succeed in falling into his cave."

"You might be right, Dante," I answered, "but I *want* God!"

"Well, you will not find him in books, or running after gurus," he said.

"How shall I find him, then?" I asked.

"By standing still!" he replied.

Dante was an artist, the husband of a life-long friend. Even after I had left England for Canada, I used to see them in London every few years. It became an established custom during those visits that Dante and I would go to museums and art galleries together. Or, it would be better to say, Dante took me to see what he felt I should learn to see. At first, we used to talk a good deal and I would ask many questions, but, during later visits, we often stood silent before a painting, a sculpture, or a vase, and then we would just smile at each other and leave.

It was during one of those visits that I experienced a moment of the purest joy, and I think came closer to ecstasy than ever before or since. We were in the British Museum, in front of a three thousand-year-old Egyptian sculpture which Dante particularly loved. He thought it was the work of a great spiritual Master and contained deep wisdom which one needed to absorb. We had visited it many times in the past, and it had become very familiar to me. But now, suddenly, I realized that I had never really seen it before. For a moment, I don't know how long, it became alive, perfect, full of beauty and wisdom, radiating compassion and peace. For the first time in my life, I felt totally focused and still. At that instant I knew what it meant to "find God" and that he was indeed a "tiger." In that one single moment out of time, I had been given a glimpse of a reality which could never *not be*, a pledge of eternity at the core of all being.

But we do not live out of time. Moments of ecstasy, however significant and profound they may be, must pass, and their memory alone cannot sustain our everyday spiritual lives. We must find a way of living eternity within the dimension of time. For most of us this means a very great struggle. It means the breaking down of protective walls we have built around our time-bound egos and opening them to what is beyond: not only in moments of ecstasy but every moment of our lives. In other words, it means the painful process of *learning to love*. Truth, beauty, joy—the presence of God—can only be found in a living encounter with another, in a relationship of love.

Christian tradition has been for me the most real and the most natural path to that relationship. Not because I believe it offers a "final solution" to the mystery of being, or is the only path to God, but because at its very core it is a *religion of love*. It is true that Christianity is a narrow path and anyone who walks on it faces the danger of falling into exclusiveness and pride. No religious path, perhaps, is free from that danger. But, as I tried to follow in the footsteps of him in whose face I recognized the fullness of the Divine Presence, that danger receded and I became, I hope, more open to truth and beauty, wherever they could be found, not less. I was led to see ever more clearly that at the heart of all true religion is "good news," a call to the joy of Bethlehem, a proclamation that God—the infinite, unknowable reality—makes himself present in the world and summons all of us to that same encounter and that same relationship of love with himself and all of his creation.

For God never comes to us alone, but brings with him the whole universe. He opens our eyes to the beauty of everything that is. He brings with him every human being who has ever lived. He breaks our hearts open to what is *not self*. He shares with us his own joy and his own total, all-embracing love.... This is why the great Christian teacher and saint, Seraphim of Sarov, having spent thirty years alone in the silence of his cell, used to run out to meet every person coming toward him, bow down to the ground, and say, "My brother, my sister, my joy!" This is why all true saints have always loved every creature which came from the hand of God. Love does not discriminate or categorize; it does not insist on being right. Love embraces all things in that great, empty silence beyond words or thought, which is the wide-open door to ecstasy and to unending joy.

Irma Zaleski was born in Poland in 1931. After World War II, she escaped with her family to England where she completed studies in Medieval History at the University of London. She emigrated to Canada in 1952 and is the author of many books, including Living the Jesus Prayer, The Way of Repentance, *and* The Country of Death. *She divides her time between her home in Cobermere, Ontario, and the Toronto homes of her son and daughter who have provided her with four grandsons and a granddaughter.*

KIM TINSLEY

* * *

The Sound of Healing

A trip to Morocco triggers a journey
of a deeper kind.

THIS IS THE STORY OF HOW AN ANCIENT SOUND AND AN INDIGO shawl from Morocco saved my life.

I am not really sure how to tell this story because it is still unfolding, and I do not have enough perspective on it yet to understand it's full meaning and implications. I am also not sure just where in time this tale actually began, although I would like to believe that it started hundreds and hundreds of years ago with an unknown ancestor, a woman in a faraway land whose daughter was taken from her and sold into slavery. I would like to believe that, in her grief, this woman prayed that one day she would have a descendant like me—a daughter who would keep the spirit of her culture even though she had no conscious recollection of its origins, no one to tell her explicitly where her beliefs came from, a daughter who would eventually find her way home and see herself, remember herself whole. This is the way I will tell it, at least.

The story began around the time that I made my very first movie to submit with an application to NYU's Graduate Film program. That's when I started having desert dreams: a series of dreams that felt more like vivid rememberings—colorful , detailed, rich...and bearing no resemblance to my hectic waking life in

New York City. In one of the most magnificent dreams, I taught people how to irrigate the desert. After overseeing a vast irrigation project, I took a walk in a lush oasis garden built on steps. As I headed down the steps, a tree with silver leaves and branches reached out to me and carried me throughout the rest of the garden. The flowers and trees were so beautiful and the sensation of being carried on the branches of the silver tree was so thrilling that I did not want to wake up.

That is the dream I told my traveling companions as we flew to Paris. I was working on the screenplay that I hoped would become my thesis film—a story about African-American expatriates that I'd written because I was heartsick about the racism I was experiencing in grad school. In my distress, I was considering the possibility of my own expatriation from America. I'd done a lot of preparation for my trip—taken months of French classes, read everything I could get my hands on that was written by and about Black expats in Paris, interviewed people who had tried expatriation for a while and had returned to the United States for one reason or another. But the guiding principle for my story was James Baldwin's admonition that "there are no untroubled countries," so I went away knowing the only thing I am ever sure about when I write a film—how it will end. I knew that the expatriated heroine of the story would eventually have to return to the States and face her wilderness, so to speak.

What I couldn't have known at the time is that I would have to face my own wilderness before I could write the story. But I'm getting ahead of myself. Off to Paris I went on Christmas Day, to take location photos, find old expatriate haunts, and to answer the question: What is it about the "city of light" that seemed like blessed relief when compared with the brutality and pain of racism in the United States? I had only a week to explore a few of the possibilities.

I never got the answer.

As it turns out, my *luggage* spent a week in Paris while I went on what I've now come to think of as the "healing waters tour." The day after I arrived in Paris I wandered south—first, to the shrine in Lourdes, then on to the sulfur springs at Cauterets (where a spa treatment cured me of a nagging hip ailment that hasn't troubled me since) and finally, finishing the week at the Spanish seaside resort of San Sebastián with the Atlantic Ocean roaring just outside the terrace of my room. At the time, I didn't understand why I was being led to these water sites, wandering farther and farther away from Paris, farther and farther away from the story I'd come to write. I would have to travel an even greater distance in terms of both miles and years, before I'd even come close to understanding that the "detours" I took were what my trip and my proposed expatriate story were really about.

The excursions to the water sites were relaxing and restorative. Because I know that sometimes delays can prove to be beneficial, I wasn't very upset about getting off course and off schedule. When I headed back to Paris at the end of the week, I thought I'd just add a couple of days to my trip and do the scouting I'd come there to do, albeit at a much more hurried pace. But for the next couple of days, every effort I made to change my ticket and head back to New York was met with an obstacle—busy phone lines, overbooked or cancelled flights, miscommunications. Finally, I arrived at a travel agency to pick up a return ticket to New York just moments after it had closed. That's when I saw it—the advertisement for Marrakesh.

That night over dinner, I discussed with my traveling companions the possibility of yet another detour. The restaurant where we were eating, Galerie 88, was a Moroccan restaurant. No further encouragement was needed. With kindly travel advice from Naima, the young Moroccan woman who owned Galerie 88, I was on my way to Marrakesh. The night before I left, I visited a shop in Les Halles and bought an indigo shawl with beaded fringe and a mysterious, sweet fragrance. Even though I had nothing else in my wardrobe that was blue (either in my luggage or back at home), I just had to have this shawl. I wore it constantly throughout the rest of my trip.

I knew nothing about Marrakesh before I went there except that I'd purchased many cherished items of Moroccan jewelry from my friend, Jane, who spent part of the year there and considered it her real home. On the flight I read brochures that described the city as an oasis on the edge of the Sahara desert known for its gardens, including one built on steps. With the hope that this might, coincidentally, be the garden I had dreamed about, I planned to arrange for a tour as soon as I got to the hotel.

I don't think it was just my excitement at the prospect of a new adventure—something strange really did happen to me as soon as I set my feet on African soil for the very first time. Every vertebrae in my spine shifted, realigned. It was as if I'd lived my whole life without ever really standing up straight until the moment I stood in Marrakesh.

The day after my arrival, a calèche driver took me on a garden tour. I couldn't get into the one I most wanted to see—it was at the palace of King Hassan II and closed to the public when he was in residence. Unable to visit what I thought surely must be the garden of my dreams, I settled for lunch at La Mamounia, a former palace and the best hotel in the city. As it was also reputed to have lovely gardens, I was more than satisfied with the diversion. Before lunch, I walked among red roses with thick, fragrant petals. Brilliant flowering vines clung to the walls and trunks of palms whose fronds formed a shady cathedral overhead. The air was soft and warm. Sunlight, filtering through the trees, dappled the stone walkways. I looked up toward a shaft of sunlight and that's when I saw the silver trees: the ones I'd dreamed about. I had no idea that the leaves of olive trees glint silver in the sunlight. I never expected to literally see silver trees. I burst into tears when I recognized them. I knew right then, that in spite of the fact that I had not gone where I'd planned, I had to be in the right place. Everywhere I went that day I saw another detail that I recognized from my dreams.

The first time a tour guide led me through the souks to buy souvenirs, I was overwhelmed by how familiar everything there seemed to me, as well—the shops with their array of pungent spices, the donkey carts negotiating narrow, meandering streets, the apothecaries with incense and perfumes and dried herbs and potions. In fact, I had to go back to the hotel and rest after a very short visit because the experience of recognizing a place I'd never been to before was absolutely dizzying. I was steadier on successive visits and kept meeting merchants who told me that I looked like a member of their families. The people who said this to me always identified themselves as Tuareg. I was also told that the indigo shawl I was wearing, the one I'd purchased in Paris, was of Tuareg origins. The beads on the fringe were from a city in southern Morocco called Goulamine, where Tuareg women are known to do a dance called the *guedra*. I didn't think much of these revelations while I was there because when I'm in New York, Ethiopians think I'm Ethiopian, Bangladeshis think I'm from Bangladesh, etc., etc. But I appreciated the stories the people told me about their families and the courtesies that were extended to me because I seemed familiar to them. For instance, I learned expert haggling techniques from a man who said I looked so much like his own daughter that he had to call his sons from other stalls in the souks to see me.

I stayed in Marrakesh almost three weeks. The only pictures I took while I was there were of the silver trees. The rest of what I saw was far too beautiful to capture on film and besides, having dreamed the place long before I knew it's name, Marrakesh was part of me in a way that could never be lost or misplaced as photographs sometimes are. I did, however, make a note and a drawing in my

---

I stood by the hut and looked out at the water as if what lay beyond it embodied who I was before and every place I had been. Here and now I cast myself apart, had found my place. Something was happening inside me, something unaccounted for that uprooted me from all sense of the present moment and carried me through unexplored regions of the mind. I felt overwhelmed by ancient memories of a place to which I had only just arrived.
        —Laurie Gough, *Kite Strings of the Southern Cross*

journal concerning some men I'd seen in Djema El Fna, the town square whose goings on—with musicians, vendors, acrobats, snake charmers, and food sellers—reminded me of 125th Street in Harlem. The men who fascinated me wore cowrie shell hats and played an instrument that looked like a large double castanet. Able to maintain many rhythms at once, the circular movement of their heads kept a tassel on top of their hats twirling while with their hands, they played the large double castanet at a much faster tempo. They kept yet another rhythm with their feet, managing, at intervals, to leap upward and extend their legs straight out in front of them. They hung then, suspended in the air as if levitating. I described them in my journal and drew a picture of the instruments they played. When I got back home I put my picture of the silver trees in plain view near my bed, but I didn't look at this trip journal again until over a year later.

I experienced a kindness and graciousness in Marrakesh that defied boundaries of religion and language. Sadly, I spoke no Arabic at all and my command of French, even after months of arduous study, was comic. But I found that my hosts were willing to work with me—and to laugh with me too, when my French turned into an unwitting stand-up routine. I have no other travel experience that compares with it except, perhaps, trips to my maternal grandparents' house when I was a little girl. I felt that safe and relaxed and at home. When I left, I carried with me a profound sense of peace—and the knowledge that my rerouting meant that the story I'd set out to tell would have to change. I just wasn't sure how.

I got sick the day I returned to the United States in February, which may have been a blessing in disguise. That and the jet lag I experienced for nearly a month kept me close to my apartment and allowed me to shelter the peace I'd returned with for a little while, at least. I think my trouble started the first day I went outside to rejoin the rest of the world. Over the next year I watched virtually every aspect of the life I had known unravel. Events seemed to conspire against me at every turn. Then one morning in the spring of the next year, just days after I'd graduated from film school and done my first professional gig as a director, I woke up crying and couldn't stop. I went home to my parents in Detroit and collapsed: I was having a nervous breakdown. Even in my state of extreme depression and agitation, I would not consider Western therapeutic methods because I knew instinctively that my problem was spiritual, not the province of the priesthood of science, not something that could be measured or tested. My pain was unspeakable. It couldn't be talked away. There was no medication for it, no magic pill to take. I just didn't know *what* the solution was. Nothing that was familiar to me, nothing I'd ever tried before to handle depression or anger was comforting to me. I couldn't bear to hear the sound of English sung or spoken. I couldn't eat or speak or read. Sunlight hurt. Every part of my body ached. I could hardly get out of bed and when I finally would drift off to sleep out of sheer exhaustion, I was tortured by nightmares. Inconsolable, I cried most of every day and night for three months.

One day I was so tired of being unable to rest, of the relentless pain and sleep deprivation, of not knowing what to do to help myself, that I tried to take my life. My unsuccessful attempt to separate the pain from my life created new discomforts. Finally a friend insisted that I go see her cousin, a psychologist. I went though I knew deep in my heart that it wasn't the right way to address my problem. I thank God that the psychologist irritated me beyond the limits of what I thought were possible! Even though it was definitely not the appropriate treatment for me, I had at least "picked up my bed and walked," taken action on my own behalf and made the first step toward healing.

I left the doctor's office and drove directly to a record store. I couldn't bear sounds of any kind and hadn't been able to listen to music for months, but I obeyed the inner directive to go to the record store. I didn't even know why I was going until after I got in the store and found myself asking one of the sales clerks to direct me to the world music section so that I could find something from Marrakesh. I needed a sound from the last place on earth where I had known peace.

I bought a recording by Hassan Hakmoun called *Gift of the Gnawa*. There wasn't much information on the CD cover except that Gnawa music is used for ritual healing and trance. I was so miserable and desperate, I figured I had nothing to lose by trying it. I took the CD home and played it that night. For the first time in three months I slept without having a nightmare. The next day I went back to the record store and bought every Moroccan recording in stock. Some of the liner notes had more information about the trance healing rituals; this was the first and only material I'd been able to focus on long enough to read since I first became sick.

The Gnawa Brotherhood is a Sufi order, established by former slaves who were brought to Morocco from throughout sub-Saharan Africa beginning in the sixteenth century, after the collapse of the Malian and Songhai empires. The cultural traditions of many peoples are preserved in the Gnawa repertoire—Hausa, Fulani, Boussou, Bambara, Mossi, and countless others. In addition to Islamic prayers sung in Arabic and prayers sung in Bambara, many of the Gnawa songs also contain rhythmic and melodic remembrances and lyrics which describe the anguish of slavery and forced exile. Even though I could not understand the text of the songs and had access to scant translations, this music spoke to me very clearly, very deeply. As a descendant of stolen and enslaved people and someone

Sometimes funny, sometimes serious, Xuan Ke asked us to close our eyes: "It is important to quiet your mind and let the music enter you. Do not think of other things, please." After a long silence, he asked us to watch as he pointed to places on his body where the music might enter: between the eyebrows, in the palms of the hands, the solar plexus, behind the knees, on the bottom of the feet. "If the music is allowed to enter you, you will become healed. Look at us! We are never sick in Lijiang!"

—Gretel Ehrlich, *Questions of Heaven: The Chinese Journeys of an American Buddhist* who had literally been sickened by racism, the Gnawa songs touched the roots of my suffering, the rhythms soothed my frayed nerves. This music provided me with an avenue, not of escape or expatriation, but of transcendence—a possibility I did not even know existed.

The Gnawa trance healing ritual—the "trance of seven colors"—bears some resemblance to vodu, Candomblé, and Santeria healing rituals in the Americas in that each of the seven rhythms played during the healing ceremony are associated with something particular such as a saint, color, fragrance, food, etc. As I listened to the Gnawa repertoire it became apparent which rhythm I was most responsive to. I either fell asleep when I heard it or couldn't keep still. Not surprisingly, it was the blue rhythm, the suite of songs associated with water and the saint, Sidi Musa, Lord of the Waters, which had the greatest effect on me. Now the first part of my trip abroad—the "healing waters tour"—made sense. I was being guided to the element that would heal my wounded spirit.

I had always loved music—especially jazz vocals—and I grew up knowing that so many of the musical forms now thought of generically as "American" have African roots. I also knew that the world views, cultural values and customs of many ethnic groups from the African continent have been kept alive globally under the guise of "entertainment" or religion—Christianity in the Americas and the Caribbean, Islam in North Africa and the Middle East.

But until I heard Gnawa music, I don't think I understood in such a visceral way just how powerful and effective music can be as a survival strategy. I don't think I ever appreciated the degree to which our sound environment influences our ability to cope with the trials of life. And I'd certainly never felt quite so palpably, the healing power of prayer. When I consider the few things I know about my family's history and experiences both with slavery and racism in this country, I would have to conclude that only a phenomenon as powerful as prayers of transcendence could have given them the strength to survive. Gnawa history is my history. Gnawa songs are my songs. I played the trance music every night to help me sleep and to relieve my anxiety during the day.

When I returned to New York, I ran into a friend I hadn't seen in twenty years—a musician. I asked him if he knew anyone who knew anything about Moroccan music. I didn't tell him what had happened to me or why I wanted to know. A week later he handed me a piece of paper with Hassan Hakmoun's name on it and the names and numbers of three people who could help me get in touch with him. Apparently, Hassan had moved from Marrakesh to New York around the same time I'd come to New York from Detroit in the mid-eighties. We are about the same age, as well.

I called him up and nervously told him my story, not quite sure how it would be received. I was relieved when he didn't laugh or treat me like I was crazy. Instead, Hassan responded with understanding and compassion and invited me to see him perform with his brothers and other musicians from Morocco at a club downtown called "The Cooler."

At the club, we talked a bit before the performance and when I showed him the music I'd been listening to, he told me that I'd done the right thing—the music I had found, "the trance of seven colors," is played especially for women who have had life crises, nervous breakdowns, or suicidal depressions, and it is performed in an all-night ceremony—a *lila*—during which the woman who is ill goes into a trance when her rhythm is played and either dances or falls into peaceful sleep, just as I had done.

At the Dance Research Library at Lincoln Center, I filled my emptiness with films of trance healing rituals from Morocco and other North African and Middle Eastern countries. And, at last, I read the journal I kept while I was in Marrakesh. I had forgotten all about the note I'd made of the performers in Djema El Fna. They were Gnawa musicians, like Hassan Hakmoun. The instrument I had drawn, the *qraqsh* or *qraqreb,* is the primary instrument of trance. When I returned from Marrakesh in 1994, I had no conscious recollection of what Gnawa music sounded like and no idea that these "entertainers" were actually participating in an ancient healing ritual that I would one day depend on for my very life. Perhaps the feeling of peace that I experienced while I was in Morocco was due to the fact that I was exposed to this healing sound daily, each time I passed through Djema El Fna. Perhaps the whole time I was there, I'd been entranced.

I also gathered information about the Tuareg, since so many people in Marrakesh thought I bore a resemblance to them. It seems that I have purchased many Tuareg objects over the years without being aware of their origins. And, coincidentally, many of the attitudes and values that I was raised with bear similarity to some of those held by various groups of Tuareg nomads. In fact, by making movies, telling stories, I am doing what is traditional for Tuareg women, who have long been known for their storytelling skills, written and oral poetry, and songs. There was also a time when the Tuareg were known for their oasis gardens, for being able to find water in the desert and thus to inhabit places that were inhospitable to less resourceful others. My most beautiful desert dream was about that very thing, managing water in the desert, teaching other people how to do the same.

Perhaps the most surprising discovery of all, however, was this: Tuareg women do not normally veil themselves except during the "*tende n goumaten*" ceremony—a trance healing ritual for depression during which the woman is completely covered in an indigo veil. The fragrance of the indigo is thought to have a calming effect on the nerves. Could it have been ancestral guidance that led me to buy the indigo shawl in Paris?

Sadly, I also discovered that the Tuareg were instrumental in the slave trade, leading camel caravans of humans, gold, salt, and spices across the expanse of the African continent. The losers among warring Tuareg factions were often sold as slaves. Is this the circumstance that first brought members of my family to North America? It is a distinct possibility. I may never know for sure.

I am in the world in a very different way than I was when I left the United States on Christmas Day. I have lots of blue clothing in my wardrobe now. From time to time I still wrap myself in the folds of my indigo shawl whose color and scent have faded with constant, comforting wear. I seek the water when I feel troubled, and when I cannot make it to an ocean, lake, or river, I immerse myself in a warm bath and surrender to its liquid embrace. I soothe myself with Gnawa music and continue to look for ways to be the opposite of what hurt me. I am doing the work of transforming rage and depression into forgiveness. It is not an easy task.

I am still distressed by racism, by the experiences I've had with it and by any act of hatred or violence that one human being inflicts upon another. All hurts are my hurts. I feel that much more strongly now as a result of my own breaking.

I have always prayed, but since my trip to Morocco, I've come to appreciate more deeply the healing power of collective prayers—especially prayers carried in song. And I've come to believe that some prayers are answered before you utter a word, that sometimes solutions appear before you realize you have a problem, that healing tools are made available to you

Sitting there in the quiet company of my friend, I think: The river is only itself. It follows its way and doesn't bruise itself on those stones. I have been feeling bruised these past weeks. An emptiness that hurt....

It doesn't matter, I think. We flow, our lives are flowing, from the source back to the source. Even the stones are flowing, back to what they were, only to be formed again, later, much later, some other way. "The stones also are the river," I say aloud.

"What?"

"It's from a poem."

"Look," Jutta says. She points to a violet growing in the crevice of a boulder near her. I walk over and touch its delicate head and pointed fingers. So stubborn. So amazing. The beauty of being alive, of being *here*.

—Sharon Balentine, "The Stones Also Are the River"

long before an illness takes hold. Knowing what to do with those tools is a matter of trusting your deep inner knowing, the God within. Healing then becomes a matter of faith, a matter of faith in your deepest longings, in your truest self.

Earlier I said that I never got the answer to my question about Paris and expatriation. That's not quite true. I had at least part of the answer before embarking on my trip: Expatriation is an unacceptable way for me to respond to the agony of racism. There is no physical place I can go to escape human suffering—my own or anyone else's. There are no untroubled countries. However, as the result of traveling my inner roads, following my dreams and intuitive leanings, I now know that I can be transported to a place of peace via the healing power of Gnawa trance music. That sacred place of inner calm is my home in the world. It must travel with me wherever I go.

I never finished writing my expatriate story. The story changed radically. So did the teller.

I still don't know what to make of all that has happened. I cannot explain why I dreamed of the desert long before I went to Morocco or why prayers sung in languages I don't understand gave me the only relief I could find from my mental distress. Perhaps it will remain a mystery to me always, a miracle, a blessing for which I will be ever grateful.

Kim Tinsley is a filmmaker who has been studying the life-crisis rituals of non-Western cultures ever since Gnawa trance healing music helped her work through a period of debilitating depression. She continues to wander off on unplanned excursions and is trying to figure out a way to integrate her filmmaking skills with the new and unexpected direction her life has taken as a result of her trip to Morocco.

PART FOUR

WALKING THE SHADOW SIDE

JOAN HALIFAX

* * *

Prayer for the Wounded World

Buddhist rituals help a daughter grieve
for her mother—and Mother Earth.

I SAT IN A WASH HIGH ABOVE OWENS LAKE, NOW A DESICCATED pallete of pale, shifting color. Owens Valley stretches its long, open body east of the Sierra Nevada in California. In its middle is the alkali floor of what was once an immense river-fed lake used by steamboats to transport salt from the Saline Valley and silver from the Inyos. Now great clouds of gray dust blow in the four directions from its basin, emptied in the early 1900s by the water lords of Los Angeles.

Close companions were fasting in the rugged canyons branching off from the rocky depression where we had made a base camp. These friends were taking refuge in silence and solitude. It was a time for them to separate themselves from their everyday lives, a time they had given to themselves to mark change in their lives, as people of many cultures have done, to renew their relationship with creation. Each spring for years, I too have gone into wilderness alone to fast, to empty, and restore myself. Now, however, I was to "bear witness" for my friends. With teachers Steven Foster and Meredith Little, I would pray for these men and women as they went out, each one alone, without food or shelter, into this seemingly empty terrain.

Sitting in the rocky, windy land, my mind turned to Los Angeles, the vast city to the south that had sucked Owens Valley dry. Thousands of dead trees stand as silent witnesses to the destruction. The skies also witness this changing time with drought. Deer have retreated far into the higher reaches of the Sierra, and hunters complain. Old-timers around these parts say even the snakes are dying out for lack of water.

On our first afternoon in the south Inyo Mountains ("Dwelling Place of a Great Spirit") before people left for their fasts, the heavens were roaring with the sound of fighter planes training for our nation's most recent war. They were so close we could see the missiles clinging to their wings like dark lampreys. I wondered if the military would play war games all weekend, or would we have quiet instead, in this big, rugged commons? The human fingerprint is found today in every drop of rain. Is there any place on Earth where the voice of technology is not heard?

Early the next morning, my friends left in an unexpected rainstorm for their lonely vigils in the bare mountains just to the north. For most of the day and throughout the night, rain raced in all directions. Usually, rain makes me smile. When I was growing up in Florida and North Carolina, bad weather meant rain. But I lived for twelve years in Southern California, and bad weather in California during the seventies and eighties meant *no* rain. I wondered what the rain would do for my fasting friends. How would it affect their internal weather?

I have always loved the smell of rain in the desert, with the bitter-fresh smell of ozone impregnating the atmosphere. The old, dry sage plants resurrect with rain. The rocks seem to give off a perfume as they show their true colors. The desert floor changes its contours before your very eyes. I still listen with interest to the voices of rain, sometimes harsh and driving, sometimes lyrical.

In the midst of this horizontal rain, I bedded down in the back of a covered pickup and listened till sleep came. At dawn, high and dry, I enjoyed the view of the drenched desert, waking up to light on the surface of each stone and pebble. After sunrise, a bright rainbow tied the world together. Then followed the silence of a cloudless day.

Silence makes the secretions of the mind visible. At first my "mental secretions" took the predictable form of an analysis of the "decline of the West" as well as everything else. East and West, North and South are a continuum, I reminded myself. The Paleolithic continuity, the world of tribal peoples, the wilderness they lived in, and dead Owens Lake are not separate and distinct from Los Angeles and Las Vegas. By emptying myself when I fast, emptying myself in solitude, I might discover myself full— of history, wilderness, and society. And I can see my identity co-evolving with all of

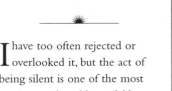

I have too often rejected or overlooked it, but the act of being silent is one of the most precious and readily available panaceas of which one can avail herself. Cold mornings spent in front of a warm fire reading a favorite book or just gazing at the dancing flames can magically reknit a broken spirit. Yoga, long evening walks, and other gentle exercises are effective aids in clearing and energizing the mind. The heart, I have found, is best repaired through prayer and intimate chats with God.
—Nimbilasha Cushing,
"Revival of One"

creation. I reminded myself as I watched the clouds collecting over the Sierra that we don't know the end of this story. The current state of events, however, had left little doubt in my mind about how pervasive suffering is in creation's continuum.

After these ruminations, I began to look around me at a rugged "unromantic" landscape—no flashy red rock twisted by the wind, no mushroom-shaped stones, no flower-filled meadows or lush forests, just scree, gray washes, and ragged mountains. This land would probably not induce visionary inflation in the fasters, I thought. Yet its beauty was subtle, with worn rock, bits of obsidian flakes from former inhabitants, a flash of pale pink in the cut or turn of a canyon. Yet most people would call this a wasteland.

When we first entered the area, I had to look hard to see where my friends might put themselves; there seemed to be nothing here. But on a second look, I could see the shadows of Earth where it turned upon itself. Hiding places to take refuge from sun, wind, and rain. I was satisfied with this secretive environment; no one would bother to come here except a few hungry fools.

As a Western woman, whatever I have learned about the nature of the self, both the local and the extended self, has been by going inward and down into the fruitful darkness, the darkness of culture, the darkness of psyche, the darkness of nature. The most important secrets seem always to hide in the shadows. "The secret of life," say the Utes, "is in the shadows and not in the open sun; to see anything at all, you must look deeply into the shadow of a living thing."

I have entered this shadow world mostly unwillingly. Having found the gold of compassion in the dark stone of suffering, having tasted the fruit of sanity in the tangled grove of the self, I also willingly entered the Valley of the Shadow through solitude, silence, stillness, meditation, and prayer. In those quiet places I discovered a mindstream whose depths were luminous.

The third morning in Owens Valley, Steven swore that something or someone had come to camp in the early hours. I walked around camp, checking the kitchen and vehicles, and all looked quite normal to me. Steven made coffee, and we settled into a good talk as we waited for Meredith to return from town.

A little after nine, she arrived. I could see from a distance that her face was tight with concern. Steven saw it as well, and he approached the car quietly. It was she who bore the news that my mother had died unexpectedly that morning.

The first thing that I could see was my mother's face, a face that had always turned away from her own suffering even as she faced the suffering of others. Her life had been one of service. As a tall and beautiful woman in her twenties, she had mastered the craft of making books for the blind. And I was to learn later that on the last day of her life, twelve hours before she died, she had delivered magazines to the sick in the very hospital in which she was to bleed to death.

My mother was dead. On hearing the news, I turned my back to my companions and awkwardly walked south of camp to stare at the dead open body of Owens Lake. As I took rough southward steps, I absently wondered why it was still called a lake. Stopping, confused and raw, I felt as though there were no skin between me and the wind. That morning, the sky had turned over and called my mother's name. Now she was gone. I then looked north at the rugged wall of mountains where my friends were fasting. The stones and mountains, the clouds and sun all looked empty. The sky looked empty. I looked at my right hand; it too was empty, and it also was something that belonged to my mother. It was then I remembered these words:

> Here on this mountain I am not alone.
> For all the lives I used to be are with me.
> All the lives tell me now I have come home.

I went from her funeral to another California desert. As I entered Joshua Tree National Monument at midnight, lightning turned the landscape bone white. I went out into this second desert, intending to be alone and to fast to mark grief. As I wandered around among the rocks and crevasses for hours looking for a protected place, I realized that the protection I sought was her. The womb that had given birth to me was gone. That protection was gone, and my back was now naked. The body I had been written from was dead, and I was without authority. It was too much for me to handle so soon after her death; I returned to base camp and the fire, the hearth, another place where mother-comfort is found. There I watched her life in the fire.

That first night, I was afraid and so slept next to the fire as coyotes walked boldly through camp. After the moon set, I had the following dream: My mother is on an operating table. A friend, a surgeon in the dream, has his scalpel on her belly. I turn away in horror, but he reaches across her body to comfort me as he cuts into her. From the pool of blood in her abdomen rises a small human figure with its eyes wide and awake.

Coming out of a dream with a start, looking at the night sky and tasting the desert in my mouth, I decided to continue the journey of mourning for my mother. I also discovered I was grieving for Earth. At that moment the two, the Earth and my mother, were one body.

In the traditional belief systems of native people, the terrestrial call is the voice of God, or of gods, the creative power that lives on Earth, inside Earth, in turtle, stone, and tree. Knowledge comes from, and is shaped by, observations and knowledge of the natural world and natural cycles.

In fact, the word *God* in the dictionary definition means to call, to invoke. Like creation, it is an act of language, as if the creator and the creation are one, the primal pull of land is what summons.

—Linda Hogan*, Dwellings: A Spiritual History of the Living World*

A short while later, I traveled to Nepal. I walked for a month in the mountains and internally carried my mother's body up and down the rugged trail. Grieving along the rivers and in the mountains, I for a time severed myself from family, friends, community, culture, and place of the familiar. I needed strange land and atmosphere in order to come to know her as an ancestor. Desert and mountains are old landscapes of space. It was in these places that her ancestral body was made, and it was to her that I offered prayer.

One evening along the trail, an old man with bright eyes and a large string of prayer beads passed through our camp. He was a *dami*, a local shaman who had come to a nearby village to heal a family. In the last light of a long, cold dusk, I asked him if I might attend the ceremony. Late that night, I and a few friends squeezed into a crowded, smoky Gurung house and watched the *dami* evoke gods of the region with drum and chant, dance their dances, handle fire, and suck out illness.

At three in the morning, I had a startling vision: my mother is wrapped up in black cobwebs; she is completely terrified and does not know what has happened or where she is. I was frozen with shock and could not move internally or externally. After a few minutes, she disappeared, and I realized with a sense of horrible regret that I had missed the opportunity of reaching through the veil that separated the living and the dead to help her. I was inconsolable.

Returning to Kathmandu, I told friends about this vision, and in compassion they arranged a Shitro ceremony in the humble Sherpa Buddhist monastery in Boudhanath. Fifteen monks and lamas with their long horns, cymbals, and offerings called my mother's "soul" back into an effigy, that she might be purified from the patterns that had caused her suffering and death. I repeatedly put my body down on the dark buttery floor as I prostrated in the *gompa*'s shrine room, and the lamas worked their prayers and offerings in her behalf. At the end of the day, her effigy was cremated. That night I boarded a plane to California.

Two days later, in Ojai, the community gathered in the evening as a Zen priest conducted the final ceremony for my mother on the forty-ninth day of her journey through the Bardo, the intermediate state between death and rebirth. In that last night of the Bardo transit when we spoke to her across the threshold, an uncommon wind extinguished the candles on the altar, and our last words to her were punctuated with falling stars.

The journey in the Bardo of Death, according to Buddhism, is forty-nine days. During those days, I had traveled ceaselessly. My sorrow was not only for the loss of my biological mother, but also for the world. I saw the material wealth of America and its relative spiritual impoverishment. In the mountains of Nepal, I witnessed great joy in the midst of material simplicity. Meditation, fasting, living close to the Earth, walking day after day in the mountains as I worked out this sorrow, my mother's secret body was made. It was stitched together in the steps of the journey, a journey that was a rite of passage for both her and her daughter.

Joan Halifax is a cultural ecologist and Buddhist teacher who has long been at the forefront of cultural and spiritual exploration. She is the author of Shaman: The Wounded Healer; *coauthor of* The Human Encounter with Death and Faces of Compassion: Classic Bodhisattva Archetypes and Their Modern Expression; *and editor of the anthology,* Shamanic Voices. *This story was excerpted from her book,* The Fruitful Darkness: Reconnecting with the Body of the Earth.

LAURA HARGER

✦ ✦ ✦

The Desert

Traveling in Niger, a woman journeys
into the depths of her loss.

AT NIGHT I SLEEP WITH A DAMP KERCHIEF DRAPED ACROSS MY face. Even the darkness is hot here: ninety, a hundred degrees, and there is not a trace of water in the air. I wake in the middle of the night with my eyes swollen with trapped salts. I sneeze dusty blood into my palms. I lie awake on the sand for hours, staring out at the sky while Bill sleeps. I search for stars that I know and can name, but the constellations are unfamiliar and too close. On my back on the sand in the Sahara, I sense for the first time that I am lying on the belly of the planet and looking into space. There is nothing between me and the galaxies here. The desert air is as still and quiet as the air inside a room closed for years.

We are traveling 300 miles north from Niamey, on the only highway in Niger, watching the scrubby Sahel bleed away into blank sand. We sleep at night by the road or in the compounds of Lutheran missionaries and Peace Corps volunteers. Bill has no vehicle, so we have hitched rides on water trucks and *vingt-et-un* buses—stripped-down, blunt-nosed VWs that do not depart until twenty-one riders have boarded. This may require several days, but no one really cares. In the desert, people wait, they sit, they sleep. Violent motion, high speeds, and action are dangerous here; they

195

call attention to oneself. At any moment, the ponderous glance of the desert, I think, may swing to you and absorb you into itself.

In my weeks here I have been lulled into a timeless frame of mind, and the difference between five o'clock and nine o'clock, between Tuesday and Saturday, is blurring. At Bill's house in Niamey, I sat by the pool all day, drinking beer and watching my feet trace patterns under the blue surface of the water. Mamadou, his houseman, brought me late lunches and teas. I became the colonial lady, drifting and mindless, very quickly.

Bill is different. He retains a sense of purpose. He paces and swears under his breath in English when the buses are late, when the driver stops to pray or brew tea, or swerves off the highway and drives 50 miles over the packed sand to visit a relative. In Niamey, Bill darts around the markets and the fields like a busy animal, charming and irritating the merchants and farmers. They take him for a Frenchman at first and are cold—the French colonists idly slaughtered Nigeriens in a failed attempt to build a railway across the Sahara, and their descendants still clog the capital, the Frenchwomen blithely ignoring Muslim etiquette and appearing in the markets in belly-skimming Spandex, tiny shorts, high heels. Bill explains he is American and is usually forgiven.

He is an economist with USAID and spends his days in the

> Soon there was nothing but the empty road ahead. The station platform was deserted. I was unsure where I would sleep that night. I was almost sure that probably I would never return again to where I had just been. In everyday emptiness and ordinary waiting, you are suddenly back simply with yourself, which feels to be nothing more than a pool; some empty space that fills and empties, is calm or angry, dark or light, grasping and clawing, or quiet, almost stable and content.
>
> —Jennifer Lash, *On Pilgrimage: A Time to Seek*

fields around Niamey, weighing bundles of millet, discussing drainage and erosion with farmers. Sun creases have appeared around his eyes. Although he has been here only two months, he looks like a farmer himself; most traces of the New Jersey Italian kid have vanished in the sun.

He is twenty-eight. I am twenty-one, and no longer sure if I recognize the person who has been my lover for the past two years. He sent a ticket to me in Washington a month ago, and I took it. I am out of school, unemployed, and running at top speed away from my own life. On the map, Niger is a beige blank in the middle of Africa. Nobody at home seems to know where Niger is. That is why I have come here.

We are headed for the Aïr Mountains, a small range that walls the western edge of the Sahara proper. A canyon, called the Tamgak, runs through the center of the range. It is an easy walk, 50 miles, up the canyon to its egress point in the Ténéré, the dead center of the desert, where massive dunes wander slow as animals from east to west to south. Almost no one lives or travels in the Ténéré but Tuareg nomads.

To get to the Aïr, we pass through Arlit, a uranium-mining town at the far northern end of the highway. The town is crouched on a flat pan of sand and surrounded by looping scrawls of tracks, dug by the enormous, cleated wheels of French mining equipment. Huge machinery, delicate and strange as insects, perches on the sand. Armed soldiers check passports at the guard-houses outside town. The bottom has recently fallen out of the uranium market, the miners are angry, and they are picking fights with the local government.

The town itself is crowded and dusty, and as we walk through its streets I am reminded of an old Western just before the sun-down shoot-out. Hard liquor and drugs can be found in this town, filtering down from Algeria, and drunken Germans fill the streets, hawking stolen cars that they have driven around the Mediterranean to sell. We drink beer and eat beignets fried with pounded red pepper on the street, and spend an uncomfortable night in a mud-walled auberge. There is a slaughterhouse next door, and its reek and wails keep us awake past midnight. A strike has knocked the electricity out.

We wake to find stones and bottles filled with gasoline bouncing into the auberge's courtyard. There are mobs of miners in the streets, hurling things at whatever is nearby. We bribe the driver of a date truck to take us out of town, toward the blue Aïr looming in the distance far beyond Arlit. On the way out of town someone, unaccountably, throws a stuffed Mickey Mouse doll at the truck. It bounces off the windshield and skates over the hood, grinning at us. In a small village at the base of the Tamgak, we hire two camels and a French-speaking Tuareg guide, Bala. We pay the local butcher to slaughter a goat for us, and sling the skinned carcass up in a burlap bag on the side of a camel, next to my bright blue pack. We pour water into goatskins and hang them from the saddles of the camels. Walking behind the camels into the mountains, I look at the collection of outlandish objects and smile, because they are unfamiliar and exotic, because I cannot recognize myself in my surroundings anymore.

The Tamgak itself is a rough channel, choked with boulders, about a quarter-mile across. White goats, small-hoofed and wary, circulate in little troops among the stones. Steep cliffs of broken sandstone wall us in on either side. Nothing grows on these mountains; their faces are blasted all day long by the sun. In the rainy season, which lasts one week here, the canyon becomes a wash, Bala explains, and the Tuareg herders living in the canyon must pick up their grass-walled homes and move. A few palm trees grow in the center of the canyon, drawing up what residual moisture they can. The camels stop to chew at scrub, calmly gnawing their way through three-inch thorns.

Bala is a tall boy of about sixteen. He is beautiful, as most of the Tuareg are, thin and long-limbed, haughty-eyed. He speaks French because he has spent time in Niamey, he tells us. He wears a heavy turban of dark blue cotton, which has bled its indigo onto his cheekbones and forehead, a white *jellaba*, and a pair of American running shoes, which he removes frequently to worry at an infected toe. Near the mouth of the canyon, he stops us and points to a nearby rock face. I take off my sunglasses and squint, the glare defeating me for several minutes. Then thin lines appear on the cliff, in the shapes of animals. There are monkeys, giraffes, slender-limbed antelope.

"Who drew these?" Bill asks.

Bala shakes his head. "Those animals used to live here, many years back," he answers. "Now they're all gone. We find bones here and there still." He hits a camel on its rump and moves on ahead of us, up the canyon. Bill shrugs and follows him.

I stand for a moment and watch the drawings shimmer on the rock face, changing shape slightly as the superheated air ripples over them. I imagine the animals dropping, one by one, into the advancing sand as their world heated and dried. The water and the grasses disappeared, the rivers dove below the ground and became inaccessible aquifers, the rain clouds separated and the hot blue sky glared out between them.

Halfway up the canyon, we stop at a cluster of small huts. Bala tells us that his family lives here, sisters, a cousin, his grandparents. A young woman in a black lace overblouse and a printed skirt wrapped over a hugely pregnant belly comes out to greet us. Her fine-boned face is smeared with red henna. She and Bala clasp hands and go through a ten-minute ritual greeting in Tamachek—how did you sleep, how is the family, and yourself, and the animals—until each detail of their lives has been queried and answered. It appears that she is his sister; certainly beauty runs in the family.

We sit down to make tea. The tea is brewed in small pots, set in the coals of a fire. The woman leans over her belly and strains water back and forth between two pots crammed with green tea leaves and sugar cubes, until the tea pours like honey. We drink it in a series of three shots from small glasses, presented on a tea tray that is printed, in florid color, with the face of Ali Saïbou, Niger's military ruler at the time. The cells in my body expand, absorbing the liquid hungrily, and a caffeine rush as strong as amphetamine envelops me.

I look around me, and the yellow sand and emerald palms waver in my wired vision. In the distant village, a muezzin wails rising and falling scales. The world is suddenly beautiful. The young woman rouses herself and asks Bala a question in Tamachek.

"She wants to know if we have any medicines," Bala says to Bill.

"Medicines for what?" he asks.

"For pain," Bala answers. "She's in labor."

Bill and I look blankly at each other. He rummages through the pack strapped to the lead camel and pulls out our medicine bag. We dump it on the sand: aspirin, antimalaria pills, antibiotic, and a package of Flintstone Band-Aids. The woman looks at this, waiting politely.

"Have you got anything?" Bill asks me. I shake my head, and then remember something. I reach back into the pack and find a blue plastic bottle. I shake it and a few pills rattle.

"Here," I say, handing it to Bala.

"What is that?" Bill asks in English.

"Midol."

He laughs.

"It's better than nothing," I retort. The woman swallows a handful of the pills with her tea, patting her stomach absently, then vanishes into one of the houses. I can hear her breathing, short bursts that sound like overworked machinery; freed of social niceties, she is apparently now allowing herself to feel the contractions. I sit down against the house, leaning my back against a pole and looking at the mountaintops burning under the white noon sun.

I know little about labor, or its pains. A month ago, I had climbed down off an operating table, my lower stomach aching, taken two Valiums, and went to wait my evening shift at a cafe in northwest Washington. In between taking orders, I went into the kitchen and stole sips of overpriced wines, until the tranquilizers and the alcohol had mixed and I no longer felt any pain at all. Lightness and emptiness moved in to replace it, as if what had been removed from me was not merely a six-week fetus, but my organs and my bones. I floated from table to table. I smiled, and recommended the trout.

By the third day, the goatskins hang shriveled on the camels' backs. Half an inch of warm, iodine-flavored water sloshes in the bottom of my canteen. We need to find a well. Bala says that there is a *guelta*, a rainwater basin, two miles up a side canyon. I look up the side canyon, sheltering my eyes with my hand—it rises at a thirty-degree gradient of broken, burning rock.

"Come on," Bill says, taking my hand and pulling me up the canyon. He has always been stronger than I am, and the lack of water and the heat have not affected him at all. On he goes, leaping from rock to rock, his strong,

> "Cleaning things up" is a habit you learn early, before you have a chance to ponder the extent to which it will constrain your life. It's all well and good to clean things, but when we turn to tidying up the past, whitewashing the events and people who have profoundly shaped us—all of them—we've laid our hands roughly on something priceless: the knowledge that we can walk through pleasure or pain, joy or sadness, with equal grace or clumsiness, as the case may be, that what counts is that we get through somehow.
> —Hannah Nyala, *Point Last Seen: A Woman Tracker's Story*

bicycle-racer's legs flashing in the sun. After half a mile, visions of ice-choked pitchers of water, of lemon halves glistening with frost, have begun to float before my eyes. I can hear, quite audibly, the sound of ice cubes stirred with a chilled glass straw, held in a woman's delicate hand. There are places in the world where cold water gushes out of walls at the touch of a hand. This is remarkable, it is fantastic; I will never cease being grateful for it again.

I place my boots on rock after rock, one after the other, dust swirling around my feet. The canyon walls lean inward in this side canyon, exhaling heat softly at each other. I am too hot to sweat.

Bill is a dot bobbing far above me, a long distance off. He cups his hands to his mouth—"Come on, Harger! I'll drink it all!" he shouts down.

At last, he has vanished entirely. The canyon narrows and ends a few hundred yards ahead. Perhaps there is no well here, perhaps Bala was mistaken. I plod on. If I die, my body will keep moving without me. I round a corner and stop. At the juncture of the canyon walls, the earth has fallen away and a green pool has taken its place. Sunlight fractures on the rock faces and sifts into the water, which returns the light to the air, a softer green. In this column of light a lavender roller is tumbling, testing its wings against the suddenly cooled air.

Bill has climbed onto the far canyon wall, above the pool, his feet set on a shallow ledge. He takes off his t-shirt and throws his boots onshore. As he braces to dive, I sit on a rock and watch the lines of his body, a body I have slept with for two years, a body which in this quiet cathedral light, a thousand miles from anything I know, seems entirely unfamiliar to me. I look at the muscles of his thighs, the blond hair on his outstretched arms, the ragged hiking shorts. I am trying to memorize him, but I don't know why. He dives.

He surfaces with a whoop, wiping the water out of his face. "What are you waiting for?" he calls to me. "It's amazing in here!"

I take off my blouse and shorts and boots and edge out onto the ledge. The sandstone whispers across my spine and my bare toes clutch the rock. I am high up, fifteen or twenty feet above the *guelta*. "Is it deep enough?" I call.

"Plenty deep," Bill calls back. "It must go all the way down to the base of the mountain!" The idea does not comfort me. Instead, it makes me uneasy, the idea of this pale green water descending somewhere to the roots of the desert. I lean out over the water, uncertainly. Bill beckons me in.

I pull out of the dive at the last moment, something catching me short, something about the way the water looks, and I strike the surface on my side. I sink. There is something soft surrounding me, long threads touch my bare legs and back and arms, I am in something. It's algae, feet and feet of mud-thick growth lying in a green bed just below the clear surface of the water. I clamber frantically for air.

I haul myself onto a rock near shore and huddle, scraping the green muck off my legs and arms. I can't seem to get control of my breathing. "Hey, Harger, it's just pond scum," Bill says, confused, from the center of the pool. "It won't hurt you. There's nothing wrong."

I look at him, floating calmly on his back in the middle of the algae. He seems a long distance away. I hold my knees to my chest, feeling disoriented and frightened, and start to cry.

That night we spread out a sleeping bag on a flat rock. Bala is a ways off; I can see the tip of his cigarette flare and fade in the darkness. Bill rolls over to me. He kisses my jaw, the side of my neck, my ear. "Is it safe?" he asks. I nod. I have walled myself off with hormones, plastic, and foam. I am thoroughly barricaded. As we begin, I pass my hand over the rock, searching for the damp kerchief. It touches my palm, a comforting cool weight, and I drape the wet cloth over my face.

On the fourth day, we reach the end of the Tamgak. The canyon floor rises steeply for a hundred yards, then falls off in a sheer cliff. The camels reach the end before we do and shuffle nervously. They don't like what they see. Bala calms them while Bill and I edge out onto the lip of the canyon. The Sahara rolls out before us, endless and gold, clamped under its lid of burning sky. We are a hundred feet above the sand, but distant dunes bulk in the distance, pushing mindlessly south.

I sit down on a boulder, rubbing my sunburned knees. The sand looks hungry to me. It will eat the remainder of the Sahel, it will eat Lake Chad and the Niger River, it will eat West Africa, chasing animals and humans and grass to the borders of the oceans. If it could, it would eat the world. I experience the same sensation here, on the lip of the Ténéré, as I did sleeping by the highway at night—I am staring into a universe that knows nothing about me. This eternity of burning sand, its hunger and its

death, are the natural and the normal. What is ephemeral and fool-
ish is me, is us, the sloshing waterbags called organic life, with our
restaurants and our love affairs and little jobs and running water.

"Look down there," Bill says. "Is that a telephone pole?"

I squint. About a quarter mile distant a slender metal pole is
planted in the sand, casting a long shadow. Bill calls Bala over. Bala
smiles and says it is not a telephone pole. "Go see," Bala says.
"You'll be surprised."

We scramble down the face of the cliff, scalding our hands on
the rocks. The sand, when we reach it, is surprisingly solid beneath
our feet. I run down the surface of a dune toward the pole, part of
me hoping that it is a telephone pole, or part of a building, or
something recognizable and familiar.

I reach it first. It is a steel column, six inches around and twenty
feet high. A plaque is set on its side. In misspelled French, it reads:
*The Ténéré's last acacia stood in this place. It was struck by a Libyan
truck and destroyed in 1973.* The column is studded with gnarled
protrusions of metal here and there, perhaps meant to suggest
branches. It glints harshly in the desert light, and I cannot imagine
a tree standing in its place. The burning metal oddity seems entirely at home here.

On the way back down the canyon, I stop eating. The taste of
the goat, now withered to jerky in its dusty burlap bag, repulses
me. I live on sugar biscuits and shots of Tuareg tea. During the
weeks I was pregnant, I vomited constantly, four or five times a day,
unable to keep down even water, crouching by the sink in the cafe,
by the sink in my apartment, darting up from restaurant tables or
barstools when I was with friends and running to bathrooms. I
dropped fifteen pounds; people complimented me, taking it as the
result of constructive labor with weights and Stairmasters. I had
gained the weight back in Niamey, during those long solitary
lunches by Bill's pool, which had begun to feel like healing. I ate
French chocolate, elaborate salads full of fruit and cheese, drank
bottle after bottle of thin, cold Nigerien beer.

Now the flesh is melting off me again. My stomach is a concave valley between the peaks of my hipbones. At night, when Bill and I make increasingly perfunctory love, I imagine I can hear our skeletons grating and sliding against each other. During the days, I walk down the canyon behind him, jumped-up and humming with caffeine and sugar, the canyon a welter of heat and electrified color around me. I am running on pure energy. I seem to have exited my own skin.

On the ninth day, we reach the cluster of huts where Bala's family lives. Bala takes us to his own hut and I collapse on a blanket spread on the sand floor. A little girl, with a shaven and perfectly shaped skull, gold hoops in her ears, brings us a metal pail of water. I put my mouth into it and drink, and Bill follows me. We leave rings of dust rippling on the surface of the cold water. The little girl whispers something to Bala. She will not look at me.

"She says that my sister would like you to see her baby," Bala says to me.

I'd forgotten about the baby. "Did the pills help?" I ask him.

He shrugs; it's clear that the topic makes him uncomfortable. "My sister would like you to take a picture of the baby," he continues. "It's a girl."

I look over at Bill. "I can't come with you," he answers. He is leaning back on the blanket, eyes closed. "No men allowed."

I take the camera and go back out into the burning sunlight, following the little girl. She is barefoot and the soles of her feet have been decorated with black lines of henna. Blinded by the sun, I follow the tiny black feet through the dust to another house.

Inside, a crowd of women surround me. Without men nearby they are bold, and they look at me frankly, tugging on my earrings and ruffling my short hair. There are five women, young and old, in black and red lace blouses. Silver gris-gris charms, gracefully carved squares meant to keep away scorpions, dangle from their necks, and their hair is caught up under twisted lengths of blue and black cloth. Once again, I am overwhelmed by their beauty; all of them are long-necked, dark-eyed, with stripes of red henna on the tops of their cheekbones. I am aware of the dirt on my bare legs, of my shirt sticking to my spine.

They ask me questions, in Tamachek. I shake my head, and they glance at each other, vexed. One cradles an arm to her hip and then looks at me inquiringly. I shake my head, no. "No children," I say. The woman looks at me sympathetically, and then raises her hand proudly, spread in the air. She has five. I look at her; she's about my age. The woman points out the door, in the direction of Bala's hut, and clasps her hands together, looking at me. I puzzle for a moment, and then realize that she is asking if Bill is married to me. "No," I say, shaking my head. "*Un ami*," I say, "he's only a friend."

The women look at me more closely then, and I see myself through their eyes: dirty, thin, with cropped hair and short pants, no children and no husband, wandering loose around the world, an object of pity. I hoist the camera defensively, and the women part ranks then. Behind them Bala's sister sits cross-legged on a raised bed covered with blankets. The infant, wrapped in a white cloth, sleeps in her arms. Its complexion is a creamy beige, with the peculiar, still-coalescing look of infant skin, and it has an impressive mop of silky black hair. The woman smiles and hands me the child.

I sit down before the bed, holding the child awkwardly. "She's beautiful," I say, and she is. The baby opens her mouth searchingly for a moment, then falls back asleep. The mother smiles proudly. I trace the round of the baby's cheek with my finger, smiling and cooing, which I hope translates. Her skin is hot and dry. Her mother leans over then, with a serious look on her face, and unwinds the cloth from the lower half of the infant's body.

The baby is perfectly formed, with little pink feet and fat legs. But above the cleft of her tiny infant vagina, a bloody bulge emerges from her abdomen. The umbilicus has been improperly tied, allowing a loop of intestine to slip through the abdominal muscles just below the skin. I have seen these lumps, the size of teacups, on children in Niamey before. If they do not catch them on anything, if the skin is not broken, the child is safe. But this baby's skin has been broken somehow, and the lump is now infected. I touch her sleeping face again, and wonder if she has peritonitis; she is far hotter than a baby ever should be. I wonder how long she has to live.

I look back up at the woman's grave face. She knows what's going on. She asks me a question in Tamachek and I shake my head, then indicate that she should keep the cloth tightly wrapped around the baby's belly, to keep the intestine from emerging further. There is no time to get the baby to Arlit, to a doctor, as I am sure the woman knows; trucks run a few times a week, if that. And there is nothing in my bag to help her, no toy medicines or placebos that will make a difference this time.

The woman wraps the baby back up again and points to my camera questioningly. She arranges the baby in her arms as I lift the camera to my eye. I look at her through the lens and she smiles at me, then glances back down at her sleeping daughter. I press the shutter. I do not cry until I am outside the house, following the little girl's flashing feet through the deadly white heat and the dust, back to my own, separate life.

Laura Harger grew up on the East Coast, acquired her undergraduate degree at the University of Michigan, then received an MFA from the Iowa Writers' Workshop. She now travels the world vicariously as a senior editor at the University of California Press and is the author of the Lonely Planet guide, Washington, D.C. Laura lives in Berkeley, California, with her husband Matt.

CAROL STIGGER

✦ ✦ ✦

Home for the Dying

A death hostel in Jamaica
seemed an unlikely setting
for a moment of grace.

WEARILY, I RANG THE DOORBELL BENEATH THE LITTLE SIGN, "Missionaries of Charity, Home for the Dying." This was my last stop. Crescents of dirt beneath my fingernails attested to my Midwest paradigm of expecting Third World restrooms to provide soap.

A nun, barefoot and wearing the plain, cotton sari of Mother Teresa's order opened the wooden door and invited me inside. The home is a two-story quadrangle set in a slum and built around an atrium of flourishing plants. In this anteroom to eternity, the nun's steps were silent, her pace serene. Her hands, in repose beside her white, unbleached skirt, were coated with flour.

The men's ward was walled in stone, floored in rough concrete. Metal cots were aligned in military order, each with a thin pillow, clean sheets and a chamber pot beneath. Aged men populated the room: some prone and barely breathing, others visiting or shuffling along, talking quietly without haste or anxiety. Two men played cards in a puddle of light from the high, unpaned window. The queen of hearts looked as if she had been waiting through the rainy season for her creased and faded king. In the dim room, the nun's sari reflected the ambient light as she patted a gnarled hand then moved along to advise a card player to draw from the deck. I realized I had been subtly sniffing for the soap I needed to wash my hands and for the institutional olfactory competition between urine and Lysol. But all I smelled was bread baking.

"We host twenty-two men and twenty-six women," she explained. "They are our family." Her calm, quiet voice carried from wall to wall. Heads nodded. I heard a sigh, a labored breath, the creak of metal springs, but not the swish of her sari as she led me down the stone corridor to the woman's hall.

She introduced me to another nun and excused herself to return to her kitchen duties. The women's room was the same size as the men's, furnished with the same cots, and emanated a similar peace, but the women, asleep or sitting alone, were silent. I saw expressions of ease and expectation. Had the sisters promised them a special treat? Perhaps the bread. I trailed behind the sister, wondering at the light that here, too, seemed to hitchhike on a sari. She stopped beside a cot and said that this was a special day. Lily, who had been waiting for a long time for God to take her home, was going home today.

Lily seemed unconscious, but I detected a slight motion

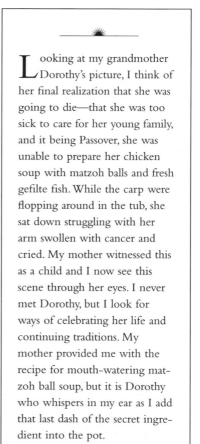

Looking at my grandmother Dorothy's picture, I think of her final realization that she was going to die—that she was too sick to care for her young family, and it being Passover, she was unable to prepare her chicken soup with matzoh balls and fresh gefilte fish. While the carp were flopping around in the tub, she sat down struggling with her arm swollen with cancer and cried. My mother witnessed this as a child and I now see this scene through her eyes. I never met Dorothy, but I look for ways of celebrating her life and continuing traditions. My mother provided me with the recipe for mouth-watering matzoh ball soup, but it is Dorothy who whispers in my ear as I add that last dash of the secret ingredient into the pot.

—Lisa Bach, "The Consuming Pilgrimage"

of her lips and heard a faint popping, like bubbles from a small fish. Lily's brown skin was yellowed, taunt over facial bones and hanging loosely from skeletal arms. Her coverlet was not the white sheet of the other cots, but a silk shawl embroidered with scarlet hummingbirds, purple and yellow flowers.

The nun motioned for me to sit beside Lily, right on the bed. She awakened the dying woman with a soft, but matter-of-fact "Lily." Lily opened her eyes and appeared to see me. I gently squeezed her hand.

"Lily," the nun continued, "your daughter has come to kiss you goodbye."

The hand in mine moved slowly, as if we had time to invent a life together. I kissed her forehead and whispered, "Goodbye, Mama, goodbye." Her eyes closed, her hand grew limp. Her breath no longer rippled the silence. Still holding her clean, brown hand with my grimy white one, I remembered my mother who died so suddenly there was no goodbye. I remembered my years of distress and anger at the sudden wrench, not bridged with a kiss. I cried there, the scarlet, purple, and yellow of the shawl becoming a misty palette. I cried long enough for all the anger to flow out of me and for the emotion to return as a simple love that does not need to understand.

I felt a hand on my shoulder. The nun had returned. She led me to a basin of cool water, provided a sliver of soap and a clean, worn towel. I washed my hands, bathed my streaked face.

Outside, in the brutal heat and clinging stench of Kingston, I suddenly remembered something that stopped me in my tracks. My mother's name was Katherine: to her husband, children, and friends, she was Katherine. But on her birth and death certificates, her first name is recorded as "Lily." She disliked the name Lily, never used it except to enter life and to leave it.

Carol Stigger is a writer specializing in poverty and social justice issues in developing countries. Her work has been published in numerous magazines and newspapers, both domestic and international. Carol lives in Forest Park, Illinois.

LUCY REES

* * *

Maenid Furies

A journey of loss—
and hope found again.

THESE ARE THE BARE BONES OF IT. QUITE A SKELETON. I TRY TO refuse to give it closet space, but equally it refuses to die entirely, leaping out from a look, a glance, a phrase.

It was not until my fourth miscarriage that I really began to doubt the doctors who shoved their hands up me, patted my knee, and said there was nothing wrong, keep trying, next please. I stopped trying to have any, but they kept coming anyway. Two or three later, advances in technology enabled a determined surgeon to discover that I had a partially divided uterus. By that time I was divorced.

You can sit down and talk to yourself until you accept the inevitability of childlessness with cool rationality; but persuading a fertile body to relinquish its inner drive is another matter. Mine was devious, refusing to tolerate reliable methods of prevention and making me inept with others. It was not difficult to clock up a couple more losses, nor to deal with them: early ones are not bad, especially when you have trained yourself not to hope.

Years later I met a man...Oh, I was wrong, I was culpable, but learning to deal with culpability without the attendant guilt that makes you squirm, feel ashamed, run away, make excuses and misrepresentations, that was the hardest. It was only when we were heavily involved that he revealed that by "I've left my wife," he had meant, "emotionally, not physically, you understand." I should have got out then, but I did not. It was not as if anything were being destroyed: his marriage had become total war, without the Geneva Convention. But I muddled that with a disregard for truth. You cannot build a healthy structure on shifting sands; but I came in for ceaseless vindictive bombardment, too, and in steeling myself to rise above that, I also disregarded the subtler but more destructive flaw.

To me, on the other hand, he behaved well after he left her, until, a year later, I became pregnant again. He left me while camping on a hillside in Spain, shouting, "How do I know it's mine?" I moved on fast, lest he find me.

I knew I would lose it, of course. I worked part time on an avocado farm, living in a tent almost wholly on oranges and avocados, licked my wounds, and waited for the inevitable. I was quite calm. It was a time of great peace and beauty, the hillsides sweet with lavender and rosemary. I shared bread and garlic with two old men, learning the Andalusian dialect, stroking the inside of the avocado canopies to find the heavy, swollen fruit.

Time passed, and it did not happen. The later a miscarriage, the more serious. I did not want to end up in a Spanish hospital, but I could not afford the airfare home. When I said I would hitch to Madrid for the bus, they turned the hens out of a wonderful old jalopy, a twenty-five-year-old Deux Chevaux, and spent two days dragging it up and down with the tractor until with triumphant shouts of "*¡Arriba!*" it purred into action.

"I can't accept a car," I said.

"It's not a car, it's a henhouse," they said. "It won't go far. When it dies, just bury it."

Oh, *la belle* Titine! Her name was painted on the steering column amid a shower of hearts. There were no seats: the driver's seat was an avocado crate. The windshield wipers were manual, worked by a knob you turned furiously until your arm ached. The headlight dip, too, was manual: you turned another knob, which turned two rods going sideways, which turned two rods running forward, whereupon the headlights, slowly, gravely, bowed their heads until you winched them up again. The hand brake worked, but was so loose you had to jam it fast with a sardine can. She jumped out of first unless you forced the gear lever in place. The roof was a torn, faded American flag. But she went *anywhere*, all day on a bottleful of cheap petrol, even if it took an octopus to drive her.

We went more or less straight across Spain, Arkansas-style, without benefit of roads, for I suspected that the flimsy scrap of paper they dug out did not constitute legality. We took mule tracks, cart tracks, sides of fields or hills in our stride, which was a brisk walking pace. Once I camped in an enormous olive grove that covered several hillsides. I had just boiled my tea in the dark when headlights came over the hill. Hastily I doused the fire and hid behind a tree away from the car, which was hidden, too. The headlight drew nearer. Torches. Voices. They found the car, and called.

"Why doesn't he come out?" they wondered, starting to swear. They discussed this curious behavior. One of them had an inspiration. "Could he perhaps be a woman?"

"A woman! She would be afraid."

"Don't fear, señora," they called. "We are honest men, doing our job."

At that, I had to come out. They invited me to spend the night with them. I said thank you, but no, thank you. They were, they said, the guardians of this land. "And we will guard you, too. No one in the bar will know you were here, until tomorrow when you are gone. It is not safe for a woman alone."

"That's what I was afraid of," I said.

"Ah, but we are honest men. The others, now..."

They woke me in the morning. They had already made a fire, and coffee. There was a spotless white napkin laid on the ground, with bread, cheese, and chorizo.

In a week we were in the Pyrenees with the eagles and the skiers. Driving through farmyards we were greeted by dogs like fleecy white bears that poked their heads through the rents in the flag to slobber on my hair. I cannot recall how I talked my way through French customs. It was the smallest frontier post, and Titine had French plates, but it took hours even so. I telephoned my insurance company in Porthmadog: maybe the sound of Welsh convinced them I was so *complètement folle* that they were better off without me.

A week later, only thirty miles from the ferry, the police caught up with me. I had followed pig tracks through the chestnut woods of Périgord, driven through miles of vineyards and sampled their wares, shivered in the dank plains of the battlefields. They could not believe I had got that far without being stopped, for I had no *carte verte* (green insurance card) on the window. I said I had seen no police, but they could not believe it of France. And my documents were *complètement, inutiles*, a farce. They added up my fines: over £250. I stuffed my £30 ferry fare in my bra and held out my 15 francs.

> Having soaked up three weeks' worth of kindness from strangers, in virtue of being relatively young, quite alone, foreign, female, and open to everything that came my way (except bulls), I felt my sadness lift like morning mist. I now longed for the kind of silence that comes with night. Not absolute quiet, mind you, which you'd have to be dead to hear anyway. Nothing so stark and naked as that. I wanted to hear sounds one stands still to listen to. Like tiny insect scratchings in long, dry grass, and breezes rustling things up a bit.
>
> —Janine Jones,
> "I'm Going to Galway"

"I have no more."

"But you must have."

"I haven't. Here, look in my wallet."

"Then we cannot let you pass. *Il faut*, you understand, you *must* pay now."

Impasse. "In that case," I said, "all I can do is give you the car. It must be worth something, it's antique." Reading his label, I filled his name in on the useless form, gave it to him, took my rucksack, and started to walk across Normandy in the dark. He ran after me.

"You cannot abandon your car there, it's forbidden."

"It's not my car, *m'sieur*, it's yours."

I had gone perhaps a mile before they drove after me, siren wailing.

"We will send Interpol to Penrhyndeudraeth, madame. Meanwhile, go, *with your car.*"

I drove to a café, opened a magazine, and found myself looking at a butter advertisement showing a cow on a field the exact shade of green of a *carte verte*. I cut a square the right size, inscribed it with my insurance information, drove past hordes of police onto the ferry and home to Wales. It snowed all the way. My wrists hurt, but I was still pregnant.

Two weeks later, four months gone, I started to bleed one night. I phoned the doctor and got the wrong one on duty. He told me not to worry. I said, "I'm old, I've had nine miscarriages, I'm half a mile from a road up a steep mountain, alone, and forty miles from the hospital."

"Take an aspirin and phone in the morning," he said, and rang off.

I was on my own, as if in a small open boat, in the middle of a stormy Atlantic night, and land had voted itself out of existence. Trembling, I waited for the big one. And waited.

What came instead was a call from the local schoolmistress, to whom I poured out my troubles, which no one else knew. That afternoon the district nurse arrived, panting from the steep climb, a woman whose sense and friendliness seemed, despite the spotlessness of her uniform, to bring the comfort and warmth of a farmyard: the tradition of hundreds of years of care that infuse those solid-walled barns thick with straw, where generations of animals have safely struggled into life. The sense of haven in her touch almost made me break down.

She sent me to the hospital.

They did a scan, pointed out arms and legs. It did not change anything. Yes, at present there was this growing inside me, yes, it was called "my baby," but there had been others, too, and I had studied my embryology, I knew what it would look like and what was going on. They did an amniocentesis, plunging a huge needle into my belly, because I was old and because I did not want a Down's syndrome child on my own. I would make the same decision again. As the needle went in I was overwhelmed by terrible panic, but told myself not to be silly. Of course it would look alarming: yes, it did slightly increase the chances of miscarriage, but they were almost certainties anyway. Afterward, they did another scan. He was thrashing about as if in a tantrum.

"No, no," I cried, "they've hurt him."

"It's all right," the nurse said, laughing. And I fought to remember that he was not much different from a stickleback whose pond has been stirred. Even amoebae retract from things as if they were mortally offended.

They gave me a room of my own, for which I was thankful. The heat of the ward, the terrible semiconsciousness that many pregnant women happily drift into, would have made me rude. I joined them for the wholly unsuitable meals they ate with relish: chips, pies, chips, jam roly-poly. A gypsy woman used to come in for secret smokes. "Gawd, Luce, you're the only one alive in 'ere." We sang an old music-hall song beloved of my grandfather, who danced to it while feeding the hens:

> Treat my daughter kindly, say you'll do no
> harm,
> And when I die, I'll leave to you my little
> stock and farm.
> My horse, my cow, my ox, my plough, my
> cottage and my barn—
> And all the little chickens in the garden.

Exhausted interns came in for a nap, curling up at my feet like dogs: "Wake me in ten minutes, don't forget."

I bled very slightly, on and off. It was, they said, a low placenta: nothing to worry about unless I suddenly went into labor, in which case things would have to happen fast. It could be any time, which was why I was there. But I could go for a walk every day. The fields were full of lambs and oxeye daisies.

Pregnancy, even when you refuse to allow yourself to imagine its consequences, profoundly alters the way you think. It is no longer a question of how you can understand the world, but of how the world relates to your child. Politics, ecology, the state of the world, all become personally involving in a way that they did not before. How are you to bring up a child in a world where people behave as they do? Greed, heartlessness, or any other of the

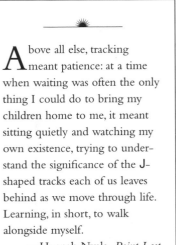

Above all else, tracking meant patience: at a time when waiting was often the only thing I could do to bring my children home to me, it meant sitting quietly and watching my own existence, trying to understand the significance of the J-shaped tracks each of us leaves behind as we move through life. Learning, in short, to walk alongside myself.

—Hannah Nyala, *Point Last Seen: A Woman Tracker's Story*

wrongs that we perpetuate, become not merely irritations or disappointments but threats to your child. How are you to teach him to love, and trust, and be open, when people do such terrible things? Even now when I look at the photos of those starving babies in war-torn countries, I look at the eyes of my child.

I tried to do things right for him, but I did not let myself dream. "When this is all over you'll find it was worth it," the nurses would say. "I've got to get there first," I'd reply, but honestly, not grimly. It crept on, day by day.

My friends, and even people who live in the same valley but whom I do not know so well, made the long trip to bring me their goodwill. The whole valley seemed to put its arms around me. The schoolmistress came and talked for hours about the children she had taught. She remembered every one. Brought up in a tiny rural Welsh community, she left home for the first time to do her teaching practice in Liverpool and Manchester. Shocked by the squalid rawness of poor urban life, she remembered, forty years on, the name of every child, which one's father was a drunkard or beat him, which one had no father or several, who brought what for lunch, and her efforts to comfort them. When she left she apologized for talking about herself, but it was the best of presents, knowing that others would cherish him, too.

I went for walks, and began to write a bread-and-butter book that my publisher, with great kindness as well as his usual astuteness, had suggested. And waited. They treated me not as a late miscarrier, but as a pregnant woman. They weighed me, and listened to his heart. The conceptual leap from the blood and pain of a miscarriage to a—what? chubby charmer? destructive toddler? pimply adolescent? was baffling.

I had to get to twenty-eight weeks before I could dare to hope, for at seven months, a baby, though very premature, is decently viable. But we all knew that at any moment my uterus might decide it had had enough. To our surprise, it did not. He was very lively inside me: I could feel every movement, feel him asleep, or stretching, or rollicking about. Simon, a friend from the valley who had moved nearby, brought me music. As time passed I realized how much he could hear, down there inside me. Rock 'n' roll had him rocking and rolling, the frantic disco beat made him twist about unpleasantly, but Mozart held him absolutely still, yet alert, as if he were concentrating.

At twenty-eight weeks they sent me to Liverpool, for they said he was bound to be early, and we would get the best care there. My daily strolls took me down streets of boarded-up shops, fish-and-chips shops, or barricaded shops selling liquor or ripped-off car radios. It seemed a city at war. But there were art galleries, Stubbs's Molly-Long-Legs with her wicked eye, and Augustus John's perceptive portraits of Liverpool aldermen, and squares of rose gardens to lie in, and a kestrel nesting in the roof of the warehouse opposite my room. And we were safe, he and I, safer as day succeeded day.

However, I seemed to be wetting myself slightly. It had happened all the time I was in the hospital, but it was getting worse.

They said it was quite common: stress incontinence, caused by pressure on the bladder. But I had excellent control over my bladder, I protested. They tested my dribbles, for I wondered if it was the waters leaking, but their little test-stick said not. But it bothered me.

Twenty-nine weeks. Thirty weeks. I began, very cautiously, to hope. I had made no plans; I had nothing for him. But he would have to stay in the premature unit for some time anyway. I knew I would manage when the time came. Meanwhile, I let myself enjoy him being there in my strange huge belly, listening with me, letting me learn him. The only thing missing was his father's seal of goodwill. I knew he had tried a reconciliation with his wife, and though I could not believe it would work, I had no wish to disturb him. But I did wish he would at least send us some small message, overcome the guilt that doubtless hounded him and compounded itself, just one small sign; but guilt is a demon master.

The miracle went on. Blessed, *bendigedig*. Ben. Miracle. Impossible reality, kicking away vigorously.

One night I crept from my bed, raided the supply cupboard for one of their little sticks, and tested myself. It was as I had thought. I was losing amniotic fluid.

I told them the next day, but I started labor too. Thirty-one weeks. I could barely believe it. I welcomed each great roll of my belly, a paean of triumph raging through me, stronger as the day went on. They would not let me drink: there had never been any question but that I would have a caesarean. The rolls got wilder, closer, a storm. Dawn was breaking when they said: "We'll take you down now."

I welcomed the needle like a friend, babbling nonsense until their laughter faded into darkness.

Being wheeled around. Doors. Curtains.
"Is he all right?"
"Just a minute, dear."
"Is he all right?" But she'd gone.
"Is he all right?"

"Wait a moment, dear."

"Is he all right?"

"She's to go there. Give me a hand."

But I knew.

He was absolutely calm, the poor man they chose, handsome as an angel, careful, and infinitely kind. He spoke slowly, trying to find out how conscious I was. I said: "I come around very fast, lots of practice. He's not all right, is he?"

"We can't be certain yet, but I'm afraid he may not be. Let me try to explain. Late in development, a baby's lungs gain elasticity by breathing amniotic fluid, what's called the waters, in and out. If there is not enough fluid, the tissues of the lung do not develop that elasticity, and the lungs cannot expand fully after birth. Do you understand?"

"Yes, I was losing my waters, so he couldn't breathe."

"Not well enough. We are—" *are*: He's alive. "—giving him oxygen. It may be that in the next few hours his lungs will respond better, and that he may—" *may, may, may* "—pull through."

"But you don't think so."

"It's too early to tell. How well do you feel?"

"Fine. I could get there."

"Not without a wheelchair."

He was tiny. Not wizened, just tiny. Beautiful. Strong, from all that activity. Round-limbed. He lay on a pad with tubes coming out of him, oxygen going in. I stared. His limbs moved in rhythms I knew from inside me. The heat was unbelievable. The morphine *froze* time, froze me. I watched, willing each movement of his chest. He was so strong but so fragile, so miraculous.

"You can hold him if you'd like," the nurse said. I wanted him to have the best chance. Perhaps I was wrong, but I felt it would disturb him, increase the demand on those flagging lungs. I shook my head, stroking him instead.

"We can take the tubes out, if they disturb you," she said.

I was furious. "No, it's not that—"

As soon as he heard my voice, he rolled his head over and

looked at me. And in that one look, wide-eyed, slightly puzzled, everything in me, my whole body, my soul, my will to live, *everything* went out to him. I had not thought...Of course, all those months, my voice...

Hours later, I was still stroking him, in that dazed incomprehension that morphine brings, when a man came in. It was Dave, a Liverpudlian friend of Simon's, a lighthouseman from Bardsey Island. Ynys Enlli, island of the saints, otherworld of cold air and sea, gull cries, clarity, peace...I realized I was falling, falling...a blinding headache...

"Dave, it seems awful to leave him, but I've got to go out for a while."

He wheeled me around in cool corridors, found cups of tea. It was a day and a half since I'd drunk anything, in that heat.

"It's a bad show, Dave."

His hand on my shoulder. Gentle man, gentleman. Confused and embarrassed maybe, speechless maybe; but rising to this impossible situation, a friend of a friend, in the depths of unknown womanhood they find themselves most incapable of dealing with capably. Good as gold.

Revived, we went back. He was even smaller, his grey eyes huger, but he moved less.

"What do they say?" I asked.

"He's putting up a good fight."

I stroked him. A few hours, the doctor had said. But many hours had gone, and he was still there. I thought of Enlli, of a child running on the cliffs. My child. My son. But I was confused too, muddled by wishes and heat and exhaustion and morphine. My head didn't work, only my heart, willing him.

They said: "Do you want to hold him?"

"I can, but don't take the tubes out; please, please don't hinder him."

I slid my hands carefully under him, and held his small weight, and I knew it was no good. Growing up on a farm, you nurse many newborn things: pigs, calves, lambs, puppies. You know when they're not going to make it, and when there's even the faintest of hopes. I tried, my head tried, my heart tried, everything in that look tried, but my hands told me.

As the hours passed he lost his rosy flush, growing limper and greyer.

We were back in my room, talking of Enlli and laughing at a story of Dave's girlfriend, when a head popped around the door and said he'd gone. We went straight back to the conversation for a minute. Effectively he'd gone when I left an hour earlier: he'd been co-matose, blue. Should I feel I abandoned him? He wasn't there.

When a ewe has a still-born lamb, she looks around at it, sniffs, nuzzles a bit, loses interest, shakes herself, and goes off to graze. When a ewe has a live lamb, her nuzzling provokes movement, which stimulates more nuzzling and licking. It is called bonding. If the lamb is sickly and dies, she will stand for two days in the field bawling over the spot. Even when the body is removed she will come back to bawl.

Bawling. Bawling. The whole body howling, right down to the roots, the roots that make life possible at all, the link that must be forged if life is to go on, the raw end of the severed link gushing out passionate incomprehen-sion. Basics. A gap in an arch, bridged with one look, a slender key-stone, and shattered again. Bawling. No, basics. Setting the thing in motion is trivial in comparison, an act that may be graced by love

> B ut, of course, the dark doesn't go away. The world is made of dark and light, as are we. If we seem to succeed in banishing it, it pops up in an-other place, sooner or later, often with greater force, and takes us by surprise.
>
> Sometimes we instinctively or unconsciously avoid seeing something until we are ready to see it, until the time is right for us to see it, when we can "make something" of it and not be simply confused or over-whelmed by it.
>
> —Sharon Balentine, "Eyes, the Soul, Knowing"

and beauty but that works perfectly well without. Mere mechanics will do for procreation. But for what is procreated only love will do, especially when times are harsh, to rise above the doubts and fear, the pain and the problems, for survival.

(It's easier this way. How else am I to write it?)

And that look, that touch, that tiny key to the totality of acceptance must, absolutely must, complete the link if the helpless life is to survive. That transference from self-protection to baby-protection, from self-interest to baby-interest, must be switched on fully, instantaneously, from the first moment. If anything, it must be strongest at first, waning as the baby develops his own self-protection. Most women, of course, ease themselves into it more gradually, with months of dreaming, knitting, and talking. I had not. The impact was not one of shattered dreams. It was of the blind fury of nature itself, raw, savage, elemental, cheated out of a destiny for which she had quietly been preparing unwitting me. Maenad furies howling, bawling, bawling.

The cries of babies being taken past the door made me want to batter myself against the walls. Milk would pour out of me. There was no escape. I could not even run away and gallop furiously over mountainsides. They said it would be a fortnight before I could leave. But every moment was an infinity, a maelstrom of torment. Printed words meant nothing. Music was all his, empty without his echoing dances within me. There was no time: when people spoke, each past word dropped into nothingness, so that I lived in an eternal present.

His surprise, to find himself evicted from his merry pond into a world that slowly crushed him to death, its only recognizable feature my voice.

Dave, who lived nearby, called Simon, who came. First, though, he sent word to the father, who called and said he could not come. Would not come. How guilt makes cowards! How cowardice makes people guilty!

Simon was extraordinary. Sympathy and kindness we can all give to our friends in distress; but tact, the ability to know exactly what can be done and when, is a real gift. Skillfully, patiently, with infinite delicacy, he succeeded in creating moments when I did at least function, however stupidly.

After three days I was walking to the bathroom, furious at the double-over, self-pitying shuffles of my fellow caesareanees, when I met a woman I'd talked to in the prenatal ward. She had had two stillbirths, and had been awaiting her third baby with the same reservation as I.

"What happened?" I asked.

"I had a little girl," she said, almost shamefaced, for she knew the savage, jealous anger. But for her I had none. Almost to my surprise I felt happiness sweep over me, the first pleasure I had had since the needle went in. Suddenly I knew exactly what would stop the pain.

"Will you bring her to me?"

"Do you think that's a good idea?"

"I know it is. Don't you see, she's the only baby I could face."

She let me hold her for hours, anxious but knowing that being in such a state does not follow the logic that others suppose; and my body, its wild hunger satisfied at last by the only thing it wanted, found peace. Living in a succession of eternal moments has its compensations if even one of them is right. The baby slept calmly on my chest.

Lucy Rees is an author, horse trainer, and behaviorist. She is the author of numerous books of both fiction and nonfiction, including The Horse's Mind, Horse of Air, *and* The Maze: A Desert Journey, *from which this story was excerpted. When she is not traveling, Lucy lives in Wales.*

PEGGY PAYNE

* *
*

Fire and Holy Water

On the Ganges River, a woman learns
the fate of the body.

RICKSHAW DRIVERS FOLLOWED ME, OFFERING TO SHOW ME THE
sights of Varanasi, the riverbank cremation grounds: "Madame...
come...this way, madame." On my first day in this Indian city, I
wanted to walk and be left alone. As one man gave up, others
showed up to take his place, leaning close to me, trying to steer
me. "Rickshaw, madame, here, please, come...this way to the burning place."

I kept walking, got out of the area of thickest crowds. I took one
branching lane after another, looking into doorways, hole-in-the-
wall vendors' stalls, nodding at people who stared blankly at me,
watching me pass. The city seemed dense and endless. The heat
made New Delhi's scorching sun feel mild.

It was almost noon when I came out on the river, at the edge
of the city, near the end of the stone bathing ghats that rise like
stairsteps from the water up to the narrow lanes. The Ganges. The
river seemed flattened by the heat, stretching out wide, bluish-
gray-faint-green to the empty white sand and distant forest on the
opposite shore. And quiet; it was hours past the early-morning ritual baths.

I picked my way down the big stone steps to the water, each

225

step the equivalent of two to three steps on an ordinary flight of stairs, the drop to the river, several stories. There was no one close by, a few people here and there at a distance. Halfway down the ghat, the paved stairstep bank, I saw to the left the postcard view. The whole curve of shore, the ghats reaching down to the water, the spires of temples and domes of a mosque, the massive riverfront palaces. The sight seemed to float before me, to seem less real as I stood looking at it, instead of more so. It was too still. I stared, waiting for something to move. The heat seemed to have burned the landscape into a brilliant still photograph, now fixing an image of me onto that same photographic plate.

I stirred myself into motion, shifted my feet as if they'd gone to sleep and I was trying to get the feeling back. I turned to take a closer look at the Ganges water, inches from where I stood, sliding smoothly along the concrete lip of the ghat.

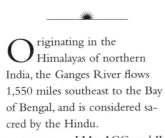

Originating in the Himalayas of northern India, the Ganges River flows 1,550 miles southeast to the Bay of Bengal, and is considered sacred by the Hindu.
—LMc, AGC, and JL

This was the holy river. It was dirty, garbage floating at the edge, dead garlands of flowers, and what looked like household trash.

I walked a few steps along the edge, crossed to the next ghat, the next set of steps, passed a pipe trickling a sewage-smelling liquid, walked for maybe 500 yards. Still no sign of people or movement, and the center of the city was like a painting I was walking toward, far in the distance. The riffle of the water's edge, a bird overhead only made the stillness seem more absolute. There was nothing to do. No one to watch. I didn't like it.

The river's bobbing garbage, the weight of the heat, the silence felt ominous. I turned, began the climb to the top of the ghat, back to street level.

I reached the top step of the ghat, plunged back into the traffic, glad to see it again. Onto the bench of the first empty rickshaw, I told the man "Dasaswamedh," the name of the main bathing ghat in the center of town, a place where I'd be able to look at the river surrounded by people and noise.

At Dasaswamedh, just beyond the vendors' tents, on foot again, I paused to look out at the river shining in the sunlight before making a second descent to the water. Here there were people along the water's edge, bathers, long rowboats, the wide shade umbrellas for the rupee-charging holy men, ready to offer a blessing or keep an eye on a bather's shoes.

A man stepped up beside me, small and dapper with a cocky air, a straight-backed and lofty bearing. Would I like to have a boat ride? His name was Mamta. His sweetly complacent smile made him seem sure of himself and sure also of his welcome. We started down the long steep steps to the river and the rowboats.

At the edge of the water, we stepped from boat to boat, to reach the one farther out where Mamta's oarsman was waiting. It was a long wooden open rowboat, just like all the others. We set off down the river, the boatman, shirtless and dark, pulling on long bamboo paddles. Along the shore here, people were bathing, even though the peak hour had long passed. Men in what looked like hand-wrapped jockey shorts, or thongs. Wiry men with dark muscular butts. The women managing to bathe fully dressed in saris. All along the edge of the water, people were shampooing their hair, soaping their bodies, or scrubbing pots or clothes.

Trash kept floating past the side of the boat—a coconut shell, pieces of charred wood, unrecognizable bits of stuff—the water gray and sudsy. "It looks dirty," Mamta said, "but push that aside," sweeping away bits of trash, "and you see it is clean." He scooped up water in his cupped hand and held it out to show me.

Then we came around the walled edge of a ghat—Manikarnika, the funeral pyres. Three fires burning, three bodies, in front of me at the water's edge. The boatman stopped rowing; we sat and looked. One who dies in Varanasi and gives the ashes to the Ganges becomes part of the eternal and is freed from the cycle of earthly rebirths, that is the Hindu belief. Two more bodies had just been brought here for cremation, each of them wrapped tightly in thin silk, left lying on the bamboo ladder on which the body was carried here. I could hardly believe I was seeing this. Corpses, lying out in daylight in the sun. They'd been lowered into the Ganges water, Mamta said, and then left on the pavement to dry before burning. The shapes of faces, limbs, knuckles, feet, showed through the silk. They'd wrapped the faces so tight you could see the nose, the hollows of the mouth and cheeks and eyes. If someone were still alive, they would suffocate.

Within the high-piled wood of one of the pyres was the bright-colored wrapping of a body, the kindling beneath just beginning to burn.

From the end of the next pyre, I saw what looked like two feet sticking out—could that be? Or was it two pieces of wood I was looking at, bent at the ends? They looked like ankles and feet. I didn't want to ask Mamta; it seemed prurient to want to know. Whatever they were, I watched as they caught fire and began to burn, turning slowly from "toes-up" to twisted-to-the-side, to downward-turned.

I wanted to scream at that person to wake up, get up from there—fast!

The bodies that lie there aren't going to wake up, the burning shows you that. That pair of human feet blistering, searing, to fat, to charred sticks, then ash, as people stared.

The sound of a chant from the top of the ghat—another body was carried into view, up high at city level, at the top of the stone stairs. The four young men carrying the stretcher calling out a singsong, *"Rama nama..."* It had a beat.

A two-line chant:

"Ra...ma..na...ma...Sa...tya...hai."

Again and again. *"Rama nama...."*

I knew what the words meant: "Rama is the true name, the name of God is truth." A marching beat. Alluring. On the seat of the rowboat, I felt myself rocking from the waist to that beat.

Down the steps to the water with the body. The four young

men lowered it in. It floated. They splashed water on it to make sure it had been completely covered, then pulled it out to dry on the steps with the other wrapped corpses.

A few steps back from the water, a man dressed in only a loin-cloth, bare-chested, rushed back and forth, through the smoke and haze of burning, tending the flaming pyres, a man of the untouchable caste of Doms. Yet another pyre flared, ignited with a blazing bundle of twigs waved in circular motion, the flame taken from fire that had been burning at this site for hundreds of years.

I saw no obvious grieving among the groups of men standing at the edge of the ghat. It is said to cause bad fortune for the dead. There were no women in sight. "Women," Mamta said, "do not want to see their husband or their child burn."

I stared at those solemn groups of impassive men.

I pictured my husband Bob's long skinny feet.

Someone among those men was watching as his beloved burned. At home, my office in Raleigh is between two funeral parlors, two blocks apart. I see funeral processions every day. Cars. Moving slowly in a line, following the hearse. Nothing to see from my window but sun on the tops of cars.

I felt wrong to be out on the river, intrusive. At the same time I wanted to convince myself that what I was seeing had nothing to do with me, that I shouldn't be here, seeing the final bows of these bereaved men as, one by one, each approached the corpse, bent low, then moved away.

The night I stood beside my father's coffin, looked at his body there for the first time, my knees gave way. Standing quietly, my face composed, I felt myself start to drop toward the floor. My brothers, one on either side of me, each caught me by an elbow. We were grown by then, all three of us in our twenties. We had known for a long time that Daddy might have a heart attack. We'd known for so long that I had grown used to the idea of death as something that loomed but never actually happened. He died late at night, at home; he and Mom had just come home from a party. It was fifteen years ago, the night after my return from my earlier trip to India.

I looked around at Mamta; he saw "enough" on my face and signaled the boatman to move us on.

As we set in motion again, I searched the riverbank up ahead for the sight of people doing reassuringly ordinary sights, washing their clothes. I let the faint hot breeze, the growing distance as the oarsman rowed, put the burning pyres behind me and out of my mind.

Then half a mile down the river, beyond the place where we first put in, the boatman accidentally let an oar slip out of his hand into the water. Carried quickly out of his reach, it was coming past me where I sat toward the back of the boat. I reached over the side, grabbed it, passed it back to him, dripping. The man stared at me, shocked, as if what I had done was astounding, and not a reflex. I gave my hand a wipe on the long blouse of my *salwar kameez,* childishly pleased with myself that I had unthinkingly reached in. It was now baptized—this hand—in the holy river, dipped halfway to the elbow in gray-green water I had not intended to touch, so murky, full of garbage, laundry soap, bits of charred bone and human ash.

Peggy Payne is the author of the novel, Sister India, *a story that emerged from a winter she spent in Varanasi on an Indo-American Fellowship. She is also the author of the novel* Revelation *and co-author of* The Healing Power of Doing Good.

KUKI GALLMANN

✦ ✦ ✦

A Bed Like a Vessel

In Africa, a ritual from the heart
soothes a grieving mother.

EVEN IF, IN THE WEST, WE NO LONGER NORMALLY BELIEVE IN THE truth of auguries, they are part of Africa and of its traditions. I have chosen Africa, and have grown to accept and to respect its rituals and beliefs, as they are rooted in the very nature of its people and in their simple lives, still close to the source of all things. They are, in their essence, indistinguishable from the instincts, which allow tribes to survive in harsh conditions, or migrate periodically to other grazing land, and which protect them from predators, or guide them to water.

There have been occasions in my life when I have been especially close to the depth of the African spirit and have felt, with humbleness and pride, that Africa has accepted and, in its inscrutable way, has chosen me too.

Like the time when the Pokot women came to offer me a special wish.

It was the afternoon before Christmas Eve, when [my husband] Paolo had been dead three years. Emanuele had followed him a few months before, sent to the country beyond by a snake which could not know what it had done; Sveva, our baby, was about three

years old. I was in the kitchen, preparing some complicated chocolate log with my cook Simon.

Rachel, the Nandi maid, had come to call me: "*Kuja! Wanawake
ya Pokot iko hapa. Unataka kuona wewe.*" "Come! The Pokot
women are here. They want to see you."

I wiped my hands on a cloth, took my baby on my hip, and
went out, licking the chocolate from my fingers.

I could see them all from the veranda, some already squatting,
at ease below the fever trees, some standing, some dancing round
like long-limbed ostriches lifting their legs high. There were old
women, covered in soft skins, their hair in dark greased ringlets,
toothless, their craggy, lined faces worn like ancient wooden
masks. There were the girls, and it was they who sang. They were
so young, so frail, like birds who have not grown feathers: sticklike
legs, thin arms, gleaming with brass bracelets, and their little round
faces on pert necks, plastered startlingly with a mixture of white
ashes and chalk in ugly patterns. But their merry eyes, glinting
with mischief and teasing anticipation, denied the very purpose of
their disguise. They each held a long ceremonial stick which they
had gone to cut for themselves from some special shrub in the forest; they oscillated them now in rhythm with their voices.

They sang; and when they saw me, their song gained strength,
momentum, as if a sudden wind had given it new wings. It was a
shrill, high-pitched lament which sounded like the call of a bird at
noon. It ran through them like a shiver as they sang in turn, rippling them into a frenzied, yet curiously composed ritual dance.

It was the song of the girls who have been circumcised, and
have borne the pain and the ordeal of this barbaric but accepted
tradition with courage and dignity, knowing that they were now
free to enter in their role of mature women, and to allow a man to
find them, and pay their bride-price of cattle and goats to their
fathers. It was the song of the women of Africa, a song of courage
and mutual solidarity, of hope of children, and proud resignation
to an unchosen, yet time-proven fate.

They spat on their hands before shaking them with me one by

one. They giggled, shyly. Some seemed so pitifully small, still almost children, the white of their eyes and teeth standing out in their tribal camouflage, intended to make them repellent to men for the duration of their recovery. In a few days, healed and ready to be seen by all eager young males, they would wear their traditional costumes of bright orange, brown, and yellow beads. Their round cheeks would be greased provocatively in red ochre, their hair dressed in complicated tresses. Their little breasts bare. Their skirts of beaded calfskin long in the back and gathered in front would reveal their agile legs, tinkling with anklets.

From now on, in the years to come, I would recognize some of them, surprised at the turn of a track, while they tended their goats and weaners, their stomachs bulging with their first and second and subsequent children, year after year, for all their fertile lives.

Suddenly that day, when all the greetings had been exchanged, my symbolic offering of tea and sugar had been passed on, and the ceremony seemed to be drawing to its end, one old woman came forward, proffering in her hands a long object. An instant hush descended on the small crowd like a last layer of leaves after a sudden storm subsides.

All the other women gathered and surrounded me in suspended silence, their faces alert in anticipation. I understood that this was really the major purpose of their visit, and the core of this ceremony. Murmuring guttural words in Pokot, the old woman offered me her gift. It was a wide belt of soft skin, smeared with greased ochre and goat fat, and beaded in a simple pattern with small, gray money-cowries like shiny pebbles. Before I knew it, with endearing giggles, they fastened it around my waist, and asked me something I could not understand, with a happy, pressing, even demanding note in their voices.

"*Nyumba yako ya kulala. Hawa nataka kubeba wewe kwa kitanda yako.*" "Your bedroom. They want to carry you to your bed," Simon interpreted for me, appearing at my side like a protecting shadow.

My bed. I remembered the day when I had sat on the floor of

the room which would be our bedroom, watching Langat and his assistant Nguare carrying in the trees that would become our bed.

Building a bed is like building a vessel to carry us through the delights and nightmares, surprises and follies, pauses to rest, and deliriums of fever during the varied travels of our nocturnal life. Our bed is the most important piece of furniture we may ever use, for so much happens in it to influence our waking hours. A bed is a *habitaculum*, a home in itself. Our sleeping body, entrusted to its protection gathers with abandon the strength, the glory of tomorrow's daylight.

Our bed was a four-poster that I had imagined and built of simple and irregular, but polished posts, linked by smaller beams and with a sensational head and foot made from offcuts shorn of their bark, to reveal the sinuous curves of their long woody muscles. This bed, where I still sleep, and will for as long as I live, was shaped in a few days inside the room. Tall, massive, and unique, it can never be moved out through the small door.

We built it together, Langat, Naguare, and I, and when it was ready, I gave them a beer, to celebrate that receptacle of dreams and sorrows. We stood together, admiringly, contemplating the result of our work, and turned to each other to shake hands on it, grinning with the pleasure of recognizing our achievement. The trails that insects had carved laboriously in the surface of the wood created a subtle, inimitable filigree, a delicate fossil memory.

One day—I was then yet to know—Paolo would climb onto the bed and hand from its central beam an empty ostrich egg, to puzzle my soul with that unrevealed oracle he had concealed inside it. I would spend sleepless nights watching that egg after Paolo died, while his baby daughter would nurse and play on the hyrax cover. A few years later, I would lay there, for his last night on earth, the tortured teenage body of my son Emanuele, and I would spend the wake, curled up on my side of the bed, rolled into cold blankets, writing for him my last song.

Show the Pokot women to my bed? The request was so odd and unexpected that I had no time to demur. With a nod, I indicated the way, and amongst cries of triumph, I was suddenly lifted high, above those heads in ringlets, by dozens of strong, skinny hands grasping me tenaciously through my khaki clothes, while a new song was being sung.

They carried me, snaking their way in circles through the garden in a live brown stream, like a procession of harvester ants carrying a large white insect to their secret pantries; before I knew it, my room was full of them, swarming at once and all together.

I was finally thrown, as gently as possible but still roughly enough, onto my bed, amidst howls and giggles from the youngest women, while the older ones proclaimed in a half singsong their prophecy, or their wish. One by one, they all fell silent, until only the oldest one spoke. Hovering over me, searching my eyes with her shining gaze, in guttural bursts she pronounced her sentence. They all chorused the last word, clapped their hands and, one after the other, spat on me their blessing in convulsive sprays of fine spittle. Then I was brought up and out again, dazzled, smeared with ochre, to see the sun.

They explained to me eventually that theirs was a special wish for me, that I should again be happy on that bed which had seen such sorrow—happy, and loved, "but no more pregnant": the best wish they had to offer, which I accepted gratefully.

And some while after, like all authentic spells, it came true.

Kuki Gallman grew up in Italy and has spent her adult life in Kenya helping to conserve its natural world. She has written I Dreamed of Africa, *a best-selling account of her life in Africa and the tragic losses of both her husband and son (made into a major motion picture in 2000 starring Kim Basinger), and* African Nights, *from which this story is excerpted.*

PART FIVE

EMERGING INTO THE LIGHT

* * *

Trusting the Trail

Along the twists and turns of the Appalachian Trail,
a hiker finds a firm foundation.

I'VE BECOME AWARE LATELY THAT THERE'S A PLACE I NEED TO GET
to. Not a physical place, but a spiritual, emotional, psychological
one. I'm definitely not there now. I'm bored, confused, discon-
tented. I've spent the past ten years—all of my twenties—wandering around, working temp jobs, entering relationships that only add
to my confusion and discontent. I'm lost and looking for something. If I can just get to that mystical place, I think I'll find it.

Although the place is not a physical location, somehow I know
that the only way to get there is to walk a great distance: a long,
slow, arduous process. A pilgrimage. I don't know what the place
is or what I will find there, but trust that it exists, that it's reach-
able, and that it's as necessary as blood or breath.

When I find a book about the Appalachian Trail, a footpath
running over 2,000 miles through the mountains from Georgia to
Maine, I know I've found my way. I spend two years preparing,
saving money and amassing gear, then take a train to Georgia and
begin walking north, toward Maine.

I come to the end of the Great Smoky Mountains, and I take a
side trip to the Mount Cammerer fire tower, a half-mile off the

Appalachian Trail. I spend a long time sitting on the mountaintop looking down into the valleys, where spring is slowly moving up the slopes, looking far off at the mountains I will cross in the coming days and weeks. A deer appears, walking delicately, like a shy girl in high-heeled shoes, and stands nearby eating leaves off a bush.

I've been out here on the Trail now, walking alone, for nearly a month. I've never felt so peaceful and right about anything I've ever done.

How can I keep this peace and trust after returning to civilization? How can I make a living, but not have a job that makes me feel as if I'm in prison? How can I keep this simple life, where it's so obvious what's important and what's not?

What's important: a warm fire, clean water, shelter from the rain, food, and the company of others I run into on the way. And the walk. The continuing pilgrimage. I have no thoughts about leaving. The world outside the Trail is like the land beyond a cliff: nothing there, nothing you'd want to leap into, anyway.

"You're the kind of person who talks to anyone and is at home with everyone," another hiker told me a couple of days ago. I was shocked. When I was a kid I was like that, then lost it in the years between then and now, when I was living a life that was false in so many ways. Now I feel like I'm coming home to myself, here in this beautiful forest.

I trust that the Trail itself will lead me where I need to go, if I give my heart to it completely. By the time I'm done, I'll know what to do next.

I bow to the deer, who tosses her head at me, then put on my heavy pack and walk. For the first time in the Smokies the Trail leaves the high, cold ridgeline and descends many miles into a dream-forest, that ethereally green, flower-filled, watery cove I've seen from such a great distance while walking along the lofty, wintry summits above. Down here it's deep into spring, the mountainsides covered with dwarf iris, fire pink, ladyslippers, bloodroot, flowering dogwoods, shadbush, golden ragwort, violets, several kinds of trilliums, flame azaleas, Dutchman's breeches, mayapples, buttercup, trout lilies, squawroot, violets, tulip trees, and striped maples. There are so many flowers it looks like the woods are going to a wedding. The path is strewn with tiny, delicate blossoms, petals, leaves, buds, green tips, and tender twigs. This generosity of the forest, its casual strewing of beauty, always touches me, as if someone has done this on purpose simply because it's so lovely and tender.

"Thank you," I say to everything: the mossy, velvet-green stump with a tiny acorn resting on it like a jeweler's display; the magnolia petals, creamy vanilla-lemon scented scoops that look like (but are not) edible spoons; the exquisitely formed maple leaves that are still as small as a fingernail. For the first time on the trip I hear a veery singing, that elusive bird of damp, rich forests. Their song, a complex, ethereal down-spiraling whistle, sounds like music from another world, where spirits live.

That night, the rough log shelter in Davenport Gap is full of people, a mix of "thruhikers" who, like me, are headed all the way to Maine; a group who hiked most of the Trail so far but then hitchhiked up from Fontana Dam; and some weekenders. The hitchhikers, who have a dog with them, could not walk through the Smokies because dogs are not allowed there. Instead of having the dog shuttled around the park and then kenneled while they hiked through, they simply skipped the Smokies entirely, hitchhiking around the mountains instead of walking through them.

"We're just a bunch of damn yellow-blazers," one of them says. He's lying in a hammock strung between the rafters, smoking a joint. His buddies laugh.

"No, man, rainbow-blazers is what we are. Rainbow."

Yellow-blazing is hitchhiking: instead of following the Appalachian Trail, which is marked by white paint marks called blazes, you're flying along on the road, which of course is marked by a yellow line. If you hike on that road instead of getting a ride, you're blue-blazing, the equivalent of using a side trail, somewhat less damning than traveling in the back of someone's pickup truck. Bushwhacking, traveling through the woods and not following a trail at all, is green-blazing, and following a trail that used to be the AT, but where the old white blazes have been painted out, is ghost-blazing. Hikers who use a mixture of the AT, blue-blazed side trails, and hitchhiking to travel up the Trail are "rainbow-blazers," and some "purist" Appalachian Trail hikers look down on them, as if their pilgrimages are somehow less valid.

I'm not concerned about who got here which way. Hikers have a saying, "Hike your own hike," which means, mind your own business, do what you're here to do, and don't judge others. I don't think there's any objective way to judge whether someone else's hike is "valid" or not; all I can do is make sure mine is valid, for me.

The rainbow-blazers pass their joint back and forth, the dog yawns and puts his head on his paws, and the weekenders hand out marshmallows for everyone to toast on the fire.

Outside the shelter it's raining flowers, creamy cup-shaped blossoms of five joined petals showering down from the canopy of trees. Limey, a British hiker, reads us a poem by Rumi, a Sufi mystic, from a book he carries in his pack:

> You reach out wanting the moon with your eyes,
> and Venus. Build a place to live
> with these dimensions. A shelter that can be
> knocked down with one kick,
> go ahead and knock it down.

We all smile at the rightness of it. It's not just a poem, some ideal of simplicity, some metaphor to longingly sigh over. It's a vivid description of our daily life. The only shelter I have, besides the official Trail ones—rough lean-tos open to the weather, like the one we're in now—is a tarp, which weighs one and a half pounds and can be taken down and packed in less than a minute. Others have tents, similarly light and easy. Most of the time our ceiling is the sky. We are never truly indoors, enclosed.

I think of my life before the Trail: enclosed, boring jobs, bad relationships. Like a house of cards on a flimsy table, it was built on the wrong foundation: Behave yourself. Find a man. Get a real job. Be normal.

Go ahead, I think. Go ahead and knock it down. Knock it down, so I can build a new life, a life that's right for me.

I lie in my sleeping bag on the hard wooden sleeping platform, looking out at the forest. The afternoon sun slants down through the trees, touching trees with gold, highlighting leaves, making some spots look special, as if, when you stand there, you'll be transformed, filled with light.

That's what I'm hoping for on this trip: transformation. And if I keep walking, living this rough and simple life, I know I'll find it.

Kelly Winters is the author of Side Roads of Long Island *and* Walking Home, *a book about her hike from Georgia to Maine, from which this story was excerpted. She says that everything in her life is a result of that transformative journey. Kelly lives in New York where she is a freelance writer and editor.*

Recommended Reading

Ackerman, Diane. *Deep Play.* New York: Random House, 1999.

Angelou, Maya. *All God's Children Need Traveling Shoes.* New York: Vintage, 1991.

Barnes, Kim. *In the Wilderness: Coming of Age in Unknown Country.* New York: Doubleday, 1996.

Bender, Sue. *Everyday Sacred: A Woman's Journey Home.* San Francisco: HarperSan Francisco, 1995.

Birkett, Dea. *Serpent in Paradise.* New York: Anchor, 1997.

Bolen, Jean Shinoda. *Crossing to Avalon: A Woman's Midlife Pilgrimage.* San Francisco: HarperSan Francisco, 1995.

Butala, Sharon. *Perfection of the Morning: A Woman's Awakening in Nature.* St. Paul, Minn.: Hungry Mind Press, 1997.

Chernin, Kim. *Reinventing Eve: Modern Woman in Search of Herself.* New York: HarperPerennial, 1994; New York: Times Books, 1987.

Colijn, Helen. *Song of Survival: Women Interned.* Ashland, Oreg.: White Cloud Press, 1995.

Deming, Alison Hawthorne. *Temporary Homelands: Essays on Nature, Spirit and Place.* New York: Picador, 1996.

Ehrlich, Gretel. Islands, *The Universe, Home.* New York: Viking Penguin, 1991.

Ehrlich, Gretel. *Questions of Heaven: The Chinese Journeys of an American Buddhist.* Boston: Beacon Press, 1997.

Ehrlich, Gretel. *The Solace of Open Spaces.* New York: Viking Penguin, 1985.

Gallagher, Nora. *Things Seen and Unseen: A Year Lived in Faith.* New York: Vintage, 1999.

Gallmann, Kuki. *African Nights.* New York: Penguin Books, 1995.

Gammelgaard, Lene. *Climbing High: A Woman's Account of Surviving the Everest Tragedy.* Seattle, Wash.: Seal Press, 1999.

Gimbutas, Marija Alseikaite. *The Language of the Goddess.* San Francisco: HarperSan Francisco, 1995.

Goldberg, Natalie. *Long Quiet Highway: Waking Up in America.* New York: Bantam, 1993.

Hadley, Leila. *A Journey with Elsa Cloud.* New York: Penguin, 1998.

Halifax, Joan. *The Fruitful Darkness: Reconnecting with the Body of the Earth.* San Francisco: HarperSan Francisco, 1994.

Hampl, Patricia. *I Could Tell You Stories: Sojourns in the Land of Memory.* New York: W. W. Norton, 1999.

Herrera, Susana. *Mango Elephants in the Sun: How Life in an African Village Let Me Be in My Skin.* Boston: Shambhala, 1999.

Hiestand, Emily. *The Very Rich Hours: Travels in Orkney, Belize, the Everglades, and Greece.* Boston: Beacon Press, 1992.

Hogan, Linda. *Dwellings: A Spiritual History of the Living World.* New York: Touchstone, 1995.

Kaza, Stephanie. *The Attentive Heart: Conversations with Trees.* New York: Fawcett Columbine, 1993.

Lamott, Anne. *Traveling Mercies: Some Thoughts on Faith.* New York: Pantheon, 1999.

Lash, Jennifer. *On Pilgrimage: A Time to Seek.* London: Bloomsbury Publishing, 1991.

L'Engle, Madeleine. *A Circle of Quiet.* San Francisco: HarperSan Francisco, 1986.

L'Engle, Madeleine. *Friends for the Journey : Two Extraordinary Women Celebrate Friendships Made and Sustained Through the Seasons of Life.* Ann Arbor, Mich.: Servant Publication, 1997.

Lindbergh, Anne Morrow. *Gift from the Sea.* New York: Pantheon, 1992.

Livingston, Patricia H. *Lessons of the Heart: Celebrating the Rhythms of Life.* Notre Dame, Ind.: Ave Maria Press, 1992.

Martino, Teresa tsimmu. *The Wolf, the Woman, the Wilderness: A*

True Story of Returning Home. Troutdale, Oreg.: NewSage Press, 1997.

Mayorga, Nancy Pope. *The Hunger of the Soul: A Spiritual Diary.* Studio City, Calif.: Vedanta, 1981.

Morrow, Susan Brind. *The Names of Things: Life, Language, and Beginnings in the Egyptian Desert.* New York: Riverhead Books, 1997.

Norris, Kathleen. *The Cloister Walk.* New York: Riverhead Books, 1997.

Norris, Kathleen. *Dakota: A Spiritual Geography.* New York: Houghton Mifflin, 1993.

Nyala, Hannah. *Point Last Seen: A Woman's Tracker's Story.* Boston: Beacon Press, 1997.

Peterson, Brenda. *Living By Water: Essays on Life, Land, & Spirit.* Bothell, Wash.: Alaska Northwest Books, 1990.

Poirier-Bures, Simone. *That Shining Place.* Ontario, Canada: Oberon Press, 1995.

Rees, Lucy. *The Maze: A Desert Journey.* New York: The Countryman Press, 1996.

Ryan, Kathleen Jo (ed.). *Writing Down the River: Into the Heart of the Grand Canyon.* Flagstaff, Ariz.: Northland, 1998.

Starhawk. *The Spiral Dance: A Rebirth of the Ancient Religion of the Great Goddess.* San Francisco: HarperSan Francisco, 1999.

Thayer, Helen. *Polar Dream.* New York: Delta Books, 1993.

Tiberghien, Susan M. *Looking for Gold. A Year in Jungian Analysis.* Einsiedeln, Switzerland: Daimon, 1995.

Vega, Janine Pommy. *Tracking the Serpent: Journeys to Four Continents.* San Francisco: City Lights Books, 1997.

Walker, Barbara G. *The Woman's Dictionary of Symbols and Sacred Objects.* San Francisco: HarperSan Francisco, 1988.

Wheeler, Sara. *Travels in a Thin Country: A Journey through Chile.* New York: Modern Library, 1999.

Zwinger, Susan. *The Last Wild Edge: One Woman's Journey from the Arctic Circle to the Olympic Rain Forest.* Boulder, Colo.: Johnson Books, 1999.

Index

Index of Contributors

Acknowledgments

I have been blessed indeed to have had Amy Carlson and Jennifer Leo as collaborators on this book—and to have had the opportunity to work under the guiding hand of our guardian angel, Lisa Bach. In addition, this book wouldn't have been possible without the inspiration—I would say "divine"—of James O'Reilly and Larry Habegger, who developed the idea for this series and whose belief in my abilities continues to spur me on. My sincerest thanks to Susan Brady for producing this book in her inimitable way from start to finish. Special thanks as well go to our type-setter Cynthia Lamb, to Tara Weaver, Michele Wetherbee, and to every-one on the Travelers' Tales team who have had a part in producing these collections: Deborah Greco, Raj Khadka, Sean O'Reilly, Tim O'Reilly, Wenda O'Reilly, and Trisha Schwartz. I would also like to thank my mother, Elizabeth McCauley, who made sure I got to church each Sunday; my father, Cleyburn McCauley, who entertained me during the services by making paper cranes; and my sister Beth, just because. And to my husband, Charles Bambach: Thank you for showing me each day how meaningful life's journey can be.

—Lucy McCauley

I come to the blank page to say thank you to my fellow weavers. Creating an anthology, as with a weaving, we must come to the loom with visions and dreams of possibilities swirling with color and flow. The web grows as the shuttle goes back and forth, our hands creating their own rhythm. Many hands have gone into the weaving of this book. I want to thank Lucy McCauley, Jennifer Leo, and Lisa Bach for their hours of dedicated focus, honest insight, and concentrated spinning. They have given truly of themselves, adding to the richness and texture of this handiwork. To all of the Travelers' Tales staff I say a great "HURRAH" yet again for all of your hard work in producing this volume. I thank Valla Howell for her love of the writing process and devotion to this art, and to all those who contributed their yarns (oooh, that's bad!). And last, but not least, I would like to thank the O'Reilly family for being so weird and wonderful, and for seeing possibility in this evolving soul. Amen.

—Amy G. Carlson

Being a part of this editorial team has been a gifted journey in itself. I first want to thank James O'Reilly for his foresight into my own path, having faith in me, and his continued support and encouragement throughout every step of this process.

Heartfelt thanks to Larry Habegger for my entry into Travelers' Tales. I have much admiration and respect for your insight into life and love— your lessons will carry me far.

To my co-editors Lucy and Amy, I'd like to thank you for your wisdom, experience, and unbound thoughtfulness in putting this book together. Special thanks to Lisa Bach for her equal efforts into making this book a reality—it is all the more complete because of her passion for women's literature, spiritual growth, and travel.

Special thanks to the Travelers' Tales staff who work hard to get the books out on time, especially Susan Brady and Tara Weaver who always go the extra mile. Many thanks also go to Cynthia Lamb, Michele Wetherbee for her beautiful cover design, Tanya Pearlman, Deborah Greco, Wenda O'Reilly, Sean O'Reilly, Raj Khadka, Trisha Schwartz, Judy Johnson, and Trigg Robinson McCloud.

I'd also like to thank my family for their patience, guidance, and undying love; to the Decker family for their continuous support; Pearl Werfel, Ph.D. for her part in keeping my distractions at bay; to the WWW writing group for their ongoing encouragement; to Katie, Matt, Alanna, and Berklee for their laughter; to Dan Buczaczer, Scott M. Gimple, Catherine Lieuwen, and Heather Walsh for their daily friendship; and to Joe Decker who stands beside me, strong and confident in all that I do.

—Jennifer L. Leo

"Go Beyond!" by Abigail Seymour reprinted from the July 1998 issue of Attaché magazine. Copyright © 1998 by Abigail Seymour. Reprinted by permission of the author.

Additional Credits (arranged alphabetically by title)

Selection from *The Attentive Heart: Conversations with Trees* by Stephanie Kaza copyright © 1993 by Stephanie Kaza. Published by Ballantine Books, a division of Random House, Inc., New York, NY.

Selection from "The Black Madonna of Mont Voirons" by Susan Tiberghien published with permission from the author. Copyright © 2000 by Susan Tiberghien.

Selection from "The Black Madonna: Primordial Ancestress" by Deborah Rose published with permission from the author. Copyright © 1998 by Deborah Rose.

Selection from *Climbing High: A Woman's Account of Surviving the Everest Tragedy* by Lene Gammelgaard copyright © 1999 by Lene Gammelgaard. Published by Seal Press, Seattle, WA.

Selection from "The Consuming Pilgrimage" by Lisa Bach published with permission from the author. Copyright © 2000 by Lisa Bach.

Selection from *Dakota: A Spiritual Geography* by Kathleen Norris copyright © 1993 by Kathleen Norris. Reprinted by permission of Ticknor & Fields/Houghton Mifflin Co. All rights reserved.

Selections from *Dwellings: A Spiritual History of the Living World* by Linda Hogan copyright © 1995 by Linda Hogan. Reprinted by permission of W. W. Norton & Company, Inc. and Sanford J. Greenburger Associates.

Selection from "The Encounter" by Jean Bucaria published with permission from the author. Copyright © 2000 by Jean Bucaria.

Selection from "Eyes, the Soul, Knowing" by Sharon Balentine published with permission from the author. Copyright © 2000 by Sharon Balentine.

Selection from *The Hunger of the Soul: A Spiritual Diary* by Nancy Pope Mayorga copyright © 1981, 1996 by the estate of Nancy Pope Mayorga. Reprinted by permission of InnerQuest Publishing Company, Studio City, CA.

Selection from "I'm Going to Galway" by Janine Jones published with permission from the author. Copyright © 2000 by Janine Jones.

Selection from "In Sunshine and in Shadow" by Deanne Stillman published with permission from the author. Copyright © 2000 by Deanne Stillman.

Selections from *Kite Strings of the Southern Cross: A Woman's Travel Odyssey* by Laurie Gough copyright©1998 by Laurie Gough. Published in Canada as *Island of the Human Heart: A Woman's Travel Odyssey* by Turnstone Press. Reprinted by permission of Travelers' Tales, Inc. and Turnstone Press.

Selections from *On Pilgrimage: A Time to Seek* by Jennifer Lash copyright © 1991 by the Estate of Jennifer Lash. Published by Bloomsbury Publishing Ltd., London, UK.

About the Editors

Lucy McCauley is the editor of two other Travelers' Tales volumes: *Women in the Wild* and *Spain*. Her writing has appeared in such publications as the *Atlantic Monthly,* the *Los Angeles Times, Harvard Review,* Salon.com, and several Travelers' Tales books. A freelance writer and editor based in Texas, she is a member of the International Women's Writing Guild.

Amy G. Carlson inherited a case of wanderlust from her Connecticut family, a malady which has led her to eat fugu (blowfish) in Japan, get chased by a Red Guard in Beijing, get kicked out of a casino in Macau, come close to starving in a London garret which writing about William Blake, and generally wander the world with only her backpack for company. Currently she has settled down with her husband, Reed, in the mountains of Washington State where she stays busy teaching poetry, giving flute lessons, writing, and researching. She is co-editor of *Travelers' Tales Japan.*

Jennifer L. Leo was working at a ski resort in Lake Tahoe when she discovered the writings of Tim Cahill in a box of old *Outside* magazines at a local mountain recreation shop. She bought every issue she could find his name in for 25 cents and decided her life must be connected to travel writing. Born in San Diego, California, she graduated with degrees in Journalism and Social Sciences from the University of Southern California. She is the editor of the humor book, *Sand in My Bra and Other Misadventures*, and her writing has appeared in in *Wild Writing Women: Stories of World Travel, A Woman's Passion for Travel, The Adventure of Food, Lonely Planet World Food Guide Hong Kong,* BootsNAll.com, and other books in the Travelers' Tales series.

TRAVELERS' TALES

THE SOUL OF TRAVEL

Footsteps Series

THE FIRE NEVER DIES
**One Man's Raucous Romp
Down the Road of Food,
Passion, and Adventure**
By Richard Sterling
ISBN 1-885-211-70-8
$14.95

"Sterling's writing is like spit-
fire, foursquare and jazzy with crackle...."
—*Kirkus Reviews*

LAST TROUT
IN VENICE
**The Far-Flung Escapades
of an Accidental
Adventurer**
By Doug Lansky
ISBN 1-885-211-63-5
$14.95

"Traveling with Doug Lansky might result in
a considerably shortened life expectancy...but
what a way to go." —Tony Wheeler,
Lonely Planet Publications

ONE YEAR OFF
**Leaving It All Behind for a
Round-the-World Journey
with Our Children**
By David Elliot Cohen
ISBN 1-885-211-65-1
$14.95

A once-in-a-lifetime
adventure generously shared.

THE WAY OF
THE WANDERER
**Discover Your True Self
Through Travel**
By David Yeadon
ISBN 1-885-211-60-0
$14.95

Experience transformation through travel
with this delightful, illustrated collection by
award-winning author David Yeadon.

TAKE ME
WITH YOU
**A Round-the-World
Journey to Invite a
Stranger Home**
By Brad Newsham
ISBN 1-885-211-51-1
$24.00 (cloth)

"Newsham is an ideal guide. His journey, at
heart, is into humanity." —Pico Iyer, author
of *Video Night in Kathmandu*

KITE STRINGS OF
THE SOUTHERN
CROSS
**A Woman's
Travel Odyssey**
By Laurie Gough
ISBN 1-885-211-54-6
$14.95 —★★★—

ForeWord Silver Medal Winner
—*Travel Book of the Year*

THE SWORD
OF HEAVEN
**A Five Continent Odyssey
to Save the World**
By Mikkel Aaland
ISBN 1-885-211-44-9
$24.00 (cloth)

"Few books capture the soul
of the road like *The Sword of Heaven*,
a sharp-edged, beautifully rendered memoir
that will inspire anyone." —Phil Cousineau,
author of *The Art of Pilgrimage*

STORM
**A Motorcycle Journey
of Love, Endurance,
and Transformation**
By Allen Noren
ISBN 1-885-211-45-7
$24.00 (cloth) —★★★—

ForeWord Gold Medal Winner
—*Travel Book of the Year*

Travelers' Tales Classics

COAST TO COAST
A Journey Across 1950s America
By Jan Morris
ISBN 1-885-211-79-1
$16.95

After reporting on the first Everest ascent in 1953, Morris spent a year journeying by car, train, ship, and aircraft across the United States. In her brilliant prose, Morris records with exuberance and curiosity a time of innocence in the U.S.

TRADER HORN
A Young Man's Astounding Adventures in 19th Century Equatorial Africa
By Alfred Aloysius Horn
ISBN 1-885-211-81-3
$16.95

Here is the stuff of legends —tale of thrills and danger, wild beasts, serpents, and savages. An unforgettable and vivid portrait of a vanished late-19th century Africa.

THE ROYAL ROAD TO ROMANCE
By Richard Halliburton
ISBN 1-885-211-53-8
$14.95

"Laughing at hardships, dreaming of beauty, ardent for adventure, Halliburton has managed to sing into the pages of this glorious book his own exultant spirit of youth and freedom."
— *Chicago Post*

UNBEATEN TRACKS IN JAPAN
By Isabella L. Bird
ISBN 1-885-211-57-0
$14.95

Isabella Bird was one of the most adventurous women travelers of the 19th century with journeys to Tibet, Canada, Korea, Turkey, Hawaii, and Japan. A fascinating read for anyone interested in women's travel, spirituality, and Asian culture.

THE RIVERS RAN EAST
By Leonard Clark
ISBN 1-885-211-66-X
$16.95

Clark is the original Indiana Jones, relaying a breathtaking account of his search for the legendary El Dorado gold in the Amazon.

Travel Humor

NOT SO FUNNY WHEN IT HAPPENED
The Best of Travel Humor and Misadventure
Edited by Tim Cahill
ISBN 1-885-211-55-4
$12.95

Laugh with Bill Bryson, Dave Barry, Anne Lamott, Adair Lara, and many more.

THERE'S NO TOILET PAPER...ON THE ROAD LESS TRAVELED
The Best of Travel Humor and Misadventure
Edited by Doug Lansky
ISBN 1-885-211-27-9
$12.95 ★ ★ ★

Humor Book of the Year
— Independent Publisher's Book Award

★ ★ ★

ForeWord Gold Medal Winner — Humor Book of the Year

LAST TROUT IN VENICE
The Far-Flung Escapades of an Accidental Adventurer
By Doug Lansky
ISBN 1-885-211-63-5
$14.95

"Traveling with Doug Lansky might result in a considerably shortened life expectancy...but what a way to go."
—Tony Wheeler, Lonely Planet Publications

Women's Travel

A WOMAN'S PASSION FOR TRAVEL
More True Stories from A Woman's World
Edited by Marybeth Bond & Pamela Michael
ISBN 1-885-211-36-8
$17.95
"A diverse and gripping series of stories!" —Arlene Blum, author of *Annapurna: A Woman's Place*

A WOMAN'S WORLD
True Stories of Life on the Road
Edited by Marybeth Bond
Introduction by Dervla Murphy
ISBN 1-885-211-06-6
$17.95

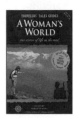

— ★ ★ ★ —

Winner of the Lowell Thomas Award for Best Travel Book— Society of American Travel Writers

WOMEN IN THE WILD
True Stories of Adventure and Connection
Edited by Lucy McCauley
ISBN 1-885-211-21-X
$17.95
"A spiritual, moving, and totally female book to take you around the world and back."—*Mademoiselle*

A MOTHER'S WORLD
Journeys of the Heart
Edited by Marybeth Bond & Pamela Michael
ISBN 1-885-211-26-0
$14.95
"These stories remind us that motherhood is one of the great unifying forces in the world" —*San Francisco Examiner*

Food

ADVENTURES IN WINE
True Stories of Vineyards and Vintages around the World
Edited by Thom Elkjer
ISBN 1-885-211-80-5
$17.95
Humanity, community, and brotherhood comprise the marvelous virtues of the wine world. This collection toasts the warmth and wonders of this large, extended family in stories by travelers who are wine novices and experts alike.

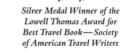

FOOD (Updated)
A Taste of the Road
Edited by Richard Sterling
Introduction by Margo True
ISBN 1-885-211-77-5
$18.95

— ★ ★ ★ —

Silver Medal Winner of the Lowell Thomas Award for Best Travel Book—Society of American Travel Writers

HER FORK IN THE ROAD
Women Celebrate Food and Travel
Edited by Lisa Bach
ISBN 1-885-211-71-6
$16.95
A savory sampling of stories by some of the best writers in and out of the food and travel fields.

THE ADVENTURE OF FOOD
True Stories of Eating Everything
Edited by Richard Sterling
ISBN 1-885-211-37-6
$17.95
"These stories are bound to whet appetites for more than food." —*Publishers Weekly*

Spiritual Travel

THE SPIRITUAL GIFTS OF TRAVEL
The Best of Travelers' Tales
Edited by James O'Reilly and Sean O'Reilly
ISBN 1-885-211-69-4
$16.95

A collection of favorite stories of transformation on the road from our award-winning Travelers' Tales series that shows the myriad ways travel indelibly alters our inner landscapes.

THE WAY OF THE WANDERER
Discover Your True Self Through Travel
By David Yeadon
ISBN 1-885-211-60-0
$14.95

Experience transformation through travel with this delightful, illustrated collection by award-winning author David Yeadon.

PILGRIMAGE
Adventures of the Spirit
Edited by Sean O'Reilly & James O'Reilly
Introduction by Phil Cousineau
ISBN 1-885-211-56-2
$16.95

——— ★ ★ ★ ———

ForeWord Silver Medal Winner
— Travel Book of the Year

A WOMAN'S PATH
Women's Best Spiritual Travel Writing
Edited by Lucy McCauley, Amy G. Carlson & Jennifer Leo
ISBN 1-885-211-48-1
$16.95

"A sensitive exploration of women's lives that have been unexpectedly and spiritually touched by travel experiences…. Highly recommended."
— Library Journal

THE ROAD WITHIN
True Stories of Transformation and the Soul
Edited by Sean O'Reilly, James O'Reilly & Tim O'Reilly
ISBN 1-885-211-19-8
$17.95

——— ★ ★ ★ ———

Best Spiritual Book — Independent Publisher's Book Award

THE ULTIMATE JOURNEY
Inspiring Stories of Living and Dying
James O'Reilly, Sean O'Reilly & Richard Sterling
ISBN 1-885-211-38-4
$17.95

"A glorious collection of writings about the ultimate adventure. A book to keep by one's bedside — and close to one's heart." —Philip Zaleski, editor,
The Best Spiritual Writing series

Adventure

TESTOSTERONE PLANET
True Stories from a Man's World
Edited by Sean O'Reilly, Larry Habegger & James O'Reilly
ISBN 1-885-211-43-0
$17.95

Thrills and laughter with some of today's best writers: Sebastian Junger, Tim Cahill, Bill Bryson, and Jon Krakauer.

DANGER!
True Stories of Trouble and Survival
Edited by James O'Reilly, Larry Habegger & Sean O'Reilly
ISBN 1-885-211-32-5
$17.95

"Exciting…for those who enjoy living on the edge or prefer to read the survival stories of others, this is a good pick."
— Library Journal

Special Interest

365 TRAVEL
**A Daily Book of
Journeys, Meditations,
and Adventures**
Edited by Lisa Bach
ISBN 1-885-211-67-8
$14.95
An illuminating collection
of travel wisdom and
adventures that reminds us
all of the lessons we learn while on the road.

THE GIFT
OF RIVERS
**True Stories of
Life on the Water**
Edited by Pamela Michael
Introduction by Robert Hass
ISBN 1-885-211-42-2
$14.95
"*The Gift of Rivers* is a
soulful compendium of wonderful stories that
illuminate, educate, inspire, and delight."
—David Brower, Chairman of
Earth Island Institute

FAMILY TRAVEL
**The Farther You Go,
the Closer You Get**
Edited by Laura Manske
ISBN 1-885-211-33-3
$17.95
"This is family travel at its
finest." —*Working Mother*

LOVE & ROMANCE
**True Stories of
Passion on the Road**
*Edited by Judith Babcock
Wylie*
ISBN 1-885-211-18-X
$17.95
"A wonderful book to
read by a crackling fire."
—*Romantic Traveling*

THE GIFT
OF BIRDS
**True Encounters
with Avian Spirits**
*Edited by Larry Habegger
& Amy G. Carlson*
ISBN 1-885-211-41-4
$17.95
"These are all wonderful,
entertaining stories offering
a *bird's-eye view!* of our avian friends."
—*Booklist*

A DOG'S WORLD
**True Stories of
Man's Best Friend
on the Road**
*Edited by Christine
Hunsicker*
ISBN 1-885-211-23-6
$12.95
This extraordinary
collection includes stories
by John Steinbeck, Helen Thayer, James
Herriot, Pico Iyer, and many others.

THE GIFT OF TRAVEL
The Best of Travelers' Tales
*Edited by Larry Habegger, James O'Reilly
& Sean O'Reilly*
ISBN 1-885-211-25-2
$14.95
"Like gourmet chefs in a French market, the
editors of Travelers' Tales pick, sift, and prod
their way through the weighty shelves of con-
temporary travel writing, creaming off the
very best."
—William Dalrymple, author of *City of Djinns*

Travel Advice

SHITTING PRETTY
How to Stay Clean and Healthy While Traveling
By Dr. Jane Wilson-Howarth
ISBN 1-885-211-47-3
$12.95

A light-hearted book about a serious subject for millions of travelers— staying healthy on the road—written by international health expert, Dr. Jane Wilson-Howarth.

THE FEARLESS SHOPPER
How to Get the Best Deals on the Planet
By Kathy Borrus
ISBN 1-885-211-39-2
$14.95

"Anyone who reads *The Fearless Shopper* will come away a smarter, more responsible shopper and a more curious, culturally attuned traveler."
—Jo Mancuso, *The Shopologist*

GUTSY WOMEN
More Travel Tips and Wisdom for the Road
By Marybeth Bond
ISBN 1-885-211-61-9
$12.95

Second Edition—Packed with funny, instructive, and inspiring advice for women heading out to see the world.

SAFETY AND SECURITY FOR WOMEN WHO TRAVEL
By Sheila Swan & Peter Laufer
ISBN 1-885-211-29-5
$12.95

A must for every woman traveler!

THE FEARLESS DINER
Travel Tips and Wisdom for Eating around the World
By Richard Sterling
ISBN 1-885-211-22-8
$7.95

Combines practical advice on foodstuffs, habits, and etiquette, with hilarious accounts of others' eating adventures.

THE PENNY PINCHER'S PASSPORT TO LUXURY TRAVEL
The Art of Cultivating Preferred Customer Status
By Joel L. Widzer
ISBN 1-885-211-31-7
$12.95

Proven techniques on how to travel first class at discount prices, even if you're not a frequent flyer.

GUTSY MAMAS
Travel Tips and Wisdom for Mothers on the Road
By Marybeth Bond
ISBN 1-885-211-20-1
$7.95

A delightful guide for mothers traveling with their children— or without them!

Destination Titles:
True Stories of Life on the Road

AMERICA
Edited by Fred Setterberg
ISBN 1-885-211-28-7
$19.95

FRANCE (Updated)
Edited by James O'Reilly,
Larry Habegger &
Sean O'Reilly
ISBN 1-885-211-73-2
$18.95

AMERICAN SOUTHWEST
Edited by Sean O'Reilly
& James O'Reilly
ISBN 1-885-211-58-9
$17.95

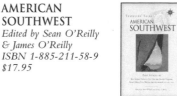

GRAND CANYON
Edited by Sean O'Reilly,
James O'Reilly &
Larry Habegger
ISBN 1-885-211-34-1
$17.95

AUSTRALIA
Edited by Larry Habegger
ISBN 1-885-211-40-6
$17.95

GREECE
Edited by Larry Habegger,
Sean O'Reilly &
Brian Alexander
ISBN 1-885 211-52-X
$17.95

BRAZIL
Edited by Annette Haddad
& Scott Doggett
Introduction by Alex
Shoumatoff
ISBN 1-885-211-11-2
$17.95

HAWAI'I
Edited by Rick &
Marcie Carroll
ISBN 1-885-211-35-X
$17.95

CENTRAL AMERICA
Edited by Larry Habegger
& Natanya Pearlman
ISBN 1-885-211-74-0
$17.95

HONG KONG
Edited by James O'Reilly,
Larry Habegger &
Sean O'Reilly
ISBN 1-885-211-03-1
$17.95

CUBA
Edited by Tom Miller
ISBN 1-885-211-62-7
$17.95

INDIA
Edited by James O'Reilly
& Larry Habegger
ISBN 1-885-211-01-5
$17.95

IRELAND
Edited by James O'Reilly,
Larry Habegger &
Sean O'Reilly
ISBN 1-885-211-46-5
$17.95

SAN FRANCISCO
Edited by James O'Reilly,
Larry Habegger &
Sean O'Reilly
ISBN 1-885-211-08-2
$17.95

ITALY (Updated)
Edited by Anne Calcagno
Introduction by Jan Morris
ISBN 1-885-211-72-4
$18.95

SPAIN (Updated)
Edited by Lucy McCauley
ISBN 1-885-211-78-3
$19.95

JAPAN
Edited by Donald W. George
& Amy G. Carlson
ISBN 1-885-211-04-X
$17.95

THAILAND (Updated)
Edited by James O'Reilly
& Larry Habegger
ISBN 1-885-211-75-9
$18.95

MEXICO (Updated)
Edited by James O'Reilly
& Larry Habegger
ISBN 1-885-211-59-7
$17.95

TIBET
Edited by James O'Reilly,
Larry Habegger, & Kim
Morris
ISBN 1-885-211-76-7
$18.95

NEPAL
Edited by Rajendra
S. Khadka
ISBN 1-885-211-14-7
$17.95

TUSCANY
Edited by James O'Reilly, &
Tara Austen Weaver
ISBN 1-885-211-68-6
$16.95

PARIS
Edited by James O'Reilly,
Larry Habegger &
Sean O'Reilly
ISBN 1-885-211-10-4
$17.95